W9-AXN-356

Praise for

Engage!

"Brian Solis has shown once again his deep understanding of the power of new media. He shows how social media can give voice, credibility, and connections to both companies and their customers."

—**Price Floyd**, Principal Deputy Assistant Secretary of Defense for Public Affairs

"What's the secret to a successful company? Seasoned business owners know that it's a combination of strong leadership and superior products. But that alone isn't enough anymore. The leader of the future needs to connect with the customer of the future when, where, and how the customer wants, and Brian Solis lays out some of the guidelines here, going far beyond the tools that are today's buzzwords."

—**Scott Monty**, Global Digital Communications, Ford Motor Company

"Social media isn't all that different from the new era of food trucks in Los Angeles: it's the wild, wild West out there where the unspoken law reigns supreme and all the established protocols of traditional media are meant to be broken. For every Jesse James, there are a thousand more who aspire to rule over the law. This book will help you succeed and thrive in an era of perceived, yet strategic, lawlessness."

—**Chef Roy Choi**, @KogiBBQ

"Brian Solis documents new media's evolution and its challenge to traditional marketing methods and corporate communications: Most profoundly, through social media the customer has become a more influential stakeholder. The book provides concrete guidelines on how companies must engage in the public conversation and how they must prepare for a new era of relationships with their clients, customers, and employees."

—**Klaus Schwab**, Executive Chairman, World Economic Forum

ENGAGE!

The Complete Guide for
BRANDS and **BUSINESSES** to
Build, Cultivate, and Measure Success
in the New Web

BRIAN SOLIS

WILEY

John Wiley & Sons, Inc.

Copyright © 2010 by Brian Solis. All rights reserved.

Published by John Wiley & Sons, Inc., Hoboken, New Jersey.
Published simultaneously in Canada.

No part of this publication may be reproduced, stored in a retrieval system, or transmitted in any form or by any means, electronic, mechanical, photocopying, recording, scanning, or otherwise, except as permitted under Section 107 or 108 of the 1976 United States Copyright Act, without either the prior written permission of the Publisher, or authorization through payment of the appropriate per-copy fee to the Copyright Clearance Center, Inc., 222 Rosewood Drive, Danvers, MA 01923, (978) 750-8400, fax (978) 646-8600, or on the Web at www.copyright.com. Requests to the Publisher for permission should be addressed to the Permissions Department, John Wiley & Sons, Inc., 111 River Street, Hoboken, NJ 07030, (201) 748-6011, fax (201) 748-6008, or online at http://www.wiley.com/go/permissions.

Limit of Liability/Disclaimer of Warranty: While the publisher and author have used their best efforts in preparing this book, they make no representations or warranties with respect to the accuracy or completeness of the contents of this book and specifically disclaim any implied warranties of merchantability or fitness for a particular purpose. No warranty may be created or extended by sales representatives or written sales materials. The advice and strategies contained herein may not be suitable for your situation. You should consult with a professional where appropriate. Neither the publisher nor author shall be liable for any loss of profit or any other commercial damages, including but not limited to special, incidental, consequential, or other damages.

For general information on our other products and services or for technical support, please contact our Customer Care Department within the United States at (800) 762-2974, outside the United States at (317) 572-3993, or fax (317) 572-4002.

Wiley also publishes its books in a variety of electronic formats. Some content that appears in print may not be available in electronic books. For more information about Wiley products, visit our website at www.wiley.com.

ISBN 978-0-470-57109-5

Printed in the United States of America

10 9 8 7 6 5 4 3 2 1

Contents

Foreword

New media is creating a new generation of influencers and it is reset-ting the hierarchy of authority, while completely freaking out those who once held power without objection. The truth is that most of the existing formulas, methodologies, and systems miss or completely ig-nore the role of new influencers to inspire action, cause change, spark trends, and recruit advocates. We are absent from the exact movement that can help us connect with those who guide their peers.

In light of the new media movement, how do brands approach this now? They spam the Web with useless rhetoric. (Who cares if you're on Facebook or Twitter?) They also distribute these horrible videos, uploading them to YouTube and then wondering why they never go viral. Look, you have seven seconds to entertain someone. If you don't grab them in seven seconds, then you can forget about someone sitting through the rest of the video—let alone having it go viral.

But if you know what people are looking for . . . if you know where people are interacting . . . if you know what moves people, you can en-gage the human algorithm to immerse viewers and trigger meaningful interaction and vibration across the social graph.

This is why we, we as in a collective of individuals who know what's best for us based on our passions, interests, and aspirations, are in charge of what compels us. In order to have any hope of attracting and earning our attention, you need to know who *we* are.

The roles are reversing and individuals and brands have the ability to reach and rouse powerful and dedicated communities without ever having to pay for advertising. I'm just part of the bigger movement of empowering the people who care enough to change the word. Social media is socializing causes and purpose, and inciting nothing short of a revolution in stature and influence, but more importantly, literacy and innovation.

As we engage, we learn. And, learning is what this is all about. But we can't grow without admitting that we have something to learn and at the same time, we have to believe in ourselves and our ability to push things forward. In the end, everything starts with engagement. This is our time. This is your time. Engage.

ASHTON KUTCHER
CO-FOUNDER OF KATALYST

Preface

We are at the beginning of something new and incredible, and its paths and processes are for the most part undefined and far from standardized. Social media is a great equalizer and it's leveling the playing field for those who can demonstrate adeptness and vision. If this is you, it's time to speak up. It's time to show executives, peers, and stakeholders that you care. With a little homework, the case can be made quite easily and impressively. It just takes a little bit of extra time and passion to do so.

You are needed now more than ever to help the brand best position itself to compete in the "now web" and for the future.

It takes a champion to rally support from within.

It takes a champion to connect customer needs with company solutions.

It takes a champion to become the customer the business needs to reach.

It takes a champion to guide decision makers within the organization on how to best implement social tools and services, how to use them, how to establish guidelines, and how to measure success and ROI.

You're a purveyor of new media, but then again, so is everyone else, it seems. Suddenly, everyone is a social media expert, but very few are indeed champions and far fewer are change agents.

So what are you going to do to rise above the fray while also delivering true, incontestable value to those you are helping?

Ask yourself . . .

Are you an evangelist or a consultant?

Are you an extension of your company brand or are you an employee?

Are you a leader or a follower, or are you meandering through your profession?

Are you confined to the role you're in now or do you represent something with longer-term value?

Everything that's transpiring around us is actually improving the existing foundation for our business, from service to marketing to product development to sales to executive management, and everything in between.

Social marketing revitalizes and empowers every facet of our workflow and its supporting ecosystem. Seeing the bigger picture and tying our knowledge to the valuable feedback from our communities will help us guide businesses towards visibility, profitability, relevance and ultimately customer loyalty.

In every single case, it doesn't take only an expert; it requires a champion to make an impact.

You are that champion.

Advancement doesn't come without investment though.

You may be saying to yourself, "I already have a full-time job that keeps me busy, more than busy, for eight to nine hours a day as it is. How am I going to squeeze in the time to learn everything required for this new role, and how will I balance my workload based on what I already have to do?"

Sorry. I don't have an easy answer or a shortcut for you.

What's taking place right now, right in front of you, is something so tremendous that to proclaim that a cheat sheet exists would actually cheat you from truly grasping this new opportunity for personal and professional growth.

This is something so much deeper than anything I could cover "for dummies." It's a matter of abridgement versus immersion. Success and maturation is tied to the latter.

The good news is that you have this book. Now let's work together to get you that MBA that will really help you excel in your career, wherever it may take you.

Think about it.

Investing extra time after hours and on weekends is the minimum ante to enroll in what I call the New Media University. With every day that passes, enrollment multiplies. The question you have to ask is whether you want to lead or follow. Please note that the risk of following is that the field will quickly become congested and choked with competition and stagnation. In contrast, when you choose to take a leadership role, you will find that challengers are scattered and in short supply. The cost, however, is that you go back to school for the near future in order to learn and acquire the skills necessary to lead your brand into the future.

While many will ask questions, few will have answers. Which side of the dialogue do you choose?

Introduction: Welcome to the Revolution

By the time you read this book, you may have already heard or will soon hear whispers, rumblings, and rantings that social media is playing out.

Tune them out.

The truth is that social media may very well cease to exist as a category one day. However, while the term and category has and always will invite debate, social media's practices and benefits are indisputable, sustainable, and enduring. And, they will always serve as an important and revered chapter in the evolution of new media.

This is not open to debate.

Influential conversations are sparked and steered by influential people right now and they exist and flourish outside of your organization. The practice of listening to and learning from these conversations in and around the social networks where they transpire is invaluable and indispensable.

Social Media. New Media. Interactive Media. Integrated Marketing. Experiential Marketing. Public Relations. Branding. Whatever we call it, it's simply a matter of digital Darwinism that affects any and all forms of marketing and service. In the world of democratized influence, businesses must endure a perpetual "survival of the fittest."

Engage or die.

In June 2007, I wrote and published *The Social Media Manifesto*. What started as a blog post intended to help marketers grasp and embrace the emerging and rapidly shifting landscape of social media, quickly ascended into the proclamation and rallying cry for a new, more cognizant, and in-touch epoch of customer-focused, direct-to-consumer engagement. *The Social Media Manifesto* introduced the methodologies, tools, and social networks that would eventually inspire a movement to evolve from top-down, broadcast programs to complementary and holistic forms of collaboration rooted in mutually beneficial engagement and exchanges. It served

Source: Original drawing in honor of *Engage!* by Hugh MacLeod, author of *Ignore Everybody* and also blogger @gapingvoid.

as the foundation to effectively redesign marketing communications and customer service organizations based on the art of observation, listening, engagement, learning, and adapting. It also introduced the mechanics and benefits for humanizing and diversifying the company story based on the unique and varying needs of customers and peers who populate disparate online communities through their channels of influence.

And here we are now: united in our efforts to discover meaning in the philosophies and processes we long operated without. We seek inspiration and we endeavor to inspire. The people we attempted to reach over the years appear before our eyes as if they are long lost friends and relatives. The faceless have revealed their identities through their role in social media. Socialized media and the people powering the convergence are accelerating an era of engagement driven by collective consciousness, yet mindful of business, in order to attract customers and preserve their affiliation. After all, customer acquisition is only rivaled in value by customer retention.

The science of procuring attention is complemented by the delicate art of earning and cultivating relationships. Social media peeled back the layers of infrastructure, data, numbers, demographics, politics, procedures, and all of the corporate red tape that dug trenches between our brand and our customers.

This is our time to engage! In doing so, it is your declaration of independence from the shackles that have bound us to hollow and vain marketing techniques and practices of yesteryear. It serves as your framework to chart your own path and create your own destiny. It is your key to unlock the doors that prevent you from reaching your customers where they're interacting and seeking solutions today *and* tomorrow.

Together we are building the foundation for corporate and personal significance. We are the architects who are drafting the blueprint for a more efficient and yearned-for bridge between our story and the people who can benefit from it.

Welcome to marketing providence. The crusade you join is growing in breadth and volume each and every day. You're surrounded by like-minded individuals who seek to improve the dynamics between people and the companies they represent. The tools, methodologies, and stories shared within this book will reveal a wealth of "unmarketing" principles, strategies, and devices. It is this idea of "unmarketing" that inevitably extends all of the goals and objectives merited by traditional marketing, while also elevating the experience for everyone on both sides and invariably stimulating advocacy in order to expand your presence and impact in the mainstream and distributed communities that influence perceptions and decisions.

While the methodologies, theories, experiences, and social tools discussed in the original manifesto still stand, a deeper and more modern look is necessary to garner support and champion change from within—specifically an examination of what to do and how to measure success. It is through engagement that we earn experience, connections, and prominence. There's no doubt that the proven tenets introduced in this book will ensure your success and career longevity. The doctrines that we examine and propose are in fact representative of best-of-breed ideals and methods unearthed and mashed-up from existing and extinct tactics to renew, edify, mature, and hone our proficiencies, conviction, knowledge, and experience.

Engage! will serve as a new manifesto, a reference point for all inward-outward-facing initiatives that incorporate two-way communication. And in the process, we'll see "unmarketing" emerge as one of the most effective forms of marketing, after all.

Until the proliferation of interactive media, traditional influence has followed a systematic top-down process of developing and pushing "controlled" messages to audiences, rooted in one-to-many faceless broadcast campaigns.

Personality wasn't absent in certain mediums, but it was missing from day-to-day communications.

For the most part, this pattern seemingly served its purposes, fueling the belief that brands were in control of their messages, from delivery to dissemination, among the demographics to which they were targeted.

It scaled and served very well over the years, until it didn't . . .

Unbeknownst to many companies, a quiet revolution has been amassing over the last two decades, one that we document clearly in this book. And, slowly but surely, the whispers eventually intensified into roars.

The socialization of the Web and content publishing disrupted the balance and is now forcing a media renaissance that is transforming information distribution, human interaction, and everything that orbits this nascent ecosystem.

It is the dawn of a democratized information economy, which is engendering the emergence of champions, facilitators, and visionaries who endeavor to manifest a more media literate society while transforming the way we publish and share relevant content.

The interactive Web heralded the arrival of mainstream consumer influence and a global ecosystem that supports and extends their observations, complaints, opinions, referrals, and recommendations.

It served as a great equalizer, capsizing the existing balance and redistributing influence—and continues to do so.

Not only is it changing how we create, decipher, and share information, it is forever reshaping how brands and content publishers think about their markets and the people who define them.

Engage.

Part

I

The New Reality of Marketing and Customer Service

Chapter 1

The Social Media Manifesto

Engage or Die

■ THE SOCIALIZATION OF MEDIA IS YEARS IN THE MAKING

In my 19-year marketing career, I've dedicated the last 13 years specifically to the practice of and experimentation in online interaction. My findings are based solely on the chemistry of failure, success, and, well, ambivalence, which by many accounts equals either defeat or promise. The constant theme throughout has been the sustained balance between the pursuit of new influencers and the incorporation of verified traditional methods. This experience, and the experiences of others, ultimately serves as the foundation for creating a new communications bridge between companies and customers.

Socialized media has:

➤ Rewired the processes by which consumers share experiences, expertise, and opinions.

➤ Broadened the channels available to consumers who seek information.

➤ Changed how companies approach markets.

➤ Altered how companies develop products.

➤ Remodeled the processes by which companies connect with and show appreciation for their customers.

➤ Transformed the method of influence, augmenting the ranks of traditional market experts and thought leaders with enthusiasts and innovators who self-create content-publishing platforms for their views.

Source: Original artwork by Jesse Thomas (http://Jess3.com).

➤ Facilitated customers' direct engagement in the conversations that were previously taking place without their participation.

A fundamental shift in our culture is underway and it is creating a new landscape of influencers, as well as changing how we define influence. By establishing an entirely new ecosystem that supports the socialization of information, this shift is facilitating new conversations that start locally, but ultimately have a global impact.

The days of "hear no evil, see no evil, speak no evil" have passed without lament.

Monologue has given way to dialogue.

The message is clear. Social media has created and magnified a new layer of influencers across all industries. It is the understanding of the role people play in the process of not only reading and disseminating information, but also how they share and create content in which others can participate. This, and only this, allows us to truly grasp the future of communications, which is already unfolding today.

The socialization of information and the tools that enable it are the undercurrent of interactive media—and serve as the capital infrastructure that defines the social economy.

Content is the new democracy and we, the people, are ensuring that our voices are heard.

This is your chance to reinvigorate the tired and aging models of marketing and service, build a corporate brand, and increase revenue, all while paving the way for a brighter, more rewarding, and more prosperous métier.

How can companies implement an integrated communications strategy quickly in this new social landscape? By focusing on multiple markets and influencers that will have a far greater impact on brand resonance and the bottom line than trying to reach the masses through any one message, venue, or tool.

Our actions speak louder than our words.

New media is constantly evolving and has yet to reveal its true impact across the entire business publishing and marketing landscape. We're only now starting to realize a small portion of its benefits and advantages. What we do know is that the current iteration of social media is only one chapter in a never-ending resource that continues to evolve as new media permeates every facet of every business. In fact, new media is only going to become more pervasive and, as such, become a critical factor in the success or failure of any business.

The life of the information offered in this book is interminable. New tools and strategies will be revealed, and they will be tied to exciting case studies that document the challenges, tactics, lessons, and successes for each.

We're just getting started.

The evolution of new media is also inducing an incredible transformation in customer service, community relations, public relations (PR), and corporate communications—its most dramatic evolution in decades. In the world of customer and product support, socialized media is putting the "customer" back in customer service, retracting the ideologies associated with cost-cutting tactics when interfacing directly with the people who purchase and influence the purchasing decisions of others. Likewise, in the world of communications, the democratization of media is putting the "public" back into public relations. It creates entirely new teams within organizations to proactively listen, learn, engage, measure, and change in real time. And we'll soon see it have a profound effect in the financial sector.

With the injection of social tools into the mix, people now have the ability to impact and influence the decisions of their peers, as well as other newsmakers. This new genre of media is not a game played from the sidelines however. Nor is this book written merely to inform you of the benefits only to have you go back to your day-to-day routing. Those who participate will succeed—everyone else will either have to catch up or miss the game altogether.

Businesses will evolve, customers will gain in prominence, and brands will humanize—with or without you.

■ THE FUTURE OF COMMUNICATIONS AND SERVICE IS ALREADY HERE

The secret to successfully navigating the new landscape of marketing and service is understanding that socialized media is about anthropology, sociology, and ethnography, and less about technology and the social tools that captivate and connect everyone today. New media marketing and services are mash-ups of new and traditional media and processes that span across advertising, PR, customer service, marketing communications (marcom), human resources (HR), sales, and community relations.

Communication, whether inbound or outbound, is now powered by conversations, and the best communicators always start as the best listeners. And, the best listeners are those who empathize while they are listening.

This is where and how the future of influence takes shape.

➤ It begins with respect and an understanding of how you connect with and benefit those whom you're hoping to help.

➤ Intent is defined by a genuine desire to evolve into a resource.

➤ Genuine participation is a form of new marketing, but is not reminiscent of traditional marketing formats and techniques—it's a new blueprint for "unmarketing."

➤ Meaningful content can earn the creator trust, authority, and influence.

➤ Conversations can forge relationships, which are measured by social capital and trust.

Figure 1.2 shows the range of people you will be interacting with, from innovators to laggards.

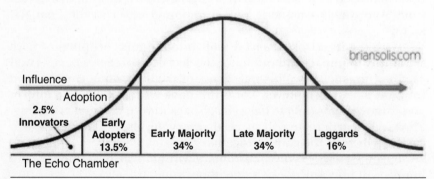

Figure 1.2

These are pretty powerful statements and they are the essence of this more dynamic form of communications required to succeed today. These methodologies combine traditional marketing with the ability to develop flourishing and dynamic relationships with important individuals and groups of people who define multiple markets, thus giving us the ability to have an impact on multiple markets in the process.

■ WE ARE THE CHAMPIONS, WE ARE NOT MESSENGERS

While we lead the transformation and socialization of our company's marketing and service infrastructure, we must also ensure that our actions are discernible. Much in the same way that we attempt to create ambassadors by empowering our customers and advocates in the Social Web, we must become their ambassadors within—representing their concerns, ideas, questions, and experiences to those on our team who can provide resolution and also internal change.

Since this is a powerful new form of *social* media, it begins with how we speak. This is the point at which most companies fall down, when they rely on traditional marketing instead of creating new dialogues.

Messages are not conversations. Targets and audiences are not people. The inability to know people for who they are and what they represent prevents us from effectively and truly seeing them—which then impedes our efforts to reach them. As Doc Searls, coauthor of *The Cluetrain Manifesto*, wisely stated, "There is no market for messages."

The market for self-promotion is finite. Yet brands, even those that experiment with social media, confuse their role and place within these new digital societies. People do not create accounts on Facebook, YouTube, Twitter, or any other social network to hear from brands. Those who are solely and intentionally seeking input from companies are joining networks such as GetSatisfaction or UserVoice, and dedicated forums such as those on Yahoo!, Google, and other bulletin boards. The bottom line is that people are seeking answers and direction, not messages or sales pitches.

People just don't speak or hear things in the same way companies speak about their products and services. In order to be heard, we have to communicate as though we were speaking person-to-person with our customers.

Social networks are a hub between the company and its customers. They represent a new genre of customer-focused engagement that fuses marcom, PR, product development, sales, and customer relations, all in one community. How we participate in each network defines our stature within them and also determines our ability to earn friends and followers while also promoting and instilling advocacy.

Everything we're integrating into the marketing mix is aimed at sparking and cultivating conversations, as well as continuously expanding a network of lasting relationships.

■ CONVERSATIONS HAPPEN WITH OR WITHOUT YOU

In his great essay entitled "We Are the People Formerly Known as the Audience," Jay Rosen introduced an entirely new concept of reaching people. In many ways, Rosen's essay served as a manifesto for the marketing, media, and advertising industries, serving as an eye-opener to the world of democratized influence and how to recognize and embrace the opportunity it represents.

In order to reach people, we have to first figure out who they are and where they go for information. In the process, you'll quickly discover that there is no magic bullet for reaching everyone, all at once. The strategy is in how to segment active communities from audiences—humanizing and materializing the people we wish to reach.

The best communications programs will reach out equally to traditional media, A-, B-, and C-list bloggers, and communities because, while newsmakers reach the masses, peers and customers also reach each other in the communities where they congregate. This approach requires a new mindset and a new era of metrics.

Social media is about speaking with, not "at" people. This means engaging in a way that works in a conversational medium, that is, serving the best interest of both parties, while not demeaning any actions or insulting the intelligence of anyone involved.

So what of those skeptics or apprehensive executives who claim that participating on social networks will only invoke negative responses and ignite potential crises?

As we're coming to realize, the social landscape is an apparent sea filled with unforgiving predators—most of whom would love nothing more than to have marketers for every meal of the day. Nevertheless, succeeding here is the future of integrated communications, marketing, and service.

The truth is that there will be negative commentary. However, that should not deter you from experimenting or piloting programs. Even without your participation, negative commentary already exists. In most cases, you just aren't encountering it. This is why I like to ask business leaders the following question: "If a conversation takes place online, and you weren't there to hear it, did it actually happen?"

Yes. Yes, it did.

Assuredly, every negative discussion is an opportunity to learn and also to participate in a way that may shift the discussion in a positive direction. If there's nothing else that we accomplish by participating, we at least acquire the ability to contribute toward a positive public perception.

The conversations that don't kill you only make you stronger. And those negative threads that escalate in social networks will only accelerate without the involvement of inherent stakeholders.

■ SOCIAL MEDIA IS ONE COMPONENT OF A BROADER COMMUNICATIONS AND MARKETING STRATEGY

It's true that everything is changing. And in many cases, it's also true that everything old eventually becomes new again. The underlying principles of customer focus and service certainly aren't new. Instead, the attention on these elements may have waned, as businesses expand, contract, shift, and evolve based on market needs and trends, profit, and peer influence, as governed by the guidance of stakeholders and shareholders.

Social media is a critical part of a larger, more complete sales, service, communications, and marketing strategy that reflects and adapts to markets and the people who define them.

Therefore, we should be realistic about how we integrate social strategies into the human-powered machine of listening, learning, engaging, and evolving.

Social media is a never-ending fountain of lessons and insight.

Social media delivers new communications tools, and also new opportunities to learn how, when, and where to use them.

Social media is both distribution channels and rivers of knowledge, education, and experience.

Social media is a means, not an end.

Social media is a revelation that we, the people, have a voice, and through the democratization of content and ideas we can once again unite around common passions, inspire movements, and ignite change.

Social media is a chapter in the evolution of New Media.

It's not a one-way broadcast channel. We are no longer broadcasters. We are now part of the community we wish to inform, and therefore we must establish prominence and earn influence in order to amass attention, instill enthusiasm, empower ambassadors, and create a community of loyal collaborators toward a more meaningful form of "unmarketing" and communications.

The previous hierarchy of messaging has collapsed. Now, in or-der to appeal to customers, clients, or potential stakeholders, we must approach them from top-down, bottom-up, and side-to-side. We must out-maneuver the elusive. We must out-think the pessimists. We must sanction and amplify the experts and the emissaries.

■ BUILDING A BRIDGE BETWEEN YOU AND YOUR CUSTOMERS

No matter what the industry, we are all, in some way, responsible for the public relations of the organization we represent.

That's right.

I'm not talking about PR or publicity intrinsically. Since our com-munications efforts are outward focused, visible, and indexable on the Web for all to see and find, everything we do now, whether we're in PR or not, reflects on, and contributes to, the brand we represent. Arming employees with knowledge, guidelines, rules, objectives, and expertise, and accordingly empowering them to participate on behalf of the brand and greater mission, creates an efficient, influential, and community-focused organization that stays in sync with stake-holders. Doing so builds an active collective of participants, powered by influential voices, in addition to employees, who will shape per-ception, steer conversations, and provide help to those seeking ad-vice. The community that once operated without us now becomes an extension of our outbound activities, beliefs, passions, and value propositions.

We are both architects and builders of strategic relationships and alliances, and we are creating the blueprints for and also constructing the bridge that connects customers and the people (you and me) who represent the companies we believe in.

In order to truly help businesses and the decision makers respon-sible for their direction, we need to learn through real work. We have to get our hands dirty. There's just no way around it. We can learn from the mistakes and successes of our peers, but actions speak louder than words. The last thing we need are more cooks in a crowded kitchen. At the same time, we need direction and lucrative move-ment. We need thinkers *and* doers. It is the only way to get smarter and, in turn, become more valuable to those you're consulting or helping.

Immersion equals incontestable experience, perspectives, and knowledge.

Let's get to work, build the bridge, and open up the gateways to traffic on both ends.

■ BEING HUMAN VERSUS HUMANIZING YOUR STORY

It takes so much more than an understanding of the tools and popular networks to inspire change and build long-term, meaningful relationships. We must not forget to fuse what works today with the strategies that reach and compel those influencers and tastemakers who live on the edge and thus promote change among those who reside in the center.

The ability to set up a profile on Facebook or Twitter, the wherewithal to update status in each network, the capacity to befriend people within each network, is in fact, child's play. This is a learned practice not unlike the sending, filing, and reading of e-mail, chatting through instant-messaging tools, placing IP-based calls on Skype, decoding the mystery of using a short message service (SMS), or sending a text message from your mobile phone.

There's a bigger, more significant opportunity to make a true impact within an organization. The tools are just extensions of you and your expertise and artistry. Everything starts with a deep commitment to the brand you're representing—its culture, personality, overall potential, and people. Without it, you're pushing the same old rhetoric in new places, which hardly helps you achieve your potential or the true capabilities of your team. And it certainly doesn't inspire anyone to concern themselves with the brand's presence in these emerging social networks that are so vital to our corporate economy.

Don't speak to me in messages!

Put down the sales sheet or the press release.

Remove me from your broadcast mailing list.

Stop calling me at home and on my cell phone.

Give me something to believe in. Give me something to let me know that you *know* who you're talking to.

I am influential. I am a consumer. I have a valuable social graph. You only wish you could connect with me. I'm the gatekeeper among gatekeepers who needs direction, insight, and answers in order for me to accomplish the tasks in my life and meet my personal and professional goals. You could be just what I'm looking for, but in social media, where I dwell, I wouldn't know it based on how you are or aren't participating.

I'm a human being and so are you.

Treat me as such.

Alas, being human is far easier than humanizing your story. Transparency is just not enough to convince me that I need to pay attention to you.

Get a little empathy going on and you'll begin to facilitate meaningful interaction. This is the necessary commitment to adopting and embodying a customer service mentality fueled by empathy and the desire to deliver resolution—one strategic engagement at a time.

Feel it.

Live it.

Breathe it.

Be it.

If you don't engage and become an internal champion, someone else will. That person may reside in your organization right now, or they may dwell in the cubicles of your competition's offices, or both. It's as simple as that. The key difference though, is that you can definitively demonstrate how your story can impact the day-to-day workflow of various important leaders and trendsetters, across multiple markets, because you, by default, have also become a new influencer in the process of socializing your company. While intent counts, value talks and BS walks. It's the poetry of relationship-building, versed in the language and delivered with the swagger of someone who knows how to speak to the people because he or she is from the people.

■ SOCIAL SCIENCE IS NO LONGER AN ELECTIVE

As mentioned earlier, technology is not in or of itself the catalyst for change. Social tools facilitate the online conversations, but it's the people who are the instigators for change.

While Generation Y (the Millennials) are entering the workforce with unprecedented knowledge of how to communicate with each other using social networks, micromedia communities, blogs, and all things social, their business discipline and work ethic are still rivaled by Baby Boomers and Generation X. And the technical aptitude of previous generations is locked into a perennial cycle of catch-up and self-education. Each generation, however, is unique and representative of the reality that everyone, no matter which generation they represent, still needs to learn how to hear and see things differently. It's psychographics over demographics, and the only way to learn about and motivate people is to see and connect with those who band together through tastes, preferences, interests, and passions, regardless of age, location, and gender.

Psychographics: Any attribute relating to personality, values, attitudes, interests, or lifestyles; also referred to as IAO variables (for interests, activities, and opinions).[1]

Demographics: The physical characteristics of a population, such as age, sex, marital status, family size, education, geographic location, and occupation.[2]

The knowledge of the tools is one thing. But it's what we hear, say, and learn that traverses seamlessly across generations and technologies—as it relates to those connected by relevant data and individuals who share their interests.

How people interact on Facebook is not the same as how they communicate on Twitter. Community interaction on YouTube is radically different from communication on MySpace. Each network cultivates its own culture—creating a unique society that fosters connections and socialization as determined by the network's terms of service (ToS), technology capabilities, and, finally, by the people who join, who produce and share content, and who interact with one another.

Social sciences instruct us to study the social life of human groups. Conducting fieldwork in the form of listening, observing, asking questions, and documenting people in the natural environments of their online habitat reveals the insights necessary to successfully navigate our own immersion into each community.

Let's take a look at the definitions of sociology, anthropology, and ethnography to appreciate the similarities in the practice of social sciences as related to our work in social media:

Sociology: The study of society, human social interaction, and the rules and processes that bind and separate people not only as individuals, but as members of associations, groups, and institutions.[3]

Anthropology: The scientific study of people, including the development of societies and cultures. It seeks to advance knowledge of who we are, how we came to be that way—and where we may go in the future.[4]

Ethnography: A branch of anthropology that provides scientific descriptions of human societies based on people in their natural or "native" environments—where they live, work, shop, and play. Ethnography is based on objective fieldwork.

Through sociology, anthropology, and ethnography, we're learning to peel back the layers of online markets to see the specific groups of people and document their behavior. As such, we can effectively visualize and personify the nuances that define each online community and the distinct subcultures within it. Through impartial examination, we gather the data necessary to effectively and intelligently cross over into societal immersion, in the networks that are relevant to our brand.

Specifically, we are looking to uncover:

➤ Material social networks.

➤ People linked through common interests that are germane to our business, industry, and marketplace.

➤ Keywords commonly used by community members.

➤ Patterns for discovering and sharing information.

➤ Influence of outside networks and also the effects of existing networks on external communities.

➤ Influential voices, tiered, and how they form distinct and over-lapping connections.

➤ The personality of networks and the specific communities.

➤ The nature of threads, memes, and associated sentiment.

➤ The language of inhabitants.

➤ The prevailing culture and our potential place within it.

➤ The tools people use to communicate in and around each network.

This critical element of preliminary fieldwork helps us adapt our outreach strategies and techniques, as well as construct the poignant information and stories we wish to share with potential stakeholders and advocates. And, through observation, we're able to find our real customers and those who influence them.

Later in the book, we'll uncover how to specifically identify the social networks and pertinent communities to your brand.

■ ARE YOU LISTENING TO ME? PROVE IT

One of the most important steps in digital sociology and digital an-thropology is the process of uncovering the voices that define and steer your markets.

Tools and networks will come and go. Popularity will shift across existing, up-and-coming, and yet-to-be introduced services. Contrary to popular opinion, your presence is not required in every network that populates the Social Web. You need to participate and contribute only in those communities where identified customers and prospects are active.

The risk and reality is that your customers and influential trend-setters could be misinterpreting your value proposition without dis-pute or resolve. Worse yet, they're receiving information and direction from your competitors. And if your brand is absent from these conversations (no matter how negative), don't breathe a sigh of relief. It means you're off the radar screens in your customers' decision-making processes.

In the current state of social media, online conversations, along with real-world activity, cannot be ignored. Identifying these discussions is only the first step, however. It takes much more than running Yahoo! or Google searches or setting up Google Alerts to unearth relevant dialogue. The process of identifying influencers, applicable interaction, and associated sentiment is a much more human and sophisticated process that supersedes the work performed by even the most expensive automated Web-based or software listening applications available now.

Casting a wide net in order to identify where your communities are thriving is the only way to truly identify which networks are important to your brand and business. Once you understand where these conversations are transpiring, you can observe the cultures, climate, and dialogue in order to create a participation strategy and navigate each opportunity to reach the appropriate person.

In my experience, it's *listening* that separates social media experts from social media theorists.

Make the time. Document important and relevant discussions. Create a Social Map that visually communicates where important dialogue is materializing, and where you and your team are needed, as well as maintain a pulse on your ORM (online reputation management) initiatives. Use the Conversation Prism (see Chapter 18).

■ YOU ARE NOT ALONE

Everything starts with unlearning what you think you know and embracing everything you need to know in today's hastily advancing and transforming social climate.

We all need to determine what we need to know to compete for the future as professionals while helping the brands we represent compete for mind-share in the face of this distributed and ever-thinning-attention economy.

Whichever department we represent, the only way to evolve is to forge rewarding, long-term connections with the very people we wish to reach and compel. Success is tied to the ability to gain influence in our own right, within each community that affects our business and markets. Winning organizations will effectually shift outward activity from broadcast, us-versus-them campaigns to a one-on-one, and eventually to a many-on-many, methodology that humanizes and personalizes the spirit and personality of our brand. What we're learning is that the ability to move and react is where most companies begin. Inevitably, however, the greatest advantages of social media reside in its ability for worthy individuals and companies to shape perception, steer activity, incite action, and adapt to the communities that establish the market, both today and tomorrow.

Engage or die.

Chapter 2

The Case for Socializing Media, by the Numbers

According to InternetWorldStats.com, there are currently 1.6 billion Internet users online around the world, compared to a world population of 7 billion.[1] Of those users, 251 million reside in North America. Comscore estimates that two-thirds of global Internet users access social networking sites.[2]

Trends indicate that online social networking is becoming the predominate form of online activity. Looking at the size of some of the most popular social networks offers an indication of the great potential for listening and learning, answering questions and solving problems, engaging potential stakeholders and advocates, and creating and cultivating valuable communities.

At the time of writing this book:

➤ Registered Twitter users number between 25 and 30 million in late 2009 and early 2010.

➤ Facebook worldwide users passed the 350 million mark in late 2009.

➤ Although MySpace is undergoing a metamorphosis, it still maintains a user base of over 260 million.

➤ Google's Orkut is hosting over 67,000,000 users.

➤ Although no longer popular in the Western world, Friendster still houses 90 million people.

➤ Classmates.com connects 50 million users.

➤ Bebo connects 35 million users.

➤ There are estimates that YouTube streams seven billion videos per month, and it is also now considered the number-two search engine, behind Google, for keyword searches.

➤ Do-it-yourself community-building network Ning claims to host 1 million communities. (Although this number is contested, the network is highly regarded as an easy way to launch, host, and cultivate custom social networks dedicated to relevant topics and companies.)

➤ Technorati tracks over 100 million blogs and indexes more than 1.5 million new blog posts in real time that introduce millions of readers to new blog and social media content.

■ GETTING OUT OF THE INBOX AND INTO SOCIAL NETWORKS

No matter how much time we spend trying to keep up with the barrage of never-ending mail in our inboxes, a Nielsen report claims that social networks and blogs have overtaken e-mail, and are now the fourth most popular online activity and growing.

While this data may change over time, the documented behavior affirms your hunch—social media is just getting started.

The Nielsen report ranked online activity as follows:

1. Searches

2. General interest portals and communities

3. Software

4. Member communities

5. E-mail

As software continues to move from hard drives to the cloud (which simply means online file and data storage and application servers), and portals and online software integrate social and collaboration features, social networking will only expand and start to rival the number-one-ranked search.

In fact, with the advent of Twitter Search, real-time search is becoming a cultural phenomenon for discovering information related to keywords as ranked by peers and time, as opposed to traditional results that are ranked and indexed by links and search engine optimization (SEO). As mentioned previously, YouTube is considered the second-most popular search engine, and Twitter and social network searches are well on their way to becoming strong alternatives to traditional search engines.

The Nielsen report "Global Faces and Networked Places"[3] analyzed data captured from December 2007 through December 2008 and revealed some very interesting statistics.

We learn in the report that two-thirds of the world's Internet population visits social networking or blogging sites—accounting for almost 10 percent of all Internet time spent. Time spent on social network sites is also expanding: Across the globe in 2008, activity in member communities accounted for 1 in every 15 online minutes and eventually grew to account for 1 in every 11.

While social networks initially appealed to younger audiences, they've become more mainstream with the passage of time. This shift has been driven primarily by Facebook, whose greatest growth has come from people aged 35 to 49 years of age (+24.1 million). Between December 2007 through December 2008, Facebook added almost twice as many 50- to 64-year-old visitors (+13.6 million) than it added under-18-year-old visitors (+7.3 million). Considering that Facebook started out as a service for university students, it is remarkable that almost one third of its global audience now falls within the 35 to 49 age group, and almost one quarter is over 50 years old.

Time spent on social networks and blogs is growing at over three times the rate of overall Internet growth.

The total amount spent online globally increased by 18 percent between December 2007 and December 2008. In the same period, however, the amount of time spent on member community sites rose by 63 percent to 45 billion minutes, and on Facebook by a massive 566 percent—from 3.1 billion to 20.5 billion minutes. Facebook has soared to become the ninth most popular brand online and now boasts the highest average time per person (3 hours 10 minutes) among the 75 most popular brands online worldwide.

In 2009 we witnessed a shift in market leadership as the seemingly invincible MySpace fell behind Facebook.

Facebook's sudden and sharp growth in 2008 and 2009 can be attributed to an organized and simple design, broad appeal, focus on activity, a supporting architecture and ecosystem for third-party applications, peer-to-peer activity influence, a sophisticated and simple system to trigger word-of-mouth and visitor engagement across social graphs, the ease of creating and promoting groups, fan pages, and events, and an ongoing focus on user privacy and user-generated governance that helps Facebook stay poignant and relevant amongst its users.

While reports are based on historical activity, we must also look to the future when preparing our social media strategies for programming, listening, and participating. For example, by the time this book is published, we'll finally have access to meaningful Twitter data and numbers. At this time, internal company projections estimate 1 billion users by 2013.

■ BUDGETS REDIRECTED TO SOCIAL MEDIA

Fueled by a combination of popularity, curiosity, necessity, strategy, and trendiness, marketers are embracing a new recipe that injects a proactive, social approach to outbound communications and engagement—with or without all of the answers before they jump in. This approach, while courageous, requires faith, conviction, and champions who don't necessarily have access to metrics and case studies at the sole proprietor, small and mid-sized business (SMB), and enterprise levels. Many of the most, and also least, effective campaigns are implemented as a method of learning. As we all know, some social media campaigns excel while others publicly flop, which fosters cynicism and fear of embracing a transparent form of open and public dialogue.

While dollars evaporate from traditional budgets previously earmarked for advertising, public relations, events, and other return-on-investment (ROI) programs, individuals recognize social media as a cost-efficient venue for maintaining visibility, especially when compared to falling completely off the radar screens of potential customers, stakeholders, and influencers.

■ THIS IS JUST BUSINESS (B2C AND B2B): FORRESTER RESEARCH

Forrester Research published a report entitled "Social Media Playtime Is Over"[4] that revealed that business-to-business (B2B) organizations were ready to increase marketing spending, especially in a market downturn.

Former Forrester analyst Jeremiah Owyang asked a direct question and the answers were incredibly telling: "Assuming that the economy is in recession in the next six months, how would you change your investment in social media overall?"

Only 5 percent responded that they would decrease spending in their social media ventures, indicating that only a minority of companies polled were using questionable methods that didn't make an impact. Forty-two percent would remain at the same funding level, which doesn't necessarily reveal how companies are practicing social media, if at all, compared to traditional efforts. Perhaps most notably, however, is that a massive 53 percent intended to increase their investment in social media during a recession.

This begs the question as to whether or not companies are embracing social media because they believe that communities can benefit from their direct participation and associated experience, or rather because social media is viewed as a lower-cost alternative to traditional marketing and advertising.

Be careful here, as you get what you pay for. You also earn the social capital that's commensurate with your company's investment of time, resources, and money.

■ MARKETINGSHERPA

MarketingSherpa also conducted research in a Social Media Marketing and PR Benchmark Survey fielded in December 2008. While it's an older study, remember that historical data increase relevance in establishing the case for social media over time.

According to MarketingSherpa, businesses across the board claim that they're embracing and practicing some form of social media in outbound marketing. Again, whether they're practicing effective, noteworthy, measurable, or even exemplary social initiatives is unclear. Yet, a round average of 80 percent reported that social media programs were indeed in effect.

Brand managers and the executives signing the paychecks continue to evaluate the effects of social media on everything including brand reputation, awareness, SEO, website traffic, leads, internal communications, and online sales. According to the MarketingSherpa study, social media had a positive impact, ranging from 50 percent to over 90 percent. Specifically, when social media is tied to influencing brand reputation, they are found to be 39 percent very effective and 53 percent somewhat effective. And when it comes to assessing the ability to increase brand awareness, 37 percent of companies concluded that social media is very effective and 54 percent attested that it was somewhat effective.

Social media was viewed as responsible for increasing website traffic, with 33 percent saying it was very effective and 55 percent acknowledging that it moved the need somewhat.

In lead generation and increasing online sales, businesses claimed that social media had a very noticeable impact at 17 percent and 13 percent respectively and were reasonably attributable to the bottom-line effects, with 48 percent and 41 percent respectively.

The study also revealed where consumers reported obtaining information regarding brands. Seventy percent consulted social communities and networks as their primary source of information, which notched higher than a company's own website. Online news and review sites ranked third and fourth. And after review, I would include wikis in the social communities and networks category, sending that number higher.

Many pundits have claimed that the benefits derived from implementing social media initiatives were clear in business to customer (B2C) cases, but wondered whether or not social media could help the B2B sector. As those who've worked in enterprise marketing or sales will resoundingly emphasize, B2B is driven by relationships, which is triggering the integration of social systems into customer relationship management (CRM). We will discuss the evolution of Social CRM in Chapter 23.

The study noted that sometimes the most effective social media tactics were also the least measurable and, contrarily, the activity behind the least effective programs was sometimes the easiest to measure. In many of the programs I work with today, the focus is on the ability to both implement effective programs and measure them specifically for each division they impact—from sales to service and marketing.

Responding to negative commentary posted online is not an exact science, nor can it be exactly duplicated from company to company. What's common however, is that listening and observing are the keys to learning.

The responses that MarketingSherpa captured are interesting and have most definitely changed over time, from companies reporting "not monitoring" and "monitoring, but not responding," to a majority reporting both "monitoring" and "responding."

MarketingSherpa sorted answers by SMBs with less than 500 employees and large businesses with 500 or more employees:

Only 26 percent of SMBs and 23 percent of SMEs and enterprise organizations stated that they don't monitor social media commentary. I can attest to this number dropping significantly over time.

Thirty-one percent of SMBs and 47 percent of larger businesses claimed that they monitor but don't respond externally. This too has changed, with companies engaging more in negative and neutral dialogue with every day that passes.

Twenty-seven percent of SMBs and 25 percent of bigger companies attempt to contact the commenter. These numbers have increased substantially as of the time of writing.

In many cases, there's merit to consumers' complaints and many times they require acknowledgment, response, and a commitment to fix things in order to improve a product or service. With the right counsel, more and more SMBs and enterprises will actively monitor comments and connect to customers in a public forum.

While numbers indicate that Social Media Marketing may, for now, be recession-proof, it is not idiot-proof. Engaging in transparent conversations in social networks to build brand-centric communities is meaningless without intelligence, sincerity, and a real-world business acumen that can tie participation to important business metrics.

Listening, observing, and learning are the keys to creating any informed social or traditional program that links insight to relevant and consequential outbound engagement.

Overall, this is exactly the level of detail that many brand, marketing, service, and public-relations professionals need to review in order to assess opportunities, risks, and benefits associated with the implementation of strategic and effective day-to-day engagement programs that are unique and tailored to each brand.

■ FACEBOOK ADVERTISING TO SURPASS MYSPACE BY 2011

MySpace has been losing "face" over the course of the last few years. With diminished traffic and attention as well as shifts in management and reductions in staff, MySpace is not only a place for friends, but also a place for skeptics.

According to a Compete.com report in July 2009, Facebook received 122,559,672 unique visits in June 2009—twice the number of rival MySpace, which realized only 60,973,908 unique visitors. In year-over-year comparisons, Facebook volume skyrocketed with 248.17 percent while MySpace slightly recoiled, down 5.65 percent. The good news for both networks is that June represented positive growth over the previous month, with Facebook visits growing by 8.45 percent and MySpace experiencing a bump of 7.19 percent.

Not only has Facebook surpassed MySpace in traffic, according to eMarketer,[5] but it also appears primed to overtake the once dominant network in ad revenue as well. Social media, and the Web in general, presents an unsteady landscape tied directly to the popularity, trendiness, and momentum of any given network at any given moment in time.

So, eMarketer estimates that U.S. spending at MySpace fell 15 percent to $495 million in 2009 from $585 million in 2008. In contrast, Facebook growth was estimated to be from $210 million in 2008 to $230 million in 2009.

After reviewing the numbers, an interesting observation surfaced. Advertising spending on Facebook and MySpace alone account for twice the total advertising dollars going to all other networks combined. Also, widgets and applications continue to grow in popularity, with funding up 6.1 percent from 40 million in 2008 to $70 million in 2009.

Even though Facebook 2009 estimates were roughly 40 percent of MySpace revenue, Debra Aho Williamson, eMarketer senior analyst and author of the new report, *Social Network Ad Spending: A Brighter Outlook Next Year*, expects Facebook to surpass MySpace revenues by 2011: "Facebook, once a distant second to MySpace, has outperformed its rival in nearly every measure of usage—and is on track to surpass MySpace in ad spending by 2011."

Williamson also predicted a brighter future for advertising spending on social networking: "The expected rebound in spending will come as more companies focus on creating and implementing an overall social marketing strategy. And it is a clear indication that the experimental phase of social network marketing is finally drawing to an end."

Indeed, 2009 painted a bleak picture, as spending was down an estimated 3 percent. The good news is that according to eMarketer, budgets will grow by 13.2 percent in 2010 and 8.2 percent in 2011.

It's just a matter of time until Twitter and other social networks change the distribution of advertising funds and which networks they are directed toward.

■ THE DECLINE OF TRADITIONAL ADVERTISING AND THE RISE OF "UNMARKETING"

A Forrester Research report published in 2009 provided a five-year forecast[6] that estimated interactive marketing spending from 2009 to 2014. The report predicts that interactive marketing in the United States will near $55 billion, will represent 21 percent of all marketing spending by 2014, and will include search marketing, display advertising, email marketing, social media, and mobile marketing. More significantly, however, overall advertising in traditional media will continue to decline in favor of less expensive, more effective interactive tools and services.

Forrester analyst Shar VanBoskirk alerts marketing and media professionals with a dire warning: "The cannibalization of traditional media will bring about a decline in overall advertising budgets, death to obsolete agencies, a publisher awakening, and a new identity for Yahoo!."

The majority of the marketing/advertising budget appears to be earmarked for search marketing, even though the search landscape is rapidly evolving to include real-time and social updates, and community and micronetworks. As a marketing professional seeking to tap into spending and visibility trends, take notice of activity in Mobile and social media over the next five years.

Mobile devices not only extend the collaboration and productivity capabilities that used to tether us to fixed locations, they also bring the rise of new, highly interactive mobile platforms and networks that will increasingly capture our attention and time. Spending growth over the next five years is compounded at 27 percent, which makes it the second most notable growth factor behind social media with $1,274 (in millions) expected to fund mobile programs in 2014.

Social media spending will increase to $3,113 (in millions) in 2014 from $716 in 2009, representing a compound annual growth rate of 34 percent—the highest percentage gain in the marketing mix. This spending activity also ranks it as the third most prominent program behind search marketing and display advertising.

Dollars that are moving away from traditional advertising are now allocated towards "unmarketing" activities that will earn stature and credibility and ultimately empower a more confident group of influential advocates through investments in innovation, research, customer services, customer experiences, and marketing-specific technology and IT staff.

■ PEOPLE INFLUENCE BUYING DECISIONS, ONLINE AND OFFLINE

Forget for a moment that an older 2008 Forrester Research study[7] suggested that only 16 percent of consumers found corporate blogs believable. This finding is most likely tied to the impressions consumers have received from years of exposure to traditional corporate marketing. In order to successfully capture mind-share and earn trust, we have to reverse the activities that have contributed to this negative perception held by consumers.

In 2009, Forrester released a survey that linked business buyers and their process of researching solutions to social media. The research group interviewed business buyers to learn about their social activity—in this case, more than 1,200 technology buyers in the United States, Canada, France, Germany, and the United Kingdom with 100 employees or more in seven major industries.

According to the responses, social media again proved to extend beyond consumers and B2C. In the real world of business-to-business research, analysis, and decisions, the Forrester data points to peer-to-peer influence and collaboration in social networks and blogs:

➤ Sixty-nine percent are "Spectators"—this group reads blogs, watches user-generated videos, and participates in other social media for business purposes.

➤ Thirty-seven percent are "Critics"—they contribute comments or react to content they see in social formats.

➤ Twenty-nine percent are "Collectors"—they use social technology to collect information and stay on top of trends.

➤ Twenty-nine percent are "Joiners" who participate in social networks. Only 5 percent are "Inactives," or nonparticipants.

This data demonstrates that social media is begetting trust as reinforced through genuine, sincere, and informative interaction between consumers, stakeholders, and brands.

■ THE WORLD'S BECOMING A MUCH SMALLER PLACE

Global use of social networks initially supported and championed the local player. However, as time progressed, certain networks garnered significant traction worldwide—connecting people not only in their respective countries, but also with like-minded individuals and those who share common interests and passions all over the world.

The world became a much smaller place as social networks began to erase borders, with the potential of creating a new genre of global citizens.

Facebook continues its global dominance in networking people in the United States and around the world. In 2009, it jumped from 200 million to 350 million users, and by the time you read this book, it may have already surpassed 400 million.

Two hundred and fifty million users is a remarkable landmark. Yet it's only a small slice of the global market. There's much more room for growth, innovation, and, more importantly, connectivity. Geographic marketing is merging with psychographic marketing. Through social networking, we can traverse borders to reach people bound by interests, without being limited by the traditional demographic blinders that we wore for so many years.

However, Facebook faces formidable competition in the countries where home-based incumbents maintain a dominant user-base or market position. As a result, Facebook is not a company's only option for reaching potential customers. In fact, to truly reach global audiences in the digital neighborhoods where they dwell, you many need to incorporate a multinetwork outreach and campaign strategy.

In China, the QQ instant messaging/social network boasts an astounding 300 million users. Russia's Facebook clone, Vkontakte, hosts a remarkable 38 million users.

In countries around the world, some local players still maintain a home field advantage:[8]

Germany: Studiverzeichnis.

Holland: Hyves.nl.

Peru (and other South American countries) and Mexico: Hi5 (Hi5 also leads in Romania and Portugal).

Argentina: Sonico (Facebook is leading, however).

India, Estonia and Brazil: Orkut.

Lithuania: One.lt.

Ukraine and Russia: Vkontakte.

Georgia, Uzbekistan, and Armenia: OdnoKlassniki.

Hungary: Iwiw.

China: QQ, Xaonei, and Kaixin01.

Japan: Mixi.

The Philippines: Friendster.

South Korea: Cyworld.

Taiwan: Wretch.

When we look at the top three social networks by country, we can observe that there are multiple avenues for reaching our target audiences. Therefore, a bit of anthropological fieldwork is necessary to fine-tune our outreach (A full list of networks by country is included at the end of the book):

Australia: Facebook, MySpace, Twitter.

Canada: Facebook, MySpace, Flickr.

China: QQ, Xiaonei, 51.

France: Facebook, Skyrock, MySpace.

Germany: Facebook, StudiVZ, MySpace.

India: Facebook, Orkut, Hi5 (Twitter is a close fourth).

Italy: Facebook, Netlog, Badoo.

Russia: VKontakte, Odnoklassniki, Mail.ru-My World.

Spain: Facebook, Tuenti, Fotolog.

United Kingdom: Facebook, Bebo, MySpace.

United States: Facebook, MySpace, Twitter.

■ NEW MEDIA IS A MOVING TARGET: HISTORY VERSUS SOCIOLOGY

As consumers, we are continually distracted as we're introduced to new content, people, networks, and shiny new applications. As we witnessed with the change in dominance from MySpace to Facebook, even the most popular communities are not immune to shifts in attention.

If you subscribe to Zuckerberg's Law, then you believe that people will share twice as much information online year after year. This idea suggests that as we embrace the Social Web as a greater society, our comfort levels will ease and succumb to the activity of our peers, encouraging us to share increasing volumes of personal and professional content online. But this premise isn't relegated to Facebook alone; it can hold true for all social networks.

We have yet to truly experience mobile networking or find the killer application for the living room. Remember that thing called a TV?

Competition for our attention is escalating and it's just a matter of time until our experimentation officially leads to distributed and uncommitted presences and attention. Our attention is demanded in so many different directions and ways that our focus is both diminishing and extending during this period of increasingly socialized interactivity. How we adopt, communicate, share, discover, and observe within social networks is still in a process of definition and documentation. Much of this is so new, we have yet to see the balance, individual adoption, sustainable activity, and long-term effects.

The excitement of having tools that allow us to instantly connect with people who share passions, interests, and contacts all over the world, combined with the psychological impact of this new genre of personal "micro" fame, is seductive, but not necessarily in line with how we will eventually fold these tools and ensuing behavior into our day-to-day patterns.

The reality is that our friends and networks of influence determine our location and participation. This is a competition not for popularity, but for you, your time, and your loyalty.

This is indeed, a very Social Economy.

■ THE DEMOCRATIZATION AND SOCIALIZATION OF BRANDED MEDIA

The democratization of content will only continue to further our global society, transforming traditional media and broadcast industries while also creating new and powerful platforms for citizens with unique perspectives and ideas to cultivate global audiences. And every business, from mainstream brands to those run by everyday people, will embrace social strategies to reach existing and potential customers and enthusiasts and demonstrate value, solutions, and expertise.

This requires dedication, practice, and perhaps, most notably, an open mind and the patience to absorb a virtual firehose of streaming information.

What you know today is quickly being leveled across an industry of people who are equally engaged and immersed—and thus becoming just as, if not more, knowledgeable than you. While new media is a great equalizer, it is also a source of motivation and inspiration to aspiring and ambitious students and professionals.

As a thought leader, you hold a power that most don't yet realize. You have influential people who follow and listen to you. This dynamic establishes authority and wields influence to further teach and change. You have the experience to create more effective teams that will work together to build an adaptive, customer-focused, and market-relevant organization. But you ... we ... are still learning. And we must practice what we learn in order to gain proficiency. We need to make mistakes, experience triumphs, and observe when, why, and how we move the corporate needle, and galvanize communities through our work.

Businesses spanning every industry will empower employees to embrace the public through real-world and online interactions, requiring a renewed sense of adeptness, passion, and commitment. It's already underway and will one day simply become a function of most roles within an organization.

Today's experimentation with socialized marketing will generate patterns, activity, results, and behavior that will serve as legitimate benchmarks for measuring metrics and ROI. It all starts with studying Web analytics and the art and science of measuring, monitoring, and improving online experiences and activity. In a genre of social proficiency, we will leverage the insight gleaned from analyzing online events to develop more meaningful and compelling engagement and participation initiatives, as well as transform our organization into one that can adapt to the real-world needs and wants of customers.

We need to be a genuine resource to the people who define the communities that are important to us. As networks become densely populated and new communities arise and thrive, we're experiencing a fundamental shift in content creation, distribution, and consumption—thus creating an active and participatory media-savvy society that is inspiring and seeding a more literate and enlightened generation.

We have to relinquish any sense of entitlement we've earned or believe we've achieved over the years as the Social Web and the impending semantic Web (or, as Tim O'Reilly refers to it, "web squared") continues to advance.

Lead by example.

Embrace those who are learning along with you.

Answer your own questions.

We are all in this together, and truthfully, we could be so much more than we are today. Let's embody the change we wish to inspire and become the experts we seek to guide us.

You are part of a new generation that is humanizing the brands you represent and championing internal transformation to reshape internal business dynamics and policies to establish, maintain, and cultivate loyalty and relationships with the people and influencers who define your markets. And, at the same time, the more you genuinely engage, create compelling and helpful content, and share and aggregate valuable information, you too will become a respected, trusted, and influential resource to your company and outside communities.

Part

II

Forever Students
of New Media

Chapter 3

The New Media University

Social Media 101

We are forever students of new media. While we learn through everything we read and practice, we should never strive to master something that evolves much faster than our ability to fully grasp its lessons, benefits, insights, and pitfalls. In the process, we learn a bit more about ourselves and our true potential.

For those versed in social media and the tools that connect us to those we wish to reach, enjoy this chance to hit "ctrl-alt-del" and restart with a fresh perspective. For those new to the socialization of media and influence, please take your time here. This is where everything begins.

Social media is a great equalizer and we share the desire and necessity to establish authority in order to help those around us.

■ INTEGRATED MARKETING: THE TOOLS

The future of today's marketing integrates traditional media with social media elements intended to impact and renovate each and every department within the organization, from service to marketing to PR, IR, and HR to sales and product development.

We're simply becoming aware of our markets, the people who define them, and our place within each community. It is mandatory and reviving a ritual of becoming socially adept.

While new media will always be "new," the principles that govern behavior, interaction, and support remain constant. They're simply interpreted differently, based on intentions, objectives, and varying levels of customer empathy or ignorance. Social media is the latest in a series of chapters that determine the course of new media. The tools described in this book will change over time and that's why they're just the tools of the trade—right now. They help us connect with people. Over time, they'll help us connect more effectively. They'll help us identify the right people and spark communities based on an understanding of what we represent and what we're looking to accomplish. The Web is becoming a lot smarter and will eventually start to help us come together as peers to collaborate and innovate.

The landscape of current social tools and networks is vast. Let's open up the toolbox in order to understand what's in it and why each tool exists, so that we can determine which tools make sense to place back in the toolbox that we will carry with us.

These tools include some that you know and others that you may not. They're listed by categories for a quick view and later we'll dive deeper into each.

The basic toolbox is organized by categories and instruments:

Blogs
WordPress
Blogger
Typepad
MovableType
Social networks
Facebook
MySpace
Hi5
Orkut
Friendster
Do-it-yourself and white label social networks
Ning (DIY)
Cisco EOS
Leverage Software
KickApps
Jive
Crowdvine (DIY)
Blog communities
Vox
BlogCatalog
MyBlogLog
Bloglines
Blogged
B5Media

Microcommunities
Twitter
FriendFeed
Identi.ca
Plurk
Yammer
Jaiku
Microblogs
Tumblr
Posterous
Micromedia (Subset of microcommunities, driven by multimedia)
12 seconds
Seesmic
Utterli
Twitvid
Twitpic
Lifestreams (aggregated activity)
SocialThing
AOL IM with streaming
Lifestream.fm

Forums
  Grouply
  Google Groups
  Yahoo! Groups
  Lefora (DIY)
  Yahoo! Answers
  Mahalo Answers
  Tangler (DIY)
Business networking
  LinkedIn
  Plaxo
Niche-working
  Magnify.net
  CrowdSpring
  TripIt
  TrustedOpinion
  Diddit
Reviews and ratings
  Yelp
  Epinions
Location
  Loopt
  FourSquare
  Google Latitude
  BrightKite
Video
  YouTube
  Metacafe
  Vimeo
  Blip.tv
  Viddler
Customer Service
  GetSatisfaction
  Uservoice
Documents/content
  Scribd
  Docstoc
  Slideshare
Wikis
  SocialText
  Wik.is
  Wikia
  PBWiki

Video: episodic or livecasting
  Veodia (corporate platform)
  Kyte (white label networks)
  Justin.tv
  Blog.tv
  Mogulus
  ustream.tv
Pictures
  Flickr
  PhotoBucket
  SmugMug
  Picasa
Social bookmarks
  Diigo
  Delicious
  StumbleUpon
  Magnolia
  MisterWong
  Evernote
Comment and reputation
  Disqus
  BackType
  JS-Kit
  Intense Debate
Wisdom of the crowds
  Wikipedia
  Mahalo
  NowPublic
  Fotopedia
  Spock
  About.com
Crowdsourced news
  Digg
  Mixx
  Reddit
  Newsvine
  Yahoo! Buzz
Audio livecasting and podcasting
  BlogTalkRadio
  iTunes
  Podcastalley
  Talkshoe

The social inbox
Xoopit (Now part of Yahoo!)
cc:Betty
Xobni

Social CRM
Bantam
SalesForce
ToucanCRM

Attention/communications dashboards
PeopleBrowsr
GoogleWave
Collecta
Tweetdeck
Seesmic Desktop

For a complete list of up-to-date tools and networks, please visit www.theconversationprism.com.

As you participate in each of these new communities, the key ingredients to warranting attention are sincerity, insightfulness, and empathy. Realize that whatever you do, it's less about the company, per se, and more about how your customers can succeed in their business or how people can simply improve their personal lives. What can they do now that they couldn't do before speaking with you?

They learn.

You learn.

It's about building a community around them—literally. The rest is just defined by the tools to facilitate the conversation.

With everything you do in social media, you must participate in order to build bridges that connect customers, prospects, peers, tastemakers, and influencers with the people who represent the company. People don't participate in conversations with brands; they converse with the people who are the ambassadors of the brands.

■ DEFINING SOCIAL MEDIA

Social media is many things to many people and represents much more than technology. It represents a societal renaissance that spawned a unique and vibrant ecosystem supported by flourishing cultures and lifestyles.

Social media is . . .

- ➤ A platform for the socialization of media.
- ➤ The online tools that facilitate conversations.
- ➤ Connections between friends, peers, and influencers.
- ➤ Collaborations.
- ➤ The redistribution of influence.

➤ A call for humanizing personas and audiences, and the stories that link them together.

➤ Compassionate.

➤ Words, pictures, video, chatter, audio, and also experiences, observations, opinions, news, and insights.

➤ An opportunity and a privilege.

When the original definition for social media was submitted to Wikipedia in 2006, it was, and still is, incomplete, inclusive, and worse, confusing. I've attempted to contribute to a more useful portrayal of social media over the years, only to find my words edited, revised, or deleted by scores of experts. I gave up and instead opted to write blogposts, publish ebooks, and write printed books to help clarify what social media is and isn't.

As I defined it several years ago with the help of Chris Shipley, Stowe Boyd, Chris Heuer, and Robert Scoble, among many others....

Social media is any tool or service that uses the Internet to facilitate conversations.

Of course, a longer version is always helpful.

Social media is the democratization of information, transforming people from content readers into publishers. It is the shift from a broadcast mechanism, one-to-many, to a many-to-many model, rooted in conversations between authors, people, and peers.

Social media is one chapter in the evolution of new media. Let's consider its affect on terminology.

■ WHEN WORDS LOSE THEIR MEANING

This is a subject that is garnering much of my attention and contemplation as the terminology that orbits the social media universe is in danger of spinning off course and into a black hole of obscurity.

We stand at a crossroads where the language of social media either matures and develops or depreciates and decays. As with anything, words become meaningless if overused and underpracticed. The words that appear in a glossary, specifically those used to capture and define the essence of social media and the tenets of successful engagement, education, and community building, are often misused, misinterpreted, undervalued, or thrown around as bragging rights.

Some of the words on the endangered species list include:

Transparency

Conversation/dialogue

Listening

Relationships

Being yourself/Being human

Engagement

Viral

Authenticity

We must hold these words and their meanings sacred to create programs that exude integrity, instill advocacy, and earn trust. Conceived or devised in any other way, our efforts may lead to misperceptions that can cause angst and backlash within important communities, regardless of intent.

Authenticity and transparency are the minimum requirements in any exchange, online and in the real world. If authority, trust, and loyalty are what we strive for, then authenticity and transparency do not, in or of themselves, attain our goals. Authority, trust, loyalty, and their ability to inspire activity are earned gradually through every exchange where those involved are informed as a result of their participation.

Relevant information, consistency, and insight are the attributes of those who build credibility among their peers. The listening that identifies relevant dialogue online and the transparency that facilitates authentic conversations by being humanly accessible is not the formula for sparking relationships that create communities that help spread our messages virally.

The essence and usefulness of each important and distinct word is slowly migrating into a hollow of obsolescence as we attach them to all things social media, without stopping to truly reflect on and observe their intent, definition, weight, and opportunity.

Before we go astray, it's now imperative to associate these words with sincerity, purpose, and action. It's not just a matter of authenticity versus authority, nor is it a race to listen and forge relationships by engaging through transparency. It's about transcending the ideas behind the words into something of significance, trustworthiness, education, and remembrance.

By way of illustration, what if we considered the differences between the following terms:

Believability versus transparency

Contribution versus engagement

Participation versus conversation

Hearing versus listening

Collaboration versus relationships

Empathy versus being human

Hearing, identified as the capability to hear, is much different from actually listening to what someone has to say, how they got to where they are, and where they need to go. Listening can have a profound affect on how we improve or evolve our services or infrastructure.

Transparency is openness, but it's irrelevant without a cause to espouse or empathy with the consumer.

Authenticity is genuine, but people can be authentically misinformed and not even know it. Being yourself may not be enough to satisfy all parties and, no matter how amazing you are, if your personality and communication skills do not connect people to the personality of the company or brand you represent, missed connections become endemic. Intentions don't necessarily count. Purpose and mission must be defined in order to impart the intended perception and spark future activity.

Conversations are meaningless without substance, insight, collaboration, or a helpful exchange that offers mutual satisfaction.

It's not conversations that build relationships and spark word-of-mouth. Interaction, collaboration, and consistency help us build meaningful interactions that deliver value to contributors. It's how we earn trust and loyalty and establish significance that defines our stature and determines our diagnosis for just how contagious we are.

Purpose, empathy, and authority are, in fact, interrelated and entwined.

Perhaps what we learn is that authenticity + wisdom + engagement + reflection + adaptation + participation = trust, loyalty, and authority.

Transparency and objectivity meets purpose and contribution.

Chapter 4

The New Media University

Social Media 201

As we advance our knowledge of New Media, its implications and opportunities, we realize just how lucky we are to live in the time of the "next" Web.

At this stage, we'll review the platforms and tools that define the terrain of the Social Web so that we may engineer and build the roads, highways, bridges, and necessary constructs of communications, community development, and good will.

But before we jump in, I'd like to introduce a concept to you—one that will make more sense as you scale your socialized communications efforts.

Building and organizing a social media program can be incredibly powerful. As people become increasingly connected and form relationships rooted in passions, alliances, and circumstances, distinct communities emerge and evolve. And, over time, these communities expand, contract, and shift as they foster and steer dialogue and behavior. Contextual networks and the social tools that bind them intrinsically emerge as the communications channels that facilitate interaction and influence.

These channels distribute information to people when and how they choose to receive, process, share, and interact with them.

You, me . . . we become media.

While once out of reach for most businesses over the years, we now effectively possess the ability to transform any brand of any size into an independent media publishing, broadcasting, and service organization.

The implications are profound. We have the power and capacity to reach people far beyond our local television and radio broadcasts and even beyond those of the most prestigious national media empires.

The difference is that this reach is not prescribed; it must be earned.

Unlike traditional broadcast mechanisms, information flows both ways; whether we choose to ignore it or embrace it, this is our choice— a choice that carries great responsibility and alternate outcomes.

We contribute to our perception through absence and participation.

We contribute to our presence.

We define our contributions and benevolence.

We are the architects who are drafting the blueprint for a more efficient and useful bridge between our story and the people who benefit from it.

■ BLOGS

No matter what we think we know about blogs, there's always something new to learn. Let's start with some interesting points of observation and reality in order to frame blogs in a proper setting.

Forrester Research published a report shockingly entitled "Time to Rethink Your Corporate Blogging Ideas."[1] To the surprise of many, it placed corporate blogs at the bottom of the credibility list. According to the study, only 16 percent of online consumers who read corporate blogs admitted to trusting them. As such, blogs ranked lower in trustworthiness than every other form of content in Forrester's list of corporate marketing and media tools, even below broadcast and print media, direct mail, and e-mail.

However, don't let this deter you from starting or further developing your blog. The primary reason for the unpopularity of a corporate blog is directly attributable to the wariness that consumers have acquired through years of being barraged by propaganda, publicity, and hype. Many companies unfortunately have used the blog as yet another vehicle to push promotion over value. It's not a place to publish press releases, nor is it intended to serve as a stepchild of service or marketing.

Blogs are completely ineffective and only contribute to consumers' leeriness when used as a corporate platform for marketing, schilling, pitching, or broadcasting promotional messages.

The lack of seriousness and understanding toward blogs has unfortunately caused reverberating effects that are difficult to overcome. With that said, you are not burdened with the responsibility of transforming an entire industry, nor the perceptions associated with it. Your responsibility is to increase the interaction and collaboration between you and your peers, customers, and prospects. Your priority is increasing your value to the communities that impact your bottom line, and blogs are an important host and library for your knowledge base. The best corporate blogs are genuine and designed to help people, by becoming an industry resource through thought leadership, unquestionable passion, and solutions for the real-world pains of the marketplace.

The blog is your hub for demonstrating expertise, sharing vision, listening to and responding to customers, communicating progress, curating relevant market and trend information, and hosting dialogues to further the company's values and principles. It requires continuity, cadence, and a voice that readers can connect with.

What's the cause?

What's the intent?

How can we fill a void and, more importantly, how can we help solve problems?

What should readers take away from the blog?

Why should anyone link back to the blog?

Of all the blogs in the world, some of the most popular are, in fact, company blogs. Google, 37Signals, FreshBooks, and Dell are among the most read and linked-to blogs in the blogosphere, and for good reason. They embody all of the points above. They live and breathe the human persona of the brand that they've created and have emerged as a frequented and must-stop destination for consumers seeking information, direction, discourse, and recognition.

It's important to point out that even to this day, executives and marketers question the efficiency and potential of blogs—even in the face of tangible evidence that proves and outlines its upside potential. Many believe that their time is better spent elsewhere and that finding contributors for regular, consistent, and insightful posts can become an unceasing chore.

One solution resides in the outsourcing of post-generation tasks to outside experts who will gladly contribute unbiased, valuable, and interesting content for a price. Depending on the individual, posts can range from $25 to hundreds of dollars per post.

Initially, marketers shied away from ghostwritten posts, where an uncredited, paid writer posts content under someone else's byline. Instead, communication and marketing professionals asked, or begged, for the participation of the influential voices of important individuals within the business, requesting them to blog as often as possible. While this is important and necessary in the art of blogging, it is not realistic to expect these busy and oft-preoccupied business leaders to assume the role of blogger. However, it is rational, and effective, to encourage infrequent, yet regularly scheduled, posts from them. There's a reason why these people are leading the company, and their vision and experiences must receive attention in the most prominent platform for sharing that company voice and persona—the blog.

It's not only contract bloggers who represent a solution for filling the editorial calendar in between executive posts—other employees and outside enthusiasts and customers are also willing to contribute. They just need direction, deadlines, and a framework. Many are more than capable of interviewing key executives, customers, partners, and influencers to feature their visions, experiences, and wisdom, without requiring them to directly write for the blog.

Everything must start with a plan, however.

Blogging for the sake of blogging, even with the best of intentions, is meaningless if the internal team cannot communicate an organized infrastructure. Essentially, someone must serve as an editor in chief for the blog or blog network. Someone must preside over the channel in order to marshal the brand and ensure integrity. In the models where multiple networks exist—for example, across product or business divisions—multiple editors must officiate the content for their dedicated channel, ultimately reporting to an editor in chief. For those organizations where tens, hundreds, or thousands of corporate-run or endorsed blogs exist, guidelines, best practices, standards, rewards, and consequences are not optional. They must exist and receive attention and governance. Otherwise, social chaos ensues, resulting in brand dilution and market confusion.

The challenges also lie outside the process of creating and publishing content. This is true for any form of social networking.

Nothing happens simply because you build a blog and publish a post. The delusions of grandeur or the fundamentally misunderstandings of how people discover, respond to, and share information through blog sites leads to disappointment, and can cause the early termination of truly promising participation strategies.

Just because we host a grand opening doesn't necessarily assure or imply that we will host any guests.

There is an element of content promotion and marketing that is usually understated and neglected—mostly due to the lack of awareness or unfamiliarity with the processes. However, it crosses over into ignorance when programs are disparaged or killed prematurely.

The truth is that everything related to content production, from blogs to podcasts to tweets, requires the active promotion of that content outside of your domain. Again, using the bridging metaphor, you must hand-deliver related information to those seeking it through unobtrusive, empathetic, and cooperative means.

With every link outward, every tweet back, every e-mail, and every comment in other forums, we point people back to our work, not simply because we published something, but in view of the fact that we mindfully contributed value and insight and were prepared to respond.

Yes, comments on other blogs are a form of both participation and "unmarketing." Make sure to pay attention to relevant posts around the blogosphere and contribute relevant comments both on your blog and elsewhere. Some of the best conversations take place in the comments section, as people react to what you wrote, as well as the feedback from their peers.

The right comments boost visibility and contribute to a resume of experience and prowess.

Services such as BackType offer a window into comments across the entire blogosphere. It's a search engine for keywords and names, specifically in the comments sections of blogs. In contrast, blog search engines scour only the posts, but do not dive into the strings of conversations that transpire in the comments sections. BackType and new comment- and reputation-tracking systems that are integrated into blog platforms can say more about you than you imagine. These services align the comments that are strewn across the hundreds of thousands of (legitimate) blogs.

As you blog, lead, or contribute to the blogging initiatives, make sure to link to all channels of influence each and every time they share something of significance—even if it's an older entry. This will send trackbacks to any outside blog post that may have inspired your post(s) and thus builds tunnels between the blogs, allowing new readers to discover your content.

Extend your knowledge and acumen outside of your domain and into the online provinces that host and promote discussions that orbit your entity. Quite simply said, go where your customers are and not where they aren't. Give them something to read. Give them something to share. Give them reasons to respond.

Create a blogroll and link out to influential voices on the Web, whether they're reporters, bloggers, customers, analysts, or just excellent resources for inspiration and intelligence.

■ BLOG EXAMPLE: SOUTHWEST AIRLINES AND DELL

Southwest Airline's blog (www.blogsouthwest.com), playfully named "Nuts about Southwest," keeps in line with the company's "Fun-LUVing" attitude. The site informs, with posts dedicated to the latest service changes or updates on its bid for Frontier Airlines. It entertains, such as by covering the wedding of two Southwest frequent flyers who prominently displayed Southwest peanuts packages at each table. And most importantly, the site aims to build a personal relationship between Southwest employees and customers. The blog extends beyond standard text posts to include multimedia. The page incorporates images; links to the Southwest Flickr group, an employee video blog; and also encourages user participation through ratings, polls, comments, and photo/video sharing.

In another example, Dell launched its blog, Direct2Dell, in July 2006, to engage customers, open up the lines of communication, and repair its reputation after dealing with a tarnished image and a firestorm of criticisms across the blogosphere. And the strategy is working. In Jeff Jarvis's *BusinessWeek* article in 2007,[2] it was reported that negative blog posts about Dell dropped from 49 percent to 22 percent.

Dell has participated openly and honestly—even posting photos of one of its exploded laptops on the blog. And the company launched IdeaStorm.com to solicit customer's suggestions, comments, and complaints. There's even been evidence that community feedback has driven product development at Dell (see http://is.gd/1YCUe).

■ PODCASTS

Podcasts are a powerful and portable way to reach people who prefer audio as a means of education, intellectual stimulation, or entertainment.

Podcasts are DIY-easy and can provide a world of value to customers, peers, and influencers. Not only are podcasts portable, they're embeddable and shareable in websites and blog posts, are promotable just about anywhere to anyone looking for insight, and are distributed by Apple iTunes, which provides access to millions of potential users worldwide. The tools for recording, editing, and publishing podcasts are increasingly affordable and readily available from computer-based audio tools to handheld recording gadgets—making it practically a no-brainer to at least experiment with this medium.

And there's reason to pay attention and speak up. In 2009, Edison Research published a joint study with Arbitron that documented a steady and unrelenting growth for the podcast audience. From 2008 to 2009, consumers grew from 18 percent of all Americans to 22 percent. Americans "aware" of audio podcasts also rose from 37 percent in 2008 to 43 percent in 2009.

The following list comes from Edison's study, "The Infinite Dial":[3]

➤ **Social Networking.** Listeners to online radio are more likely to have a profile on a social networking site (like MySpace,

Facebook, or even LinkedIn), 54 percent compared to 34 percent who have a social network presence in the general population.

➤ **Internet Video.** Internet video consumption exploded last year, with approximately 69 million, or 27 percent of people, watching online video sometime in the past week. That figure is up from 18 percent in 2008.

➤ **Portable Media Players.** More than four in ten people (42 percent) own an iPod, iPhone, or other kind of portable media/mp3 player, and among the 12- to 44-year-old crowd, that percentage jumps to above 50 percent. The "key radio demographic" of 35- to 54-year-olds is becoming more frequent among online radio listeners.

➤ **Podcast Audience.** Forty-three percent of Americans are aware of podcasts, up from 37 percent in 2008. Twenty-two percent of Americans have listened to a podcast (up from 18 percent in 2008), and approximately 27 million (or 11 percent) have listened to one in the past month (up from 9 percent last year).

Podcast content can focus on a variety of programming and can include shows dedicated to company milestones, industry trends and challenges, executive interviews, customer success stories, how-to instructions, and anything else in between.

■ PODCAST EXAMPLES: FIDELITY INVESTMENTS AND SONY ERICSSON

Financial services provider Fidelity Investments offers its clients and the general public free podcasts at Fidelity Podcasts. Current and interested investors can listen to interviews with Fidelity mutual-fund portfolio managers as they share investment strategies, expectations, and market analysis. No doubt this value-adding information keeps Fidelity in the spotlight for investors and helps establish their authority (see http://is.gd/1YBUF).

■ WIKIS

Wikis, a name that comes from the Hawaiian phrase "wiki wiki," meaning "really fast," are among the most efficient tools for tapping the wisdom of the crowds wherever ideas, information, directions and instructions, product or experiential feedback, brainstorming, process/event management, and myriad other applications are requested. In fact, one of the most successful and influential websites in existence is a wiki. You probably know it better as Wikipedia.

Wikis are designed to allow site visitors to add, edit, update, and amend information through any Web browser. They invite and promote collaboration among employees, as well as consumers and influencers.

Wikis are important to facilitate collaboration in a friendlier, more socially focused content creation and management system. It's not just about teams and document management or collaboration around a particular topic. Wikis can provide a vibrant forum for inviting content and suggestions from customers and partners to further ideas and dialog in an ongoing, trackable, scalable, and measurable fashion.

Wiki software can run on any Web server, to host custom wiki pages as a stand-alone destination or as an extension to your website. Third-party wiki platforms are also widely available if you choose to host a wiki outside of your domain. URLs can still be customized and simply point to a different location.

Wikipedia entries regarding your company and market are highly influential to visitors who visit those pages. The Google page-rank function is incredibly strong in Wikipedia, and in most cases the leading result for any search in Google will direct you to the corresponding page in Wikipedia.

I've worked with several influential and famous people who did not appreciate the user-generated content associated with their Wikipedia entries and tried, numerously and unsuccessfully, to edit them directly or through the help of employees and outside experts. Their edits always reverted back to the previous version. Wikipedia operates on an earned trust and credibility system where accredited editors outrank everyday users. Find an expert to help you before you inadvertently lock up the page, which occurs when there are too many attempts to change it.

■ WIKI EXAMPLE: ORACLE

Oracle launched its official public Oracle Wiki back in 2007. Designed for both employees and nonemployees (the main page bears the message "Oracle employees, this is not an internal site!"), the wiki is a place where members of the Oracle community can collaborate and share content on Oracle-related subjects—including installation guides, technical tips, and project documentation.

The Oracle Wiki presents an interesting example for those companies grappling with the loss of control in the very public and transparent world of social media. While the Wiki FAQs state that the site belongs to the community, Oracle (like Microsoft and others) has chosen to play the role of active moderator. The company has been criticized for removing negative statements about its products (which they claimed violated the terms of use). Of course, unlike the true community-driven Wikipedia, corporate wiki owners always have a choice of when and how to moderate content on their site. In Oracle's case, they may have wanted to prevent damaging material from reaching their competitors—yet in the process of being careful and calculated, they run the risk of public backlash against perceived censorship and loss of goodwill in the community (see http://wiki.oracle.com).

■ VIRTUAL WORLDS

Virtual worlds encompass a 3D computer environment in which users are represented on screen as themselves or as made-up characters and interact in real time with other users. Multiuser online games (MMOGs) and virtual worlds such as Second Life are examples.[4]

In 2007 to 2008, many brands and companies flocked to Second Life to build a virtual presence, a trend that spiked and then experienced a backlash and ultimately lost a large percentage of users. By mid-2009, virtual worlds were realizing a comeback of sorts. In July 2009, virtual worlds consultancy firm KZero Worldswide (www.kzero.co.uk) reported that membership of virtual worlds grew by 39 percent in the second quarter of 2009 to an estimated 579 million. The virtual worlds of Warcraft, Entropia Universe, Habbo Hotel, Club Penguin, and Second Life are respectively posting profits powered by those who were intent on getting a "second" life.

According to the study, it is the youth demographic that drove the bulk of this 39 percent growth. KZero reported that Poptropica.com, which targets 5- to 10-year-olds, boasts over 76 million registered users. As the ages increase, so do the numbers of users. For example, in the range of 10- to 15-year-olds, Habbo's virtual world population rivaled some real-world countries with 135 million users. Other networks also accommodate massive citizenry. Fifty-four million inhabit Neopets, 34 million occupy Star Dolls, and 28 million reside in Club Penguin.

Older users seem to take more interest in real-life social networks such as Facebook, MySpace, and Twitter. Among 15- to 25-year-olds usage appears to diminish—apart from Poptropica, which maintains and active community of 35 million. However, as existing, younger demographics of virtual worlds mature, their conditioning and expectations for sophisticated and immersive interaction won't dwindle. Social networks that cater to older demographics may soon need to integrate virtual features and experiences in order to attract new users over time.

Many companies are extending their presence into these active new realms. For example, World of Warcraft, a popular MMOG, is rife with branded content. In many cases, companies pay for prominent placement within the networks as they can psychologically connect with users at a peer level. There's a general sentiment that the sponsoring brand is part of the community because it supports the community. Certain brands also promote their presence using traditional media tools to connect themselves to the legions of users through outside means.

KZero breaks out the world of virtual words using a visual that resembles a radar screen. In its cartography of the virtual landscape, the company organizes the disparate varieties of communities into 12 categories:

➤ Socializing chat
➤ Casual gaming
➤ Miscellaneous
➤ Mirror worlds
➤ Roleplay/fantasy/quests
➤ Toys/real-world games
➤ Music
➤ Fashion/lifestyle
➤ Education/development
➤ Sports
➤ TV/film/books
➤ Content creation

Many brands are creating custom and dedicated virtual worlds that create unique experiences that symbolize the brand's essence, style, and personality. This requires the involvement of an interactive design team that's well-versed in creating alternative realities and online escapes that engage users while also discretely, yet persuasively, reinforcing brand attributes and encouraging user recruitment of friends and contacts to connect with them in these brave new worlds.

In some cases, participation in virtual worlds was as simple as engaging individuals or groups of people directly through your alter ego. In other more common usage scenarios, brands set up virtual presences, branches, outlets, venues, and so forth to host discussions, answer questions, and also facilitate transactions. Existing virtual worlds require observation and either direct or indirect participation as an active user prior to undertaking any form of marketing. There's just no way around spending the time to participate if you hope to have any shot at long-term viability and return. These worlds nurture unique cultures that require hands-on experience and skill at adapting to a new landscape and successfully befriending and communicating with residents—levels of experience that is only possible through residence and participation.

■ VIRTUAL WORLD EXAMPLE: IBM

IBM has embraced the virtual world of Second Life to host corporate meetings and connect with customers. They opened a Briefing Center in Second Life where customers and potential customers can explore, find answers to specific questions, and chat with the avatars of real-life IBM experts and employees. For example, interested IT professionals and other techies can take a "hands-on" tour of the IBM Virtual Green Data Center, see the IBM storage systems in action, and learn all about the key energy-efficient technologies (Figure 4.1). There are regularly scheduled data-center tours, presentations, and conference sessions.

Figure 4.1   IBM's Virtual Green Data Center in Second Life

And this Second Life data center is staffed 24 hours a day, five days a week.

The venerable technology company is also using the virtual world to take the place of expensive and time-consuming corporate meetings for its global workforce. A case study published by Linden Lab (the makers of Second Life) documents how IBM held a Virtual World Conference and Annual Meeting on Second Life. The meeting brought together more than 200 participants and included everything you'd expect—keynote speeches, breakout sessions, and various areas for community gathering. Participants were given preconference training on the basics of Second Life to help ease the adoption curve. The study reported that the Annual Meeting was executed at one-fifth the cost of a real-world event (in addition to the productivity gains, because attendees could participate from their desks, rather than catch a flight) (see http://is.gd/1YsRw).

As we close the chapter on 101 and advance to 201, we realize that our induction into new media was absent of any form of hazing, providing only the data and insight that will help us excel.

Chapter

5

The New Media University

Social Media 202

In the last chapter we reviewed the online provinces of blogs, podcasts, wikis, and virtual worlds. In this chapter, we examine the nuances, risks, applications, and also the merits associated with content communities, social bookmarking, and livecasting.

■ CROWD-SOURCED CONTENT COMMUNITIES

Online content communities exist to promote the filtering of online information (or manipulation of it, depending on how you look at it). These unique communities are basically social networks that foster connectivity and interactivity around compelling content. The mechanisms and platforms to do so effectively tap the wisdom of the crowds to source, share, and showcase news, videos, pictures, music/audio, and events, powered by the crowd-sourcing of votes to determine popularity and visibility of entries as organized by the specific categories within the network.

These communities serve as a lens into what's hot, interesting, or promising, as dictated by the psychographics that connect demographics. We'll open the curtains to reveal the groups of people powering these networks later in the book.

Leading sites include Reddit, Digg, Mixx, Fark, Yahoo! Buzz, among others. Combined, these networks receive on average 55 million unique visitors. In comparison, CNN.com receives, on average, roughly 30 million unique visitors. Niche content communities exist for almost every vertical industry as well, and here may be more than one resource for you to learn and share with people that can help you and the company your represent.

The practice of curating content is pervasive in these networks, as well as in networks dedicated to social bookmarks (see next section). Conversations transpire in the form of comments and backchannel interaction where people usually ask each other for votes or spark private dialogues based on the comments for a particular entry.

Votes serve as forms of support and endorsement, or they can represent discontent or disagreement associated with particular submissions.

These communities receive content from users who submit something that they find interesting on a news site, blog, website, or other social network (YouTube, Flickr, Vimeo, Photobucket, Picasa, Docstoc, etc.) directly into the community—usually by clicking "submit" or a similar command. To simplify the submission and promotion of content in user-curated communities, integrated (or user-installable) tools exist directly in the pages where the content is hosted. For example, if you're reading a news story or blog post, you may be guided to a "Digg This" or other button specific to a particular network of the publisher's choice, in order to either submit a story or vote it up for further visibility. Other aggregated services such as "Share This" enable publishers to offer one tool to connect users to the network of their choice.

The goal, of course, is to earn significant momentum within a finite time period in order to hit the virtual front page, or at the very least, be among the most active within your given category.

The front page of Digg, for example, can yield upwards of 20,000 to 50,000 unique visits in one week to that particular piece of content. And if it's a blog post on your corporate site or a video related to your brand or product, imagine how that traffic could directly convert into leads or prospects.

The activity that sends flurries of votes in any given direction is not always organic. In fact, in some cases, the hustle is calculated or paid. For example, in most social networks, especially Twitter, many of the votes are driven by working with people in specific social graphs to vote as a favor or as an investment, when something is needed in return. On the other hand, to make the front page of Digg, many of the "Power Diggers" will help you for a price ranging from $500 to $2,500 per event. While Digg and other networks are trying to develop code that blocks this type of behavior, the truth is that Power Diggers in Digg and power users in any other network control the majority of the stories that become popular (which can require only 200 to over 1,000 votes to hit the top). Power users are connected and there's incentive for them to leverage their networks to your advantage. Without them, it takes a very organized and orchestrated campaign to submit a story and then drive enough support for it to move naturally—pushed by the people you've aligned in advance to help.

Sometimes it's a combination of leveraging both power networks and the social graph to help push posts to the top.

We each possess the ability to earn significance within social networks—through the give-and-take efforts that serve not only our own needs, but others' needs as well. We can create our own presence and define our social graph through meaningful interaction that achieves goals through the process of always paying it forward.

With the advent of Facebook Connect and Twitter Login, it may now be a bit easier and "affordable." Those networks that allow users to login using Facebook and Twitter will push a notice out to the respective networks and the corresponding followers to alert them to your new submission or vote—thus attracting a new group of visitors to support your efforts.

The wisdom of the crowds begins with curation and is then propelled by word of mouth (WOM) and/or the physical act of endorsing or promoting content within the network and also across the social graph (in other social networks). Everything requires content promotion in order to grab the attention of those who are focused on everything else but what it is you're trying to share with them.

Earn their attention.

■ SOCIAL BOOKMARKING

A relative of crowd-powered content-voting communities, social bookmarking networks are also powered by user submissions. The more people that bookmark the same thing, the more momentum it earns to make the top lists associated with popularity and tags. Whereas earning the most votes is the primary objective of aggregated content communities, social bookmarking sites are primarily designed to help you collect relevant information from around the Web for your reference and future review, as well as the packaging of interesting links for others who can benefit from curated material.

Not unlike the bookmarks you maintain in online browsers, users save interesting sites, pages, articles, media, and clippings, highlights, and annotations (portions of sites or pages that captivate them and the notes and sections they save and highlight). Aside from the additional features and capabilities, the most notable advantage to social bookmarking networks is the socialization and curation of this qualified material.

Optimization, tagging, and descriptions are critical to establishing presence within their respective networks. That search box that you see in each network is there for a reason, and the results that are returned are governed by the descriptions and tags tied to each piece of information. Like the rest of social media, social-marking sites are grounded, categorized, and defined through folksonomy.

Social bookmarking sites, such as del.icio.us, Diigo, and Stumbleupon, provide a social network for people to save, share, and discover relevant links and bookmarks organized by keywords and descriptions. Sophisticated users looking for specific and qualified results for search topics will visit a social bookmarking site before running a general search in Google or Yahoo!, simply because bookmarks are powered by a human collective of information gatherers who filter only the most interesting items through the manual labor of saving and tagging. It is a valuable source of intelligence mining.

Relevant tags allow other people to discover information, bookmark it on their own, and also read through bookmarks. Tags also serve as the hub for information gathering. Similar to the way many users subscribe to the rich site summary (RSS) feeds of their favorite sites and content producers, subscriptions are also available for tags. I subscribe to the highly focused tags that are important to me and also the companies I represent to get a feel for what is grabbing people's attention and why. Be selective; otherwise you'll turn on yet another fire-hose of information that will make it impossible to gather any value from the experience.

This form of intelligence gathering is also a clever way to introduce branded content into the fray—carefully titled, described, and tagged, of course. Now if you tie this into a syndication system, say a lifestream, for example, each bookmark can then broadcast to other social networks where you've changed the settings to pick up the bookmark feeds (this is true for any social network you wish to extend, as well). This process promotes the saved content beyond the original network to potentially reach new subsets of audiences within the distributed networks.

Purpose-built channels are also an additional way that companies curate important information for consumption by customers, influencers, media and analysts, investors/stakeholders, and employees. This can be done through the creation of individual accounts or through tags. For example, I bookmark everything that I find incredibly interesting and relevant to my world at http://delicious.com/briansolis. I also save content in this stream that I find interesting for others in social media, using the tag "socialmedia." If I wanted to share this with peers or if followers chose to channel only this content, you'll notice that by clicking this tag in my stream, the URL changes to http://delicious.com/briansolis/socialmedia. Note the tag is now at the end of the URL. The same is true for any tag I use to describe my bookmarks. I maintain tag channels for "PR2.0," "marketing," and "Customer+Service."

Tagging not only organizes information for you and those with whom you share relevant links, but also with those who either follow you or find content because of your tags and definitions.

The backchannel is important in bookmarking networks, just as it is in any social network. Many companies and individuals use this as a way to privately share interesting links with their connections on a one-by-one or group basis.

Another interesting way to use social bookmarks is through the publishing of lists and summaries in microblogs, tumblelogs (Tumblr and Posterous are good examples), and blogs. For example, bloggers leverage social bookmarks to save and share the information of interesting information they collect on the Web for future blog posts. Using the export feature found in many bookmarking networks, bloggers can simply export their list as a blog post with the ease of cutting and pasting. The blog will automatically pick up and recognize the timeframe or parameters of the bookmarks you wish to share. This comes in handy when you don't necessarily have enough time to write or edit a post, but wish to maintain a rhythm of posting. Other ways to utilize bookmarks are through the creation and publishing of linkblogs, which can republish all of the links you collect and share them as you go. While many individuals and some companies invest in this practice, I strongly suggest you maintain a solidified presence in the bookmarking community that aligns itself with what you represent and channels those links into occasional blog posts.

■ SOCIAL BOOKMARKING EXAMPLE: ADOBE

Adobe tags useful sites and tutorials to their del.icio.us site. Graphic designers, developers, and other Adobe users can find a wealth of information—such as "30 Free Photoshop Swirl Brushes," "25 brilliant wine label designs," "Digital scrapbooking tutorials," and "Flash animation tutorials." Adobe curators collect the best bookmarks around and also accept links from the community. At the time of writing, they have 1,506 links and 2,779 fans in their network.

Adobe saw the power in leveraging the wisdom and experience of the extensive Adobe community. The company recognized that knowledgeable users were providing help and value to other users within the community and wanted to collect and share this collaboration with an even larger pool of users. They've integrated links to their del.icio.us site from the product's help features. It's a win-win-win situation, where general Adobe users can find answers and resources to make the most of their Adobe product, Adobe can keep their customer-base happy without increasing technical support, and expert users receive greater recognition within the community (see http://delicious.com/adobe).

■ SOCIAL CALENDARS AND EVENTS

Nothing beats participation and relationship building like connecting in the real world!

Social calendaring networks transform e-mail or website-based consumer invitation and RSVP management solutions (such as evite.com) and provide a platform and supporting social network for those hosting or seeking events.

Want to see what your friends are attending?

Care to view upcoming events tied to your keywords in any city around the world?

Social calendar networks facilitate this ability and form paths to identify and connect with real world communities—or, as some refer to it, IRL (in real life).

Facebook events, Upcoming.org, Meetup, Twtvite (tweetups) and Eventful serve as sites that reach potential constituents by introducing or participating in relevant events, sorted by location and by topic/industry. In the case of companies and interest groups, these networks serve as tools to invite people to demos, votes, town halls, open houses, training, webcasts, trade shows, or hosted events, customer spotlights and Q&As, and discussions, among many other occasions and gatherings.

For example, an organization or individual can host and list a particular event within a social calendar network. They can also invite inside and outside network friends to RSVP for the event. As people RSVP, their responses are visible across their social graph (those people connected to them within the social network and those whom have set up their accounts to syndicate their updates across other social networks).

You'll notice that the events in each of the aforementioned services differ in organization, intention, and reach. For instance, Meetup.com is dedicated to recurring themed events. It's a vibrant, geographically expansive network that hosts regular meetups for everything from Web 2.0 to scrapbooking, photography workshops to branded dialogue around issues and opportunities facing particular industries.

I've hosted events for companies in our home cities using Meetup.com as well as Upcoming.org to experiment with event formulas, formats, and audiences that offer the most impact and value for attending guests while still also building a community that extends from online to the real world. The idea was to create an event that appealed to customers, prospects, partners, and influencers to share and learn together—as well as to serve as an installment series that provides ongoing insight and brings up the most critical questions and concerns permeating the industry.

We invited customers and industry experts to speak about industry trends, challenges, and solutions, as well as answer questions related to the real-world experiences of those in the audience. Using Meetup.com, we're able to create a branded "event" that created a microcommunity within the larger community of users looking for related events. The goal was to find a format that proved effective, and that could be used locally on a monthly or quarterly basis, and create a template that could be reproduced by appointed ambassadors around the country in order to provide resources and solutions for communities of users IRL. You wouldn't believe the power of pizzas, beverages, beer, and wine. The value was less in the splendor and extravagance of the event, but more in the structure, flow, and information presented each evening.

We also experimented with events where we utilized a combination of Upcoming.org, Facebook events, and Twitter for additional visibility to point back to one or both of the event hubs. Each network boasts its own group of contacts. Crossover may exist, but for the most part, distinct connections are anchored to each community. Contacts discovered and shared the events within their own networks and when combined with those targeted prospects who also discovered the affairs through search, the results were always outstanding—to the point of having to close sign-up lists and/or turn people away.

Another popular trend for meetups or tweetups centers on bloggers, local influencers, and visiting authorities who are in town for an event or conference.

As companies recognize the value, opportunity, and potential of blogger relations and engagement, extending a virtual hand to introduce bloggers to key executives is instrumental in establishing effective relationships that can potentially garner attention and coverage in the future.

People are actively searching for relevant events. In order to reach them, we must earn a presence in the networks where they seek intelligence. It is imperative for every company to proactively and personally recognize bloggers as important to your business—not only for pitching stories, but also for establishing dialogue. Respect and admiration are not simply sentiments, they can be effective building blocks for strong relationships.

Building relationships within these communities, promoting events among those they benefit, and utilizing the right tags and descriptions all play important roles in creating and attracting visibility.

Hosting events in the real world, even if they're organized on the Social Web, transcends online interactions and builds bona fide, real-world relationships—in fact, it ratifies them. Creating and arranging events within social networks connects true ambassadors and advocates through the powerful and influential fusion of the social graph.

Creating an event in Facebook, Upcoming.org, Meetup.com, or Twtvite, provides a public forum for people who already looking for pertinent gatherings and affairs qualified by keywords and location. As a brand seeking to connect with local consumers, offering opportunities to connect, learn, and collaborate in-person goes a long way toward engendering loyalty and fostering communities in the online and offline worlds.

As people RSVP for the event, it triggers an in- and cross-network update that can reverberate and resonate within the existing network by automatically generating status updates that appears on the radar screens (timelines) of their friends and contacts. For instance, if you RSVP for a particular event in Facebook, I would see that activity in my timeline, "YOU have RSVPd for X event." The idea is that it would most likely motivate me to click-through to view additional details about the event. This activity can also send updates to outside networks such as Twitter and Facebook, to reach an entirely different set of contacts. Did you know that over 2.5 million events are created each month within Facebook?

If you are organizing an event, it's important to leverage the Social Web to not only orchestrate activities and guests, but also to promote the event as it's occurring. It's highly recommended that you establish a short and recognizable hashtag to encourage participants to tweet or share their updates with a classifier that helps promote the event brand. If the event generates enough updates, it could potentially set the stage for a keyword to earn a spot in the top-trending topics in any related social networks. It's also critical that a person or persons on the organizing team monitors these conversations and updates as they're published, in order to monitor for sentiment, mood, perception, spirit, and the overall tenor and flavor of the function.

■ LIVECASTING

There was a time when only the most prosperous companies had access to the tools and services to shoot, edit, and broadcast audio/video.

Over recent years, the Social Web has sparked incredible innovation, substantially reducing the barriers to entry and the associated costs for creating and publishing online audio and video. Essentially, companies are building full-fledged content networks online that can air live or episodic videos on demand.

As a result, a rising and dedicated class of video networks exists that facilitates the creation and hosting of live and prerecorded video channels that entwine conversations around media.

Live video communities such as Veodia, Ustream, BlogTV, and Justin.tv, among others, enable livecasting and chatroom interactivity. Services such as Qik and Mogulus also allow for livecasting, in addition to offering the ability to broadcast video and support chatroom functionality from a mobile phone. Viewers can enjoy the videos from any PC or mobile device.

Live audio also represents a growing opportunity to reach important markets. Services such as BlogTalkRadio provide a sophisticated, but simple, toolkit for livecasting hosted audio discussions, similar to a radio talk show format. Imagine hosting a weekly interview series with executives, customers, or market experts to share insights and direction with your community while revealing the personalities driving the business.

Livecasting networks also share many similarities with traditional social networks. Inherent in each network is a community of active and growing affiliates and associates. Users can "friend" other members to connect with each other to form micronetworks of contacts to interact in and around scheduled or spontaneous programming.

The new tools for creating and sharing content in these nouveau forums are most likely already in your technology toolbox. Today's fixed or mobile production studio can effectively run from any desktop or notebook computer, a fixed network connection, or a mobile Web broadband device for mobile casts, and either a webcam, camcorder, or mobile phone with video capability. For audio, many broadcasters choose USB studio microphones to ensure quality.

Many companies that I've worked with or observed have effectively leveraged these services to webcast training sessions, earnings reports, live chats with key personnel and special guests, HR and executive announcements, product reviews, marketing or industry events, lectures, and conference discussions, speeches, panels, and so on. Employees, partners, and customers can view and chat with one another during the sessions to ask and answer questions and solicit feedback. In every interaction, you're investing in and building a dedicated community of appreciative and loyal subscribers and patrons.

■ EVENT LIVECASTING EXAMPLE: OFFICE 2.0 CONFERENCE

Office 2.0, a conference centering around enterprise adoption of Office 2.0 technologies, was held in San Francisco in September 2008. The event was witnessed by show attendees and, thanks to livecasting, by a global audience as well. Veodia recorded and live-streamed the conference tracks and sessions. Hundreds of event attendees were able to watch sessions right from their conference-sponsored iPhones, and countless others were able to check in from around the world.

Livecasting let Office 2.0 expand its reach beyond those individuals able to attend the event in person. And the conference and Veodia made each session recording embeddable in blogs, wikis, and Web pages. A speaker could then include a high-quality recording of the session on his or her blog or company website—to keep the conversation going after the last day of the show and thus increase visibility of Office 2.0 for the speaker's own followers and audience.

Chapter 6

The New Media University

Social Media 203

In this chapter, we study social networks dedicated to multimedia and focused discussions, as well as the phenomenon of URL shorteners and their true value, along with discussing the social media press release and the Social Media Newsroom.

■ IMAGES

One of the most understated categories of social networks is also one of the most established. Online photo-sharing has evolved over the last decade and has effectively organized people around the viewing and interaction of the image, transforming pictures into social objects. Now social networks are uniting pictures and people to create communities for the sharing and discovery of relevant content that transcends the typical processes of uploading and publishing pictures to share with friends and family.

People are, right now, looking for pictures related to products, companies, and brands, interesting people, places, events, and anything else you can imagine, by using keywords within these photo networks to find, react, utilize, remix, share, and republish.

Some of the more successful companies are already sharing art and customer-focused, exclusive content in communities such as Flickr, Zooomr, Webshots, Photobucket, Facebook Photos, Animoto, or all of the above. Just to give you perspective, Flickr alone receives on average, 30 million unique visitors per month. Facebook, now technically the largest social network for photos, receives more than 1 billion new photos every month.

On the most basic level, these new image channels can publicize and potentially circulate original artwork, previews and glimpses of forthcoming and existing works, behind-the-scenes shots, events, products, screen shots, and beauty shots. Essentially all applicable media should be placed in social communities to benefit influencers, customers, stakeholders, and prospects. Create channels within the photo networks that host pertinent activity and organize the images by albums to help and empower interested parties, who will discover, appreciate, and hopefully interact and share.

The existence of these highly trafficked networks is changing our perception of how we create and distribute corporate artwork. They also broaden the landscape and reach for artists (this is true for all forms of social media as well). It starts with letting go of control in order to effectually galvanize activity around your brand instead.

Prior to the socialization of the Web, copyrights controlled and governed image usage. However, there are benefits to providing access to images and promoting free distribution. As pictures, as well as all forms of media and content, are increasing in pervasiveness as social objects, the advantages and rewards that result from the extended interaction and visibility far outweigh controlled distribution. For that reason, many businesses and artists are adopting the use of Creative Commons licensing over traditional copyrights. Creative Commons is a nonprofit organization that increases sharing and improves collaboration. The tagline says it all, "Share, Remix, Reuse—Legally."

Creative Commons (CC) promotes the spirit of the Social Web by increasing the amount of creativity (cultural, educational, and scientific content) in "the commons"—the body of work that is available to the public—and securely encourages free and legal sharing, use, repurposing, and remixing. CC tools offer users a simple, standardized way to grant permission to their creative works, benefiting everyone from individual creators to large companies and institutions.

■ IMAGES EXAMPLE: JETBLUE ON FLICKR AND THE AMERICAN RED CROSS

JetBlue hosts a public group on Flickr that encourages customers, employees, and fans to post and share their own JetBlue-related shots. At the time of writing, community members have posted 4,800 photos, videos, and drawings—ranging from shots of the plane on the tarmac to photos of the in-flight snacks and panoramas of skylines captured from the air. Sprinkled among the traveler's shots are photos clearly posted by JetBlue marketing teams and employees. Far from

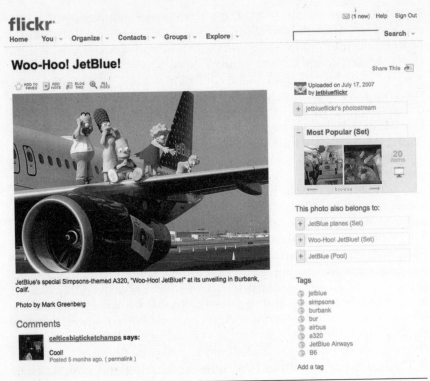

Figure 6.1   JetBlue's Simpson-Themed A320 Promotional Photo on Flickr

appearing like promotional fluff, these photos reveal the human side of the corporate brand, showing staff at corporate events or professional shots from various marketing events (see Figure 6.1).

Members of this Flickr group can comment on one another's photos. And without a doubt, employees and fans are connecting—sharing experiences and building relationships around travel memories and the brand (see http://www.flickr.com/groups/b6/).

Post–Hurricane Katrina, the American Red Cross launched a broad social media initiative to track people's sentiments about Red Cross–related issues and strengthen the organization's relationship with the public. In addition to launching a blog, using WordPress to create disaster portals where affected citizens can find resources, and sending Twitter updates with alerts on shelter locations, the organization is developing an active Flickr community where people can share their photographs. At the time of writing, there are 393 Red Cross Flickr members and 1,627 images have been posted.

The Flickr site is designed to give Red Cross volunteers a place to visually share their unique stories and experiences and connect with

Figure 6.2   The American Red Cross on Flickr

others around the country who are passionate about the organization. Communities like this one on Flickr help the Red Cross strengthen its bonds with people who are already active in the organization, as well as increase exposure to its causes and services.

Of course, remember that it's never just about one social media tool. While the Red Cross's Flickr community may be vibrant, they are leveraging multiple social media tools (Blogs, Facebook, Twitter, and active brand monitoring across the Web), creating multiple touch points with volunteers and the general public. By cross-referencing updates, available resources, and communities across all these social media points, the Red Cross can increase visibility and drive traffic among its communities (see Figure 6.2, and http://www.flickr.com/groups/americanredcross).

■ FORUMS/GROUPS

In all of the excitement surrounding social media, we can't ignore many of the online groups and forums that continue to bloom and prosper.

Message boards, discussion boards, and forums served and continue to serve as the foundations for defining and refining the functionality that powers today's social networks and online communities.

And many of the early forums continue to host millions of active and dedicated groups to every topic or interest conceivable—especially brands, industries, and products. Over the years Web 1.0 communities including Yahoo! and Google Groups, Amazon reviews, epinions, and TripAdvisor continue to persevere. These networks, among the many others that exist, enable members to create subgroups to host conversations around areas of interest, as well as collaborate on events, projects, and tasks. Forums and discussion boards represent active interest groups that can benefit from transparent and genuine engagement. To get an idea of the size, shape, and scope of some of the world's most active forums, take a look at http://rankings.big-boards.com.

While Ning and Facebook Groups represent the lion's share of niche networking, there is no shortage of emerging, dynamic, and dedicated 2.0 networks that host discussions around businesses, services, and topics. Just to illustrate this point, Yelp, a community that connects people through their experiences with local businesses, receives over 25 million (and growing) unique visitors per month. If you're a local business owner and not active on Yelp, you're missing tremendous opportunities to steer the perception of your brand while also increasing the base of happy, loyal, and enthusiastic customers and their ensuing referrals.

Similar to Yelp, many other niche networks unify conversations, interests, experiences, and opinions. RateItAll hosts reviews of virtually anything and everything. Trusted Opinion and Minekey not only allow people to share and discuss experiences, but the network also uses intelligent software (recommendation engines) to recommend relevant and matching content and people to you, based on your activity. GetSatisfacton and UserVoice power networks that unearth problems, incidents, encounters, and perspectives of customers to bridge the gap between brands and service.

Other DIY services allow businesses and individuals to set up hosted, customized, and dedicated forums.

■ URL SHORTENERS

In brevity there's clarity.

As marketers and communicators in the era of socialized media, we're relearning how to summarize what we represent so that we might quickly capture the attention of those we wish to reach.

Twitter, FriendFeed, Plurk, Qik, Seesmic, 12seconds, Facebook News Feeds, and all other forms of micromedia communities prosper through a concise economy of language and forethought. The exchange of richer dialogue flourishes through succinctness. This introspective and empathetic form of micromessaging inspires us to embrace and practice incisiveness and relevance outside of Twitter and micromedia, in the real world, to help people connect with what we do and why they should care.

Welcome to the art and science of the escalator pitch. It makes the elevator pitch seem like a luxury now.

As microcommunities are anchored in a finite set of characters or time in which to communicate, the one key word to embody is relevance. Assume you have one shot at getting someone excited about what you're doing, because, technically, you do.

The intrinsic worth of every second and character continues to gain incalculable value.

In the world of text-based microcommunities, sharing important discoveries on the Web is emerging as an art in and of itself. URLs are typically long and often exceed the 140-character limit most services employ. Short URL services are rapidly emerging to help us say more with less, especially when wrapping context around URLs we're hoping to share. Every character counts and some of these services can take even the longest URL strings and automatically condense them to 18 to 20 characters.

Although URL shorteners number in the thousands, a small group of popular solutions includes Bit.Ly, TinyURL, Is.Gd, Cli.gs, and Tr.im.

Toolbars for sharing and condensing links are also emerging, to promote interactivity around a page or site. For example, Digg offers a URL-shortening service that, when clicked, allows people to view the content and also "digg it," find related stories, share it on Facebook, tweet it, and send it via e-mail.

Perhaps one of the most important features of these services isn't just the ability to truncate URLs or host dialogue around them, it's the capacity to reveal the activity and trends behind URL sharing.

Bit.ly, the default URL-shortening service used by Twitter, is one of the more sophisticated shorteners on the market. Its value is in the real-time analytics and semantics introduced into the URL-sharing equation. Every Bit.ly URL offers real-time traffic and referrer data as well as location and metadata to review the volume of traffic and the source where it was clicked. Perhaps its most profound feature is that every URL is forever saved in a central repository and is packaged with a search interface for exploring user-qualified links associated with keywords.

Additionally, if you wanted to measure the volume and quantity of all shortened URLs that point to the same place on Twitter, for instance, Backtweets.com can identify the source URL and the aggregate number of related tweets regardless of the URL shortener used to share it on Twitter.

■ SOCIAL MEDIA RELEASE

The use of the press release is over 100 years old. For the most part, it has retained the same form and flavor for most of its lifespan. However, the press release has evolved more in the past decade than it has over the entire previous century, thanks to the proliferation of the Internet and, most notably, the Social Web. The tired and oft-disregarded press release is finally experiencing reinvention as it transforms to chase the new channels of influence, as well as adapt to the rapidly shifting behavior of content discovery, consumption, and sharing.

The Social Media Press Release (SMR) debuted in 2006. It was created by Todd Defren in response to a growing online community of journalists and bloggers speaking out against the old press-release format.

The Social Media Release was our chance to not only invigorate the traditional press release, but also provide visionaries and evangelists with the ability to embrace new tools, media, and narrative voices to tell stories more convincingly to those seeking to gain information, in their own way.

It is an effective tool for packing content and information for online journalists and bloggers, as well as facilitating conversations within the pertinent communities that host the social objects discussed in this chapter. It organizes media content in a more concise and contextualized format and also serves as a host to facilitate dialogue.

Nevertheless, the social media press release is not a miracle pill to cure the ills of poorly written press releases. It is merely a tool and is most effective when combined with a strategic arsenal of online media content, including relevant company blog posts, traditional releases, relationships, and an emerging category of press releases that tell a story.

Social media releases are designed to aggregate disparate content related to a particular story strewn across the Social Web, including videos, pictures, blog posts, tweets, content, and so on. Think of them as social dashboards that provide visitors/readers with the ability to disseminate and share information, as well as the ability to retell the story their own way with content provided in an easy-to-source format. SMRs also serve the purpose of providing new media influencers with the information they need to write a full story in one package—without having to carve out the BS of a traditional release or pitch.

News releases can tell the same story in different ways—appealing to specific markets and the users that define them.

In order for new media releases to work, they have to receive support representative of an entirely new methodology for communicating stories. It's not anything new. Corporate executives, spokespersons, and marketing and sales professionals have long faced the challenge of refining the value proposition into a compelling elevator or, better yet, *escalator* pitch.

The process of humanizing a press release also presents new answers to the question of whom we're hoping to reach. Markets are distributed and supported by mainstream and vertical segments. No one tool, publication, blog, peer-to-peer network, or story reaches and compels them similarly. Having one press release with a general set of value propositions is necessary, but also potentially limiting. Whether or not you address this in your pitch letter to varying representatives of these markets is one thing, but also think about the SEO value of distributing releases targeted directly to various customer groups who are actively looking for information on traditional search engines.

A study conducted by Outsell unearthed the fact that over 51 percent of IT professionals report that they get their news from press releases discovered in Yahoo! and Google business news searches over their top trade journals.

The press release thus becomes a social object, capable of sparking conversations, actions, and events.

The inclusion of social media elements within the release also fortifies the cornerstones for improving personal connections and attention to the release—and also enables the discovery and sharing of content. Having the ability to include videos, pictures, and audio, all served from different social networks into one centralized story dashboard, forces us to rethink how and what we share within the story.

We effectively become storytellers and the process of press release writing now transforms into an experiential and technical production, with ROI measured not only in hits, but also release and content views, trackbacks, tweets, mashups, conversations, comments, extended sharing within individual social networks, and also the call to action that we integrate into the release. Yes, we can now measure and steer experiences.

Once we move beyond the creative, storyboarding, and production process, we can tackle the creation of the press release. Because everything usually starts with good old-fashioned word processing, I've included a template to help users to visualize these new ideas. Essentially, you can "socialize" a press release simply by integrating all of the content within the release and also by adding "live" links to the content.

Ultimately the release may or may not cross a wire or garner Web visibility through services such as PitchEngine or PRWeb. They will, at the very least, attempt to earn an audience with reporters, bloggers, influencers, and also prospective customers via the corporate website, online newsroom, or e-mail. The originating template now also serves as a source of an organized story as well as a resource for storytellers to grab media in their desired formats.

What lies ahead is nothing less than remarkable. The social media release is no longer an "if" or "when." Thousands of SMRs are live and wild in the interactive Web, thanks to the inventive, resourceful, and inspired champions who've helped ensure their vibrancy, effectiveness, and residence as a permanent fixture in the day-to-day toolbox of communications professionals.

After all, it is the new generation of online storytellers and peers who are changing everything. It's forcing the evolution of interaction and connectivity—from PR to media creation and distribution. In the end, whether PR or media professional, citizen, or consumer, we are all contributors to the global democratization of content and information.

■ SOCIAL MEDIA NEWSROOM

The social media newsroom operates on the same premise as the social dashboards, which we review in the next chapter, as well as social media releases. They almost always complement or replace an existing "press room" to reduce redundancy and increase the level of interactivity and the repurposing of corporate media assets.

Social newsrooms help press, analysts, bloggers, conference organizers, and also customers discover, subscribe, and share corporate news, bios, images, video, RSS feeds, bookmarks, blogs, embeddable content, and so on, hosted in a more modern, organized, and dynamic online press room.

■ SOCIAL MEDIA NEWSROOM EXAMPLE: ANHEUSER BUSCH AB-EXTRAS

In 2009, I worked with Anheuser-Busch to create a hybrid social media newsroom and social dashboard that featured social media releases and exclusive media content dedicated to promoting the company's new commercials debuting during the broadcast of the Super Bowl. While it was originally designed to appeal to reporters covering the

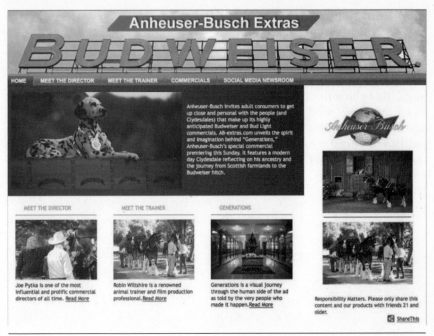

Figure 6.3   Anheuser-Busch Extras

Super Bowl and the extravagantly produced commercials that air during the big game, we realized that the value of the behind-the-scenes footage and images we captured during the making of the commercials would also offer value and fulfillment to consumers as well. So we created AB-Extras.com—a social media destination for Bud fans 21 years of age and older to reveal the human element and stories behind the ads (see Figure 6.3).

AB-Extras.com is a unique social platform for the internal PR team at Anheuser-Busch to work more effectively with traditional and digital press and bloggers, using the tools and services that they rely upon to publish and share stories. Through the experience, we learned that the site offered value beyond the reports and blogs covering the company and the advertising created for the game: It also appealed to influencers who actively discuss consumer lifestyle topics, sports, and beer.

AB-Extras.com featured exclusive content using a combination of social tools and networks such as Social Media Releases (SMRs), YouTube, Blip.TV, and Flickr, hosted on a blog platform. It served as an outside, dedicated online newsroom that aggregated and packaged disparate social elements from across the Web in a contextualized storyboard that streamlined the viewing, sourcing, and distribution of relevant information.

The press team at Anheuser-Busch is learning from individual experiences, driven by this new form of engagement, to further evolve its communications methodologies and improve the foundation for building relationships. As the team is listening and internalizing activity, analysis, and feedback, they will also define new policies and amendments to the PR and marketing regiment in order to embrace public conversations through social networks and microcommunities including Facebook, Twitter, and FriendFeed.

Chapter 7

The New Media University

Social Media 301

I know ... there's a lot to process here—not to mention that we are only beginning to discuss the evolution and transformation of media and communications overall. Take solace in your state of understanding and in your surroundings. You are not alone. We are all in this together.

Learn with determination.

Breathe it in.

Discover.

Dream.

Imagine.

Lead.

Listen and engage in discussions with empathy and understanding.

Moving forward, we'll review social media dashboards, social networks, virtual goods, and branded/purpose-built social networks.

■ SOCIAL MEDIA DASHBOARDS

The book will repeat this message throughout: We must produce and promote compelling material in the communities where our customers, peers, influencers, and prospects are active—using the consumption methods and means that they prefer.

Social media dashboards serve as a solution for arranging content from disparate networks into one cooperative digital menu.

Consumers may view one form of media, for example a video on YouTube, but they may not necessarily be aware that the company offers additional insight through other forms of content beyond the YouTube video and profile. Sending viewers back to a company website is only going to hinder our goal of effectively creating a bridge for communication and interaction. For those curious visitors seeking a social directory in our domain, how do we steer them to our external social presences?

Chances are, a directory either doesn't exist or profiles are littered throughout the site and the Web.

A social dashboard is a dedicated microsite either within an existing corporate website or hosted at a dedicated URL that aggregates the disparate corporate social profiles and media—presenting them in one visually rich, easy-to-navigate destination that promotes outside connectivity and onsite interaction.

The dashboard offers an organized view of media that's published in outside networks. Dashboards can include video from YouTube, pictures from Flickr, blog posts, pools, tweets, or other forms of updates from the "Statusphere," social network activity, Facebook Fan pages, a forum, events, and a directory to other social profiles. Each component of the dashboard can also provide individual RSS feeds or an all-inclusive feed (in online processor markup language, or OPML) for interested visitors who prefer to follow the updated content in their respective RSS readers.

In one such example, Chevy released VoltAge, a destination website to host and spark activity through a visually rich aggregated experience.

VoltAge offered unique content for visitors in the form of "behind the scenes" and custom videos and exclusive pictures of the Volt through channeled pictures (see Figure 7.1).

Chevy also integrated other forms of compartmentalized conversational content, such as a hosted forum for topical dialogue, blog posts, tweets from Twitter, news releases, polls with real-time results, upcoming events, and also Facebook Connect.

Services such as Facebook Connect and also Twitter Login provide a secure widget to integrate into your hosted network, and also blog commenting, so that visitors can access or contribute content without needing to create yet another profile or login account. By integrating (easily) the ability for people to login using their Facebook and Twitter IDs, the likelihood of participation is increased. It also aggregates the extracurricular activity of individuals outside of Facebook and Twitter, and feeds that activity back into their respective networks. This is, perhaps, the most valuable reason for using Facebook and Twitter logins in your hosted dashboard. When a user signs in using either network ID, it sends all of their updates back to the respective network for all of those in their social graph to see. The

Figure 7.1

subsequent action of, for example, commenting on a video or blog post, will send that comment back to the particular network. In that realm their followers will see it, and if it's intriguing, will respond and most likely click-through to see what has engaged their attention.

It is a very simple and effective way of "unmarketing" content from your domain to the extended social graphs of those who appreciate the content you publish (see www.chevroletvoltage.com).

■ SOCIAL NETWORKS

Social networks such as Facebook, MySpace, Bebo, Hi5, and LinkedIn offer a variety of mechanisms to discover and connect with influencers and peers. Conversations in social networks are prevalent, but they're not necessarily as easy to unearth as relevant dialogue on Twitter for example. But that's changing and by the time you read this book, social networks may become a prominent source for monitoring and engaging, much in the same way that businesses participate on Twitter and FriendFeed today.

Social networks also offer myriad other forms of collaboration and promotion. Opportunities range from comments and wall posts to groups and fan pages to events to customized applications, widgets, and games, and to virtual goods.

Community and brand managers can also create groups and or fan pages if they don't yet exist, in order to host dialogues with and solicit feedback from stakeholders. This group engagement also provides opportunities, which pave the way for interaction, direction, or support.

In Facebook, for example, each group, event, application, or Fan Page can be promoted by organic means and also through e-mail and in-network mail. However, it also provides a simple method for running a small visual ad tied to your chosen keywords, where you can promote the page on a cost per 1,000 (CPM) or a cost per click (CPC) basis. CPM is used when trying to reach the broadest range of impressions possible. CPC is used when the goal of the program is to get people to click-through (measured in a click-through rate, or CTR), and, in this case, join a group or page.

Many companies rush to create group or fan pages dedicated to their corporate and product brands without first considering the rationale for doing so or checking if one may already exist (usually started by a fan or an angry customer).

In some cases where a popular group is already thriving, it may make more sense to align the brand with the group and take an active role in its direction. For example, on Facebook alone, there are thousands of groups and fan pages dedicated to Coke and Coca Cola, with the most popular fan page hosting 4 million fans. While Facebook rules state that fan pages can only be created by the company or authorized representatives, this page was started by Dusty Sorg and Michael Jedrzejewski in Los Angeles prior to the new rule taking effect. When Coca-Cola was contemplating its Facebook fan page strategy, it realized that its greatest networking opportunity was to empower the duo to continue to run the page along with collaboration from the Coke team.

Unlike Twitter, where everyone can follow anyone, the act of proactively "Friending" is key, as most networks require a two-way connection in order to view and share information. In the creation of groups or fan pages, anyone can join them, even if you haven't directly friended them. And, as new people become members of the groups, or "fan" a fan page, their activity appears in the personal timelines of all their connections. This means that inquisitive people who see these updates may click-through to the designated page to see if it's of interest, and also what's in it for them.

That's the trick of all of this. It's the art of garnering attention and then capturing and holding it now and henceforward. Everything requires promotion through the consistent and vigorous acts of connecting profiles and pages to those who will enjoy them. With proactive campaigning, stakeholders join and augment the process of increasing visibility by willfully sharing your presences within their social graph.

Participation is key to growing the community and ensuring its integrity and associated activity.

■ COMMENTS AND WALL POSTS

Wall posts and comments on individual updates provide you with the ability to individually recognize someone for their contributions or simply to acknowledge them for who they are and what they represent. Your response resides on their page, in their notification alerts, and in your timeline. Every bit of social networking represents the potential to resonate throughout an individual social graph.

■ GROUPS

Groups within social networks are similar to traditional online groups of Web 1.0, but again, the social graph is the differentiating element that offers the potential to carry information to new people with each and every update.

Groups provide a contained environment where the host, in addition to its members, can share news, pictures, videos, links, comment on the main wall, and also start conversations, or ask and answer questions within the included discussion boards. Social networks make it incredibly easy to start and promote a group.

■ FAN PAGES

Fan pages are similar to personal profile pages, but are reserved for brands. Instead of connecting to friends, individuals become "fans." Interaction is similar to that with profiles and groups, since the fan pages facilitate dialogue around the content that is uploaded and shared on the page, as well as enable fans to participate in the flow of conversations through comments and the sharing of media files.

■ VIRTUAL GOODS

As we reviewed earlier in the book, Virtual Goods are products within social networks and represent gestures between people or between brands to foster goodwill, express affection or support, bestow rewards, and create fellowship, as well as other forms of fleeting and ongoing interaction. For example, you can send a virtual Coke to someone if they updated in the network that they were wishing they had a cold beverage at that very moment. Or, if someone had a hard day, you could send him or her a virtual bouquet of flowers from 1800flowers.com.

Brands are also working with developers to create apps based on the gift-giving of branded virtual goods.

Another example is Ben & Jerry's Ice Cream, which has a classic Facebook presence, full of user-generated content from fans and company employees. Users can send virtual ice cream gifts to friends—and the ice cream maker cleverly ties these virtual gifts to new flavors to increase visibility and buzz.

According to a study conducted by Frank N. Magid Associates, commissioned by virtual currency provider PlaySpan, the virtual goods and currency market was estimated to hit $1.8 billion in 2009.[1]

The study revealed that 15 percent of males between ages 12 and 24 and 15 percent of women between ages 35 and 44 reported that they purchased virtual goods.

Almost half of the survey participants who reported that they purchase virtual items are also active MMO participants.

■ BRANDED/PURPOSE-DRIVEN SOCIAL NETWORKS

Indeed, the most popular social networks in the world offer the ability to create, host, and participate in subnetworks, or groups dedicated to your brand and products. They are not the only networks to establish a presence, however. In the spirit of reaching out to significant groups of people where they interact, there are several services that exist to facilitate the creation, promotion, and cultivation of stand-alone networks that are either hosted independently from your main Web presence or are also embeddable within your primary site.

These communities function similarly to other groups and networks, but differ in where they're hosted, how they appear, and their intended form and function. Simply said, brands can maintain multiple presences dedicated to fostering specific conversations spanning from sales and service to education to internal collaboration and dialogue related to specific products, lifestyles, and events—or simply a place that encourages consumers to share insights, ask questions, and contribute ideas on company and product direction.

Many brands "seed" to build loyalty building networks in addition to existing social networks. And, while I don't promote any brand spreading itself thin by applying and dedicating resources to establishing presences in each and every network, it is typical to establish and promote presences in multiple, targeted networks. For example, even if a Facebook group triggers updates to Twitter, Plurk, Identi.ca, Posterous, and other social networks, friends and followers must still be active or, at the very least, registered users of Facebook in order to join and interact.[2]

Communities such as Ning provide DIY tools to build a very professional, custom social network dedicated to any theme or topic you choose. Ning is also a social network for social networks, in that it already boasts over one million niche groups and a significant user population that supports them. Ning gathers users together around common interests and therefore is an ideal location in which to establish a strategic presence and promote it inside and outside the rapidly growing network.

Other brands choose to socialize their main online presence, usually the corporate website, by adding social networking functionality on a particular page of the site. Some brands prefer the ability to aggregate worldwide Web traffic to a place where it can guide user click paths and ultimately capture leads or sales in one place. Leverage Software, Jive, Cisco, and Kickapps, among others, provide dedicated resources, services, and systems for creating and hosting inward and outward facing social networks. It's for this reason that Facebook has made its fan pages portable, allowing brands and personalities who have or will host Fan Pages to embed a widget version of the page directly into websites, other social networks, social networks, and blogs. Doing so builds a bridge between the strong Facebook network and outside visitors to strategically concentrate on promotion and community building.

Interactivity is key and by embedding the Facebook widget, site owners can augment, eliminate, or reduce reliance on custom brand building and attention-grabbing site development, while still amassing a significant following. It also extends the updates and content live, providing site visitors with the latest activity from inside the network to wherever the widget is placed. It's a simple matter of adding a bit of automatically generated code to the site, not unlike the method of embedding YouTube videos or Flickr pictures used today.

Visitors to outside branded pages can securely login with their Facebook credentials to interact with the widget to comment, become a fan, and view the latest pictures, videos, posts, and so on. As fans participate, their activity is simultaneously shared within the Facebook community, further promoting the branded content within the personal "News Feed" for Facebook friends and contacts to potentially view and click-through.

Brands currently using the embedded Facebook Fan Page include BlackBerry, NPR, World Wildlife Fund, *Newsweek*, Roger Federer, and ABC News.

Remember, just because you build it, doesn't mean they will come. You have to start by recruiting. Go find your customers and bring them to you or participate where they are currently. Make sure to maintain a concurrent presence in other social networks—where relevant—so your customers can also find you.

■ BRANDED SOCIAL NETWORK EXAMPLES: PANASONIC LIVING IN HD

In conjunction with Crayon, a New Media agency, Panasonic developed a dedicated social network surrounding its high-definition products and technology (www.livinginhd.com). Dubbed an HD playground, Living in HD (LiHD) encourages Panasonic HD customers, technology fans, and anyone else to share their insights, experience, creativity, and enthusiasm about the world of HD. To create buzz and

Figure 7.2   Living in HD

incentives for joining, Panasonic offers valuable prizes, including a contest that gave away 30 HD products in 30 days to members.

Panasonic actively engages the LiHD community. For example, Greg Harper, the Panasonic Answer Man, offers community videos in response to questions from community members, on topics such as what to look for before making an HD purchase. LiHD also leverages the experience and wisdom of its community, as members frequently post and discuss tips and advice on various HD products. And recognizing that the fan base for HD products, particularly cameras and camcorders, is likely to be creative and expressive types, Panasonic offers community blogs where members can express themselves through words, photos, and videos. They're creating a creative and collaborative atmosphere—all wrapped around the Panasonic HD brand (see Figure 7.2).

Chapter 8

The New Media University

Social Media 302

If there's one thing we're learning in the new world of socialized media, it's that our need for higher, modern education will always exist as technology advances and human behavior adjusts to accommodate the continuing rotation of pervasive applications. It's not only the study of the new tools and networks, and the intelligence that powers them, it's also the ongoing survey of the social sciences that reveal true cultures and behavior.

As our journey advances, we learn the value of aggregation and conversational threading in activity feeds and lifestreams as well as microblogs and microcommunities.

■ ACTIVITY FEEDS/LIFESTREAMS

If social media is powered by listening, user-generated content (UGC), and engagement, as time passes, our digital footprint is further scattered in bits and pieces all over the Web. If you, for a moment, assume the role of a follower, you can understand just how difficult it might be to keep up with active brands.

The content we share and the updates and information we publish is broadcasted within individual networks. Without an aggregated social media dashboard, we find ourselves projecting fragmented pieces of our brand persona. Staying in sync with contacts, either as a producer or follower, has become tedious and unrewarding.

Activity feeds and lifestreams represent a new publishing medium, usually supported by a corresponding community that enables the publishing of "byte-sized" and channeled updates and/or aggregated information into a timeline format that simplifies content consumption.

82

Lifestreams also serve as a streamlined opportunity to listen or respond to influential peers and customers who also publish lifestreams. Some channel services that have experienced breakaway success in the past year include FriendFeed, tumblr, Chi.mp, Ping.fm, and SocialThing, among many others.

Basically, these new tools are designed to share short updates, whether you're publishing new information, content, or media, or channeling the RSS feeds from a variety of disparate networks, such as blogs, flickr, YouTube, or Twitter, into one "flow" where people can read, respond, share, and mark your updates as "favorites"—and vice versa.

Brandstreams are fortified content channels dedicated to reinforcing the brand personality and value proposition across the Social Web, through one cohesive view.

Daimler AG, the maker of Mercedes Benz and other car and truck lines, uses FriendFeed (www.friendfeed.com/daimlerblog) to consolidate its updates and content across multiple points of presence on the Web—including its blog, website, and Flickr. Likewise, technology company EMC Corporation also has a brandstream on FriendFeed (www.friendfeed.com/emccorp) that includes content from its own blogs, Flickr group, and relevant industry and influencer blogs.

Facebook's news feed, combined with the new Facebook Connect infrastructure, is setting the stage for a global conversation platform that may go unrivaled. Facebook is already hosting channeled conversations sourced from Twitter, FriendFeed, and many other notable communities with an audience that is undeniably substantial, captive, and vigorous.

People "add" individuals and companies as "friends" when they want to learn about or stay up-to-date with their activities. More importantly however, they also can collect RSS feeds from almost every important network and blog that you produce and participate in. These collected streams can represent a focused channel of information specific for the people you want to reach.

Again, these are just a few examples of places where conversations are taking place. Not any one site represents a collective community for your customer base. You have to understand where your customers are, what they're looking for, and why, in order to potentially reach them.

■ MICROBLOGS, MICROCOMMUNITIES

When this category was initially conceived, it was an industry sector that went by many names—microblogging, micromedia, microcommunities, micromessaging, and micronetworks, among others. Obviously, the prefix "micro" is consistent throughout these naming conventions. And likewise, it's this kind of microagreement that serves as a motto for this important branch of social networking.

For the sake of discussion here, we'll refer to these networks as something fun, say "personal broadcast systems (PBSs)."

Personal broadcast systems and their supporting communities accommodate a unique culture of dialogue organized around short bursts of updates and the responses and corresponding voices and personalities behind them. In this category, Twitter is by far the most significant champion. Other micronetworks, including FriendFeed, Plurk, Identi.ca, Utterli, Lifestream.fm, Kwippy, Yammer, and Present.ly, among many others, are paving the way for shorter, more frequent online postings, as well as conversations and responses overall.

Online personal broadcast systems have also introduced new psychologies and behaviors into the routine of social media participation. On average, there's a greater number of people updating their social status than writing blog posts on a daily basis. More links are shared via micromessages than on any other form of digital media. PBS represents a more approachable and usable gateway to social media than any of the networks serving as its predecessors.

Twitter has not only led the way for the evolution of microconversations, it has single-handedly forced businesses to pay attention to online conversations on a mass, and growing, scale. Communications, customer service, and even sales organizations are flocking to Twitter to participate in related conversations as well as attempting to create and foster communities around their brand and core values.

The magic of microcommunications is the human nature of the dialogue. Successful communities are built upon the fulfillment that consumers experience based on their dialogues with "real" people who listen to and acknowledge their participation. It's driven by reciprocation and progressing updates, connections, and responses. The behavior associated with online engagement in these social networks dedicated to personal broadcasting will evolve. The techniques that captivate them today may no longer prove effective tomorrow. I challenge you to gaze at the horizon and determine what's coming next. Anyone reading this book or reading blogs or following influencers in social networks can design and implement "copycat" programs, but only you can customize a program that's specific to your community of users and prospects to engage and influence a powerful population of brand crusaders.

Now, let's take a look at how to leverage these powerful microcommunities for macro impact, referencing the examples of today that can inspire tomorrow's programs.

■ TOP 10 MONETIZATION TRENDS FOR SOCIAL MEDIA AND MICROCOMMUNITIES

When it comes to savvy, proven, and incredibly successful tech investors, Ron Conway is a legend. He has a gift or an uncanny sense of shrewdness, or a fusion of both, to identify the real opportunities that will transform into successful exits and also fuel and inspire aggressive innovation in the process.

To help entrepreneurs, startups, and industry leaders capitalize on the tremendous opportunity that social media presents, Conway offers his vision for the top 10 ways to monetize real-time conversations:

10. Lead generation
9. Coupons
8. Analytics; analyzing the data
7. Enterprise CRM
6. Payments
5. Commerce
4. User-authentication; verifying accounts
3. Syndication of new ads
2. Advertising—Context and display ads
1. Acquiring followers

In the spirit of sharing monetization strategies, *Forbes* magazine assembled a visual list of Top 21 Twitter Tips[1] to help enterprise and small businesses learn how to engage on Twitter through the practices of those already successfully building online communities of customers and advocates. While many of the examples and quotes from company spokespeople remain the same, the article inspired me to modify the list, based on my experiences and observations. The end result is still a list of 21 Twitter Tips, but I believe this version may be more helpful and applicable to your world.

■ TIPS FOR TWITTER AND SOCIAL MEDIA FOR SOCIALLY SAVVY BUSINESSES

➤ Number 1. Special Offers

We live in a society that is as distracted as it is informed. People are making decisions on what to read, view, purchase, visit, and sample based on the information that filters through their attention dashboards. At best, even the most qualified information sourced from the most trusted contacts will receive only a cursory overview. The trick is to concisely introduce the value up front. If the offer is compelling and affiliated with their interests, the consumer will make the connection to personal value and benefits and click-through to redeem the special or coupon when ready or so inclined.

As Conway predicts, coupons and special offers will inject commerce into the social equation.

For example, @delloutlet uses Twitter and Facebook to send coupons to customers. In just one year, Dell recorded upward of $3 million in sales directly sourced from Twitter.

California Tortilla (@caltort), a chain of 39 casual Mexican restaurants based in Rockville, MD, sends coupon passwords via Twitter, which customers must say at checkout to redeem the offer.

➤ Number 2. Ordering

While the distance between introduction and action is only separated by a link, many businesses are using Twitter to log orders. Coffee Groundz (@coffeegroundz) uses the direct message channel on Twitter to receive and prepare orders. Using Twitter as a promotion and marketing channel, Coffee Groundz reports 20 to 30 percent increased sales and market share.

As an aside, Pizza Hut offers an iPhone and Facebook application that allow hungry patrons to order pizza directly from Facebook and their mobile phone.

➤ Number 3. Word of Mouth Marketing (There Is No Such Thing as Viral Marketing)

Moonfruit offered 11 Macbook Pros and 10 iPod Touches to celebrate its 10th anniversary. In order to qualify, contestants had to send a tweettweet using the hashtag #moonfruit. One month following the completion of the contest, Moonfruit site traffic was up 300 percent and sales also increased by 20 percent—and all because of a meager investment of $15,000. The company also realized SEO benefits, by landing on the first results page on Google for "free website builder."

Wendy White, Moonfruit's CEO, realizes that there's a fine line between effective and destructive #tweetowin campaigns: "Such campaigns must be courteous and fit with a company's brand, lest you draw the ire of the Twitter-sphere."

We'll discuss this challenge in more detail later in this book.

➤ Number 4. Conversation Marketing

Zappos (@zappos) doesn't necessarily market on Twitter; instead, it "unmarkets" via conversations and engagement. At current count, 436 Zappos employees use Twitter, including CEO Tony Hsieh. For the record, Tony has over 1 million followers.

Aaron Magness, director of business development at Zappos, acknowledges that proactively sharing the company culture and values creates a humanizing effect that invites people to be part of the community, and also acts as a sales driver. "It's easier for them to embrace openness," he said.

➤ Number 5. Customer Service

Frank Eliason of Comcast (@comcastcares) and Richard Binhammer of Dell (@richardatdell) are paving the way for service-focused organizations on Twitter.

Eliason, whose title is director of digital care at Comcast, uses Twitter to help 200 to 300 subscribers a day. Frank and his 10-person help desk receive direct questions, but also proactively seek out complaints. His key to success lies in his desire to earn relations, not bark advice or chat people up. "If they want assistance, they'll let me know," he said.

➤ Number 6. Focus Groups

Wisdom and creativity are widespread in social media. Tuning in to the frequency of conversations related to the brand or marketplace can serve as a real-time focus group for innovation and adaptation.

Over 3 million mentions of Starbucks populated Twitter in May 2009 and, as the company learned, the price for paying attention is less than that for a caramel macchiato, but the value is priceless.

Brad Nelson who leads @starbucks recognizes the inherent wisdom and insight in Twitter: "There is a major element of Twitter that's about listening and learning. Twitter is a leading indicator," he said.

Morgan Johnston, Manager of Corporate Communications at Jet Blue, was inspired to change policy because of Twitter. He helped eliminate a $50 fee for carry-on bikes after hearing complaints via Twitter.

Johnston listens to the people who are active on the Social Web in order to improve company processes and customer service. "Think of Twitter as the canary in the coal mine. We watch for customers' discussions about amenities we have, and what they'd like to see made better."

➤ Number 7. Direct Sales

Brian Simpson (@BSIMI) has helped The Roger Smith in New York monitor dialogue related to hotel stays and travel in order to offer specials in the hopes of attracting new guests. Using Twitter search, he can identify prospects and offer them a 10 percent discount on the lowest-rate rooms. Simpson estimates that Twitter and other forms of social media have netted between $15,000 to $20,000 in additional revenue.

Simpson also professed the necessity of cultivating community in social networks: "It validates us more when other people talk about us than when we talk about ourselves," he noted.

United Airlines and JetBlue use Twitter to provide customer service, in addition to using the micronetwork to offer followers first dibs on discounted fares and last-minute specials. Dubbed "cheeps" by JetBlue and "twares" by United, these tweets provide an already active and extemporaneous network with the ability to pounce on great deals by simply following these airlines and all the other companies that will soon follow suit.

➤ Number 8. Business Development

Twitter, along with blogs, blog comments, and other social networks, is abundant with conversations that broadcast and echo dissatisfaction with brands and products. One company's crisis is another's opportunity.

Monitoring conversations (social reconnaissance) related to competitors provides the ability to "save the day" with better service or monetary incentives.

A word of caution on this front, however: Responding in the public timeline can be viewed by your competition. In my experience, following someone and offering to help via direct message has proven effective. Empowering your community to publicly respond is also powerful, as they can do so across networks and communities without regard for the ramifications of competitive awareness.

➤ **Number 9. Curation**

I've written in the past that Twitter is not necessarily most advantageous when used as a conversation platform. Sometimes you can say more with less. Embracing it as a broadcast channel or a dumb pipe is also beneficial when used strategically.

For example, Google maintains over 1.2 million followers, but only follows 160. It employs a strategy that I refer to as a "curation" feed. It compiles links to content and company posts elsewhere and aggregates them into one channel. I recommend that companies use this for information collected from customers and influencers, as well in order to truly curate the best, most helpful content from around the Web while building good will in the process.

However, Twitter accounts can also create and portray a persona around an inanimate social object. For example Albion's Oven, a bakery in London, notifies followers when fresh croissants are ready.

➤ **Number 10. Information Networks**

Unlike a curated network that keeps followers in sync with trends, services, and solutions, Information Networks can serve up helpful alerts and notices to help followers avert problems, change plans, and also pursue new opportunities.

The Michigan Department of Transportation uses Facebook and Twitter to alert friends and followers of traffic and road closures. Oakland County Parks uses Facebook and Twitter to spread the word about events and news and also conducts polls to improve local programs and services.

In 2009, I established @microjobs along with Christopher Peri (@perivision) to connect employers with job seekers on Twitter.

In business, customers could also benefit from updates and alerts that they might not have otherwise have encountered on their own.

JetBlue tweets flight delays.

Comcast tweets updates on service interruptions.

United Linen, a linens and uniform company in Bartlesville, OK, alerts customers to delays in deliveries when weather becomes a factor.

➤ **Number 11. Dedicated and Branded Channels**

Sometimes the pipes in social media become overloaded with general information, making it difficult to truly create and foster communities dedicated to particular topics, interests, or industries. Establishing exclusive channels or subchannels to share specific information increases signal versus noise.

On Twitter, Ford Motor uses distinct accounts for sharing information about specific models and products. For example, @forddrivegreen focuses on sustainability, whereas @fordmustang, well, you guessed it, shares content related to the Mustang.

Scott Monty, head of social media for Ford, recognizes that social media reveals the people who formerly comprised the audience: "We give customers a choice as to how they want to consume information."

Whole Foods maintains independent channels, as well, to better serve customers. For example, the healthy foods retailer channels specific information and updates for wine and beer, cheese, and recipes.

➤ **Number 12. Mobile and Geo Location Marketing**

This will prove to be among the most oft-discussed examples of social media, and most specifically with Twitter. Local businesses are using social tools to identify customers within the area to attract new business and also extend the online interaction into a full-blown community in the real world. Because I was there when this story was just about to unfold, I will reference my good friend Mike Prasad and the great work he's done for Kogi, a mobile force of Korean BBQ taco trucks.

One night in Hollywood, Mike and I were talking about getting a late night snack. He told me about the company he was working with and how if we sent a tweet out requesting their presence, there was a good chance that they'd stop by the neighborhood to serve us dinner. Thirty minutes later, Kogi was indeed outside our hotel and a group of about 25 to 30 people immediately began proclaiming their appreciation for @kogiBBQ on Twitter. The rest is history in the making and will serve as the standard for local businesses building communities IRL.

Prasad echoes this sentiment and is helping to lead the way: "We try to foster a culture by interaction with the people around us. Now, Kogi isn't about getting a taco, it's about having an experience."

Expect to see this trend continue in mobile social networks dedicated to locale and accessible via mobile phones.

➤ **Number 13. Hosted Conversations That Generate Traffic and Referrers**

Social Media Dashboards are the future of hosted and aggregated conversations. As we're observing, those sites that integrate Twitter chat functionality can not only thread conversations in one place for easy following, but also send out tweets in the Twitter stream for all followers to see, and hopefully feel compelled or curious to join, as well.

During the NBA Eastern Conference Finals between the Cleveland Cavaliers and the Orlando Magic, Turner Broadcasting integrated Twitter into TNT.com with the help of Gigya Socialize. Visitors could log into the site with their Twitter ID and respond directly in the hosted timeline. As such, their tweets not only appeared on TNT.com but also in Twitter, attracting more fans into the site.

➤ Number 14. User-Generated Change

As we've seen and will continue to see, in social media tiny online social revolutions can manifest and ultimately ignite change.

Historically, the 2009 Iran Election will serve as an inflection point for the rise of user-generated change. While the results of election itself weren't altered, the Iran government was forced to respond.

Two services mentioned in the *Forbes* Top Twitter Tips article, Twitition and TinyPetition, are dedicated to organizing people on Twitter to call for change officially.

➤ Number 15. Vendor Relationship Management

A form of relationship management introduced by *Cluetrain Manifesto* author Doc Searls, Vendor Relationships Management (VRM) flips the workflow of CRM (customer relationship management) from companies to customers. Social media is a powerful vehicle for forcing or encouraging companies that have yet to embrace the Social Web to engage and participate through listening and evolution.

Whereas people are relegated to faceless customers when e-mailing or calling into the service department, social media takes the power once held exclusively by the brand and injects balance.

UK-based Wiggly Wigglers, a marketer of farming and gardening supplies, was surprised to learn that British Telecom overcharged the company by $10,000. After five months of a stalemate and without any promise or hope of resolution, company owner Heather Gorringe took her story to the Twitterverse. Within 30 minutes, @BTCare responded with help and two days later, the bill was adjusted.

On a smaller scale, inciting responses on social networks is also a form of forcing companies to compete for your business in the public spotlight.

As the saying goes, a happy customer tells a few people, but an unhappy customer tells everyone. Social media serves as an amplifier to those seeking change, reform, and response.

We'll discuss VRM in a later chapter as part of the bigger discussion around sCRM (Social Customer Relationship Management).

➤ Number 16. Ideation

As we've witnessed with My Starbucks Idea (http://mystarbucksidea. force.com) and Dell's IdeaStorm (www.ideastorm.com), crowd-sourcing ideas can not only be an excellent source for innovation, but also an effective means for establishing goodwill.

IBM uses Twitter to test concepts and solicit feedback and ideas through @ibmresearch.

➤ Number 17. Employee Recruitment

Twitter is a magnet for people seeking information. It's one of the reasons that Christopher Peri and I created and released @microjobs. We realized that recruiters and hiring managers were turning to Twitter to seek referrals and applicants for open positions. Twitter and social media can spark a social effect that galvanizes community support and action. Not only can companies save a significant amount of money on listing and referral fees using traditional outlets and resources, the company essentially creates a presence through the practice of "unmarketing" itself through the process of seeking qualified candidates.

➤ Number 18. Events

As we reviewed in the Social Calendaring section of Social Media 201, organizing and promoting events are natural applications for Twitter. Tweetups transcend online relationships and become real-world connections.

Using Coffee Groundz as an example again, the Houston-based business regularly organizes tweetups to draw hundreds of customers into the store for each event.

➤ Number 19. Research and Intelligence

The Social Web is a real-time collective and assembly of valuable information that mostly goes unnoticed. A few existing services are dedicated to applying a magnifying lens into the dialogue that leads to insight, direction, creativity, and inventiveness.

For example, brands.peoplebrowsr.com and celebrity.people browsr.com provide real-time insight into the most actively discussed brands and celebrities on Twitter at any moment in time, while also revealing the sentiment that is most associated with each.

StockTwits provides an open, community-powered idea and information service for investments. Users can listen to traders and investors, or contribute to the conversation. The service leverages Twitter as a content production platform and transforms tweets into financial related data structured by stock, user, and reputation.

➤ Number 20. Fund Raising

This is a big opportunity and one that will yield amazing stories on how people are using Twitter and social media to raise money for charitable causes and capital for projects and companies. It's the art of spurring contributions through information and education, not solicitation.

When it comes to social media for Social Good, we don't have to look much further than anything Beth Kanter touches or spotlights. She's one of the most influential people in using social media for raising awareness and money for her causes. One of the projects that she remains dedicated to is helping orphans in Cambodia and, to date, it has raised over $200,000. She has also used Twitter, Widgets, and other social networks to help many other organizations and causes. In one live demonstration, which still leaves me in awe, she raised over $2,500 to send a young Cambodian woman to college while she was on stage at Gnomedex in Seattle.

Jeff Pulver, founder of The 140 Characters Conference, and I decided to help prevent a single mother and her daughter from being evicted from their apartment by using an online payment service to collect money to go toward their rent. TipJoy is basically a PayPal for Twitter and was instrumental in tying together tweets, RTs, and contributions.

These examples will only grow in prominence as time passes.

➤ Number 21. Words of Wisdom

As reiterated throughout these top tips, listening and responding is helpful and efficacious in luring new customers, empowering advocacy, and instilling loyalty.

Serving as a resource for your community or industry positions, proactively responding to online users who are posing questions, and assisting those who are seeking advice and guidance can garner trust, respect, and camaraderie for you and the causes you espouse.

There are measurable and also incalculable benefits to dedicating resources to lead individuals and organizations to resolution.

For example, @homedepot monitors dialogue related to the company, but also those individuals who are tackling home projects and seeking tips and instructions.

BestBuy's @Twelpforce has authorized its entire staff of trained employees to seek out discussions related to consumer electronics, home theaters, gaming, music, appliances, and technology, and to answer questions, whether or not they're directly tied to the BestBuy brand.

The examples are many, and the common thread is a willingness to share and a dedication to offering help.

Chapter

The New Media University

Social Media 303

Higher education inspires us to strive for the insights that yield intelligence and personal significance. And here we are learning and sharing together—not about what we think we know, but mining for knowledge we don't yet possess. It's this ambition that broadens the gap between you, your goals, and everyone else. This is your time.

Let's now draw the curtains to reveal the windows into geo location and mobile networking, widgets and applications, and the immensely gripping and popular video broadcast networks.

■ GEO LOCATION/MOBILE NETWORKING

One of the lesser-known, more interesting facts about Twitter is also one of its most legendary. Even though Twitter debuted in March 2006, it took one year and an onslaught of South by Southwest (SXSW) geeks convening in Austin, Texas, to employ Twitter in the transient activity that would ultimately bring it into the social media spotlight. For those who are unfamiliar with SXSW, it is an annual, landmark event that combines music, film, and interactives to celebrate the artistry of the people who are engendering innovation and engaging communities in the real world.

During SXSW 2007, Twitter became the glue that connected everyone together during the pandemonium associated with the conference, which is attended by thousands of geeks from all over the world. Tweets flew back and forth, with attendees alerting friends and followers where they were and what they were witnessing, to share experiences and designate the next rendezvous. This rush of early adopters congregating in one city at the same time and using

Twitter as a real-time human-powered positioning system helped to establish awareness for an application that initially struggled to find a market.

Even as Twitter was acquiring market share, it wasn't the first micromedia network designed to connect people via geography and location. At the time, Dodgeball was also competing for users as the essential network that bound together people and the locales they occupied online and in the real world. For several reasons, Twitter adoption outpaced Dodgeball, and subsequently Google eventually laid the service to rest.

Concurrently, another service contended with Twitter, not just for status updates, but also to help users connect with each other IRL. Jaiku, which eventually was acquired by Google, was honed on the Web and also on the Nokia mobile platform. Updates were viewable by user and location, allowing individuals to see what people were doing and where.

With the launch of the iPhone and other "smart" mobile devices, the rise of mobile networks flourished. Applications such as BrightKite, Loopt, and Yahoo!'s FireEagle introduced a new element to micro/mobile networking. Not only are people encouraged to update their status, they're motivated to "check in" to specific locations, tying a place with an action.

Two years after Twitter stormed SXSW, a new service also emerged as the breakout application to consume attention (and bandwidth) during the popular show in Austin. Built by one of the original creators of Dodgeball, FourSquare united location-based networking with micronetworking, and introduced a gaming element to the experience.

Like Loopt and BrightKite, FourSquare uses the phone's ability to discern a location and, based on the privacy settings, can show nearby friends and the locations that they've visited on a map. FourSquare also rewards users and ranks them by city and by location. Updates are also transmittable to Twitter for public consumption or as direct messages to stay connected to important contacts in both networks. While these mobile networks operate independently from Twitter, they are meant to extend the functionality of existing networks, not replace them.

With mobile networking, the world becomes a much smaller place. Mobile networking also uncovers new riches and interesting people within each neighborhood for discovery and exploration.

There's an interesting play here for businesses looking to promote a local presence and also attract new customers (whether they're permanent residents or simply visiting). Certainly, many of the applications mentioned in the Top 21 Tips for Twitter (see Chapter 8) will serve as inspiration. Coupons, offers, events, tips/advice, and to-do lists represent the initial opportunities to establish goodwill, create a presence, and forge loyal relationships. When tied to Yelp, local-based networks can symbolize a potential windfall—when practiced genuinely, sincerely, and creatively.

For example, in FourSquare, an individual who repeatedly visits and checks-in to a particular location automatically becomes the mayor of that establishment, until someone else overthrows them. In one instance, San Francisco–based Marsh Cafe is promoting free drinks for the Foursquare Mayor. And why not? Every time someone checks-in, they're essentially marketing and advertising a business or service—especially if they add updates, tips, and to-do's around the location. It's peer-to-peer influence at its best and very engaging.

However, as in any social network, you must embrace and participate in the community if you wish to truly be part of it.

■ WIDGETS/APPLICATIONS

Facebook, MySpace, and other social networks enable developers to build branded applications and widgets that are embeddable within the forums. With the right promotion, branding, and interactivity (stickiness), brands can enjoy viral sharing and engagement, which spurs adoption and brand visibility.

Widgets are also ideal for the Social Web in general. Many businesses are creating portable branded widgets that can travel from social network profiles to blogs to websites. They can deliver an immersive, compartmentalized experience that's shareable and potentially viral.

Most sophisticated applications and widgets require a development team. Other simple, yet functional widgets can be self-created using tools such as Sprout Builder.

The inherent value of applications and widgets is in their social architecture. These range from games to quizzes, surveys, and polls, to widgets that provide a self-contained weblike experience and are embeddable and sometimes portable across multiple networks. As users install an application on their page or profile, their friends are introduced to it either by visiting their page or by viewing updates generated from the application that are published in the general timeline. Applications and widgets are highly viral in that they're powered by sharing and in-timeline public updating.

When well-crafted and strategically promoted, apps are contagious and an effective means for establishing and broadening in-network communities.

Many brands have contracted developers to build branded apps to deploy in specific social networks to engage users through themes and interactions that tie back to the brand or brand personality.

Widgets are basically self-contained, portable Web experiences or even mini websites. According to Wikipedia,[1] a Web widget is a portable chunk of code that can be installed and executed within any separate HTML-based Web page by an end user, without requiring additional compilation. They are derived from the idea of code reuse. Web widgets typically, but not always, use DHTML, JavaScript, or Adobe Flash.

Widgets often take the form of on-screen tools—clocks, event countdowns, auction-tickers, stock market tickers, flight arrival information, daily weather, and more. In the era of the Social Web, widgets are now also including mini sites that feature games, the ability to find, follow, and interact with individuals and organizations, and also stream/host content such as video, pictures, audio, and so forth. For example, when viewing a YouTube video on a website outside of YouTube, you are viewing it through an embeddable widget. In this case, the widget is taking the form of a video player. Although the video appears on the site, it's hosted back at YouTube and the widget creates a bridge between the site and the original video.

For example, Coke developed a handy QuickCodeEntry widget for its My Coke Rewards promotion that lets people earn points by drinking Coke (and other Coca-Cola products) and then redeem them for a wide range of products and services from various partners. The QuickCodeEntry widget resides on the user's desktop and lets them quickly and easily enter a reward code and check their latest balance, without having to launch a browser and visit the My Coke Rewards website. It's a convenient tool that helps encourage user participation in their program (see http://is.gd/22W7u).

■ VIDEO BROADCAST NETWORKS

Video is the new frontier, again, and it's powered by the socialization of content, which balances the landscape for producers and viewers, each collaborating with the other to broaden visibility and incite reactions. The ability to produce and publish online video is universal and the networks that host them can extend the reach of any person or brand globally, facilitating connections based on the content in a practically limitless array

YouTube popularized the use of embed code to encourage people to automatically add favorite videos to their websites, blogs, and profiles in social networks. It is this use of embed code that further fueled the creation of other embeddable content, such as pictures, documents and presentations, animated media, and games.

The following is an example of embed code:

```
<object width = "560" height = "340">
  <param name = "movie" value = "http://www.youtube.com/v/
    xa1zvj5YDy4&hl = en&fs = 1&">
  </param>
  <param name = "allowFullScreen" value = "true">
  </param>
  <param name = "allowscriptaccess" value = "always">
  </param>
  <embed src = "http://www.youtube.com/v/xa1zvj5YDy4&hl =
    en&fs = 1&" type = "application/x-shockwave-flash"
    allowscriptaccess = "always" allowfullscreen = "true"
    width = "560" height = "340">
  </embed>
</object>
```

Yes, it looks complicated, but it's very easy to implement. YouTube, and most other media networks, provide the ability to copy the code and all you have to do is paste it where you want the video (or media) to play.

Digital measurement company Comscore released a report[2] showing that U.S. Internet users viewed an astounding 14.8 billion online videos in January 2009 alone, representing an increase of 4 percent over December 2008. By far, YouTube is leading the category, contributing 91 percent of all activity toward the gain. Comscore also noted that 76.8 percent of the total U.S. Internet audience viewed online videos in that particular month.

It's estimated that YouTube recently surpassed 100 million users for the first time. The average online video viewer watched 356 minutes of video (approximately 6 hours), which symbolized an increase of 15 percent over the previous month. In one month, 100.9 million viewers watched 6.3 billion videos on YouTube, which averaged about 62.6 videos per viewer. YouTube isn't the only network where videos are pervasive, however. For example, 54.1 million people watched 473 million videos on MySpace, which equates to roughly 8.7 videos per viewer. And Facebook released statistics that claim that over 10 million videos are uploaded to the social network each month.

Obviously the opportunity for finding online video audiences is tremendous. Getting and holding their attention, however, are different. Anyone can shoot and upload a video. However, we represent a brand, and that brand perception is defined through the content we produce and share. Quality, professionalism, creativity, and context speak volumes. Otherwise anyone, including your competitors, could win market share through the creation of amateur video.

There's a reason why I say that there's no such thing as viral videos and viral marketing. It's people that make something viral, not the video itself. Simply uploading a video to YouTube will not in and of itself earn attention, nor will it spark a flurry of views and shares. Almost nothing goes viral without preparation and orchestration, fused with a little luck.

Videos are mostly viewed as finite campaigns and not as dedicated channels to visualizing a company or brand story.

In one such instance, which must go unnamed unfortunately, I was hired by a major consumer pet food company to help save its "viral" videos that debuted on YouTube a month earlier. The marketing team was frustrated that the videos hadn't received a significant volume of views and were prepared to kill the entire campaign. However, with a little strategy, guidance, and coordination, we resuscitated the videos through an informed, targeted, and substantial outbound program.

First, we removed the videos from YouTube and created a new, more intriguing, dedicated and polished channel to house the content. We then cleverly titled and tagged the videos to promote social media optimization (SMO). This gave the videos a fresh start, with zero views and recent upload dates. Since time was of the essence, we didn't include the usual program element of assembling and managing a devoted digital "street team" to help us promote the videos across the Social Web. Note: these teams are either paid or rewarded with noteworthy or valuable stuff.

We then monitored conversations on Twitter, blogs, and other video networks related to dogs, bacon, and other key attributes of the video series and drafted clever, yet informational introductions to the video and encouraged people to view and share. For Twitter, we used Twazzup.com and Search.Twitter.com, and for blogs we used blogsearch.google.com and Technorati (we searched blogs by "topic," not keywords). The video earned 20,000 views within the first 24 hours, and that number only continued to skyrocket as time progressed. Not that views account for success, but in this case, views were used as the metric from the inception point.

In other cases we tied an action to the end result in order to truly measure the effectiveness of the video. When we were introducing a particular online social bookmarking tool, we realized that its greatest market opportunity resided with the vertical markets of users seeking to document, share, and plan activities and projects around information discovered online. We shot a four-minute demonstration video as a screencast (a video that captures what's on the computer screen) along with narration from the user perspective. The goal of the video was to inform people that a new solution existed that could help them. Our metrics were determined by how many people watched the video and clicked through to download the application. With these two parameters in mind, we drafted a script and storyboard that would entertain, capture attention, and motivate people to click-through to install the software. Again, titled and tagged strategically in YouTube as well as promoted among the people we discovered who were already looking for a solution like this on Twitter, blogs, and other social networks, we earned 70,000 views in one week with almost 60 percent of those translating into direct downloads. The campaign continued effectively and would ultimately spark a new series of videos that demonstrated its advantages to specific markets.

With reference to digital street teams, they can be a highly effective group when directed and managed. They must be held to metrics, which should be defined prior to the formation and official deployment of the team. "Viral" marketing agencies exist and they can help you produce and promote videos. They're not inexpensive, but they can orchestrate popular, far-reaching campaigns. Ultimately, it's the intent and goals of the video that determine the content and promotion strategies.

Many businesses film their spokespersons or project leads demonstrating or discussing a product or service and in most cases, it never truly connects or resonates with viewers. They're usually presented in a top-down messaging format, showcasing the features and benefits that the presenter "thinks" makes for interesting viewing. We learned otherwise. Other videos feature interviews with executives or key personnel, but much like the demo videos, most are not terribly interesting, revealing, or gripping. Online videos aren't necessarily gimmicks nor are they intended to provide the same old broadcast messages using new mediums.

This is storytelling.

This is entertainment.

This is education.

This is your chance to genuinely connect with people in ways and in places where they're evidently focused and impressionable, using a human voice or creative narrative.

Videos can range from short demos, screencasts, or event footage, to entertaining "day in the life of" snippets, collages, customer or "hero" interviews, original episodes related to your value proposition, or behind the scenes footage, to helpful guides and "did you know" segments that appeal to viewers as well as help them learn, solve, or perform something they couldn't do before watching the video.

Now before you jump over to YouTube or any other video network such as Viddler, Metacafe, Blip.tv, and so on, think about the video strategy and the associated branding of your online video presence. I highly recommend creating one master channel and also dedicated channels to specific programming and company divisions. This keeps everything focused, organized, and highly brandable without cluttering or diluting the brand through the saturation of various videos housed in one massive location.

Also, it's essential that each video is titled, described, and tagged with SMO using the keywords that are important to your market as well as the keywords that your customers and prospects are using to find relevant information.

■ VIDEO EXAMPLE: HOME DEPOT

Home Depot serves as an excellent example of a brand publishing relevant and educational video content that won't be dismissed as overly promotional or gimmicky. The company launched a Home Depot branded channel on YouTube (www.homedepot.com/youtube) that features know-how videos on relevant material—anything from programming a thermostat for optimal energy efficiency to installing

Figure 9.1   Home Depot on YouTube

a bath fan (see Figure 9.1). While a step-by-step video on retiling the shower doesn't have mass appeal, it's going to be highly relevant to a key demographic—those interested in DIY home renovation projects (and those most likely looking to buy bathroom tiles and other needed supplies).

What's particularly successful about Home Depot's approach is that the videos lack outright product pitches by blatant spokespeople. Instead, we see Home Depot employees offering practical advice and walking through each step in a very natural, friendly way. It's almost as if someone walked into their local Home Depot and asked a store associate a question. Of course, Home Depot is promoting their merchandise, but more importantly, they're establishing themselves as a trusted and friendly resource for whatever home improvement task is on the front burner.

Chapter 10

The New Media University

Social Media 401

In the 401 series of the New Media University program, we will undergo initiations that introduce us to the technology undercurrent as well as the philosophies and social sciences that govern and enrich human behavior on the Social Web.

■ SOCIAL OBJECTS

The topic of social objects will force us to think about social media as the connection of abstract objects that trigger and host related dialogues and activities.

In social media, these objects are personified by the pictures in Flickr, the videos on YouTube, the events in Upcoming, the profiles in Facebook, the links in Delicious, the votes in Digg, the places in FourSquare, the documents in Scribd, a destination or service in Yelp, a subject in Ning, a thought shared in the comment of a blog post, and so on.

Essentially, Social Objects in social networks take the form of content or media and can induce responses and reaction in each network in which they're launched as dictated by those who notice and are prompted or notified.

Subscribing to the school of thought that aligns effective social media strategies with anthropology and sociology, social objects therefore represent the epicenter for the extensive, diversified, and distributed micronetworks that are formed within larger, established social networks. Social Objects become the hubs for specialized engagement and discourse at the point of introduction and also as time, relevance, and the debut and discovery of related objects continue to support interaction.

Introducing social theory into the mix of social media allows us to understand the behaviors and movements that regulate and affect the culture and influence of objects within respective groups of individuals that share affinities and interests.

According to social theory,[1] the comprehension of natural phenomena is predicated on the understanding of social phenomena, as the interpretation of natural phenomena is a social activity. To better understand the nature and prospect of adoption and resulting activity associated with social objects, we must embrace social theory as it relates to existing and past objects of similar traits and targets online. Altogether, this is not unlike the fieldwork and observational studies performed by anthropologists and sociologists.

Typically, we view the connections established within social networks as symbolizing relationships between people. Therefore we look at the number of friends and followers as a metric for authority and popularity. However, as we discuss in Chapter 20, which visualizes "human networks," we've learned that in social media, the pattern for forging connection is migrating towards orbiting objects over the criteria usually associated with establishing traditional friendships and acquaintances.

In 2009, Bernardo A. Huberman, Daniel M. Romero, and Fang Wu of the Social Computing Laboratory at HP Labs issued a report that examined relationships on Twitter. Their findings, published in "Social Networks That Matter: Twitter under the Microscope,"[2] revealed that the driver of usage is actually a sparse and hidden network of connections that defines the declared set of friends and followers.

In the abstract, HP Labs disclosed, "The scarcity of attention and the daily rhythms of life and work make people default to interacting with those few that matter and that reciprocate their attention."

As the HP Labs report states, people do interact with those few who matter and reciprocate recognition. But they did not account for the viral potential of social objects. They did however, qualify it and helped associate credibility for the consumption and sharing of the content within their social graph as well as the respective graphs of their contacts.

The backchannel, which is practically immeasurable for the time being outside of our dominion, is also incredibly influential in the volume and extent of interaction, as well as the duration of the lifecycle and lifespan of any social object.

The backchannel represents the communication, connections, cooperation, favors, deals, and alliances that transpire, form, and take shape outside public view—usually through in-network messaging, traditional e-mail, and events that take place offline, among other forms of invisible interaction. The backchannel is instrumental in the creation and ensuing success of programs designed around social objects.

The contacts that we leveraged in these cases were distinct in their interrelationship and association with the nature of each social object. Said another way, people didn't connect to or share content in the long term just because we placed it in front of them and asked them nicely to view and promote the content. An emotional or intellectual bond must eventually exist—even in the cases of established, proven, healthy, and vibrant relationships.

Assuredly, these prevailing relationships forged prior to the introduction of social objects, reinforced by interaction and recognition, created the most successful foundations for the introduction, adoption, and distribution of relevant and related social objects. Note, what started as empirical, research-based test beds evolved into carefully crafted communities through the diligent and exacting means of curating and cultivating relations and alliances over time.

Having described the benefits of the backchannel, I should mention that its effectiveness is not without limits. While there may initially be natural enthusiasm and excitement as new objects are presented, without scrutiny, restraint, respect, and, most important, recognition and reciprocation, we unwittingly foster exhaustion and possibly resentment among our peers.

It's about awareness trumping promotion, social alliances but not socialism, and camaraderie and collaboration over hierarchy.

Building these communities to support social objects represents only one way to ensure their acceptance and incite engagement and response, albeit an effective and ethical way. Additionally, online support and promotion of social objects is readily available for hire. Service providers, consultants, and marketing agencies dedicated to creating awareness and visibility for social objects are prevalent and in truth, they have always existed. Their art, techniques, and playing fields have transformed with every technology (r)evolution, including social media.

Is it wrong or unethical to hire these hired guns? I suppose it's all in the way that they draw attention to the object and ultimately how your brand fares throughout the promotion. Studies already show that this has and most likely always will work when practiced thoughtfully and artfully.

■ GETTING NOTICED: SOCIAL MEDIA OPTIMIZATION, THE NEW SEO

As discussed, at the center of any social media program is the social object. And, in many social networks, that object takes the form of content, profiles, events, media, and other social semblances that establish conversational hubs. Content indeed serves as the foray into the conversations that ultimately define the presence, acceptance, and perception of any brand.

Uploading content into a social network simply guarantees that it will have a place to reside online. Visibility and the socialization of the content however, are not assured. Contrary to perception, objects don't inherently generate gravitational pull. The laws of attraction are not unlike those in the wild kingdom. Specifically, we have to integrate digital seduction in the objects we wish to earn attention and notoriety.

Much in the same way that SEO helps keywords and the sites and Web pages that they point to gain greater visibility in searches, SMO increases visibility for keywords and the corresponding objects within social networks.

For example, YouTube is among the largest destinations for search. Delicious continues to serve as a qualified, user-generated content search engine—aside from offering social bookmarking capabilities. Flickr is one of the default stops for image search, which also feeds Yahoo! and Google image searches. The point is that if you want your content discovered, it requires Social Media Optimization to increase its discoverability.

■ WHAT IS SOCIAL MEDIA OPTIMIZATION?

Social media optimization (SMO), at the moment, is less scientific than search engine optimization, but none less important. At a minimum, SMO refers to the deliberate acts of aligning keywords with social objects to improve the association of your content with the individuals performing the search within specific social networks as well as traditional searches and also real-time/social search engines.

To clarify...

Traditional search: Searches performed in the search engines that have existed since the dawn of the Web, such as Google, Yahoo!, and the like.

Real-time search: The emerging category of search, spawned by the adoption of Twitter search, where content is discoverable as it's uploaded online, whether it's on a website, blog, or any social network, including Twitter. Real-time search engines include Collecta, OneRiot, and Topsy, among others.

Social network search: A manual form of search within each social network, in which keywords or keyword strings are manually input into the search boxes of each network.

SMO specifically is defined by the elements ingrained in each social network. For example, when a social object is uploaded to its respective social network, you're provided with the opportunity to further describe the content through the titles, descriptions, and tags. To get a bit geeky here, this is technically referred to as metadata. Quite specifically, metadata is the data that defines other data. It is this metadata that proved instrumental in Web 2.0 to help classify and organize the volumes of user-generated content uploaded to social networks and blogs everywhere. Unknowingly, we became the Web's librarians and helped to index the volumes of social objects to help others discover them quickly and easily.

Yes, tags, descriptions, and keywords collectively contribute to the "discoverability" of social content.

■ TITLES

Titles refer to the official designation or name of the content. Specifically, when you upload a video, image, or any other social object, the headline serves as the main moniker. The art of headline writing is not unlike that of magazines or newspapers. It must grip the viewer immediately and compel them to act and hopefully share. In social media, the headline must also contain the keywords that explicitly match the search patterns of the people you hope to reach.

■ DESCRIPTIONS

Descriptions further refine the context of the social object to entice visitors to view and hopefully circulate it among their social graph. Usually the description falls either beneath the title or below the media preview. The description field is your chance to frame an object in order to further convince or entice the viewer to spend a portion of their precious time clicking through, as well as helps form how they should perceive and mentally assimilate the intended messages, desired sentiment, and strategic takeaways. Make sure that the description includes at least two or three keywords related to your business/brand and target viewers.

■ TAGS

Tags are basically keywords that further group and organize the object within the social network. Tags are based on folksonomy,[3] a system of classification derived from the practice and method of collaboratively creating and managing tags to annotate and categorize content within specific networks.

■ ■ ■

The same process of matching content based on metadata can be engineered to work in your favor in almost every social network where titles, tags, and descriptions are woven into the content fabric.

Moving forward, let's presume that tags and keywords are identical when referring to SMO, and that keywords are the social beacons that extend visibility.

Indeed, keywords are the whispers behind closed doors that secretly control the popularity and ranking of websites and media—not only in social media, but across the World Wide Web. Keyword ranking is referred to as the dark art of SEO, and it is unimaginably powerful. We borrow the basics from the black book of SEO to help us increase visibility for media within social networks. And it is these keywords that serve as one side of the social media optimization equation.

When we think of keywords, we usually conjure the terms and names related to the content we're describing. We're also usually modest about those terms, but keywords should also describe the content using associated expressions, phrases, and labels. It is essential to not only attach the words and descriptors that we think best describe the content; we must also audit the terminology frequently exercised by our communities when finding and sharing related information. This will help increase the exposure of our content, as it is driven more by how they categorize it.

One way to do so is to use an online keyword tool to help analyze the trends, obtain ideas, and most importantly, to visualize popular terms that others may use in addition to or in place of your keywords or phrases. One such tool (and it's free) is Google Adwords, which is located at https://adwords.google.com/select/KeywordToolExternal, or simply Google "Google keyword tool."

In some networks, tags also serve as grouping mechanisms in addition to keyword anchors that facilitate the categorization of social objects within a social timeline–helping people find them at later points in time. In particular, the use of #hashtags in Twitter serve as keywords or tag markers, which surface all of the discussions related to either a social object or topic through a standard Twitter search.

■ CONTENT DISTRIBUTION

On the other side of the Social Media Optimization equation is content distribution, which metaphorically establishes presences in strategic networks and points back to the original content to increase visibility and findability.

If we upload a picture worthy of viewing for any number of reasons, we would then organize community-supported activity to help attract targeted visitors—after we effectively titled, described, and tagged the image of course. The next step could employ a strategy where we promote the content within those networks dedicated to the sharing and promotion of social objects, such as a Digg, del.icio.us, and StumbleUpon.

Inserting the object into the network isn't enough, however. An organized, thorough, and significant effort is also imperative to earn votes and bookmarks (diggs in digg, stumbles in StumbleUpon, and bookmarks in Delicious). Combined with the incorporation of SMO within each network, this orchestrated campaign of promoting the object can generate tens of thousands of unique views. Perhaps I should highlight a small but important note about SMO in these networks. When objects are placed within each network, timing and placement are critical. Digg, for instance, offers channels for video, pictures, and stories, as well as other forms of media. Within each of those channels are subpassages that further categorize the object, such as News, Technology, Sports, and so forth. While many networks offer a general "main" group, in most cases, placing the content within the appropriate bracket, by someone who has a proven or trusted reputation within the network, will lend credibility and also position the object advantageously.

If you're without the resources to generate say, the 200 to 300 immediate, yet rhythmic, votes that it takes to make the front page of Digg, a simple Web search will turn up teams and resources dedicated to helping you make the top list within any network for a price. Rising too fast usually triggers bots that quell rapid escalations as the system is programmed to assume that someone is "gaming it." Any reputable team will know this and will help steer you effectively. To make the front page of Digg or StumbleUpon, you're looking at anywhere between $500 and $2,500 per instance.

The quantity of views, diggs, bookmarks, and tweets contributes to the popularity of the object within the particular network, and, with enough velocity, the object can make the short list or front page of what's hot, right now.

Through a content syndication plus SMO strategy, the social object can also earn prominence in Twitter, Facebook, and other social networks to entice views and also bookmarks, additional sharing, "likes," favorites, and comments. Much in the same way an orchestrated program can increase diggs in Digg, for example, tweets and retweets of a particular URL can also send thousands and potentially multiples of thousands to any given destination.

■ LINKS

In SEO, the quantity of inbound links increase the Google PageRank for any given website. In blog ranking, inbound links contribute to the authority of a particular blog overall. In social media, inbound links increase the weight and visibility of social objects. These links serve as orbiting satellites that beam signals (or traffic) back to the source and can be measured in views, ratings, retweets, likes, and favorites. This criterion portrays stature and engenders credibility for steering perception when someone "stumbles upon" the object. Depending on the host network, the gauges are viewable by visitors and hosts alike.

For example, in Flickr and YouTube the quantity of "views" is readily present. In Delicious and Digg, that benchmark is visible in the number of other bookmarks or Diggs. In Twitter, we can view the aggregate of retweets through a BackTweets or Search.Twitter. In Facebook, we can calculate the sum of "likes" and comments.

Of course, many of these social networks have earned prominence and visibility as measured by the ranking and authority that govern traditional search algorithms and determine the placement and ranking of specific social objects in search engine results pages (SERPs). While I focus on the proactive and organic activities that amplify and escalate the discoverability of social objects within their respective social networks, SMO fundamentally offers SEO benefits as well.

The folksonomy that served as the underpinning of Web 2.0 will be augmented as the Social Web progresses. The next generation of the Web, referred to as Web Squared (by Tim O'Reilly, the visionary who coined the phrase Web 2.0), and also called the Semantic Web, will inject intelligence or semantics into the foundation of the Web to connect data, metadata, and personal preferences based on individual activity, as well as the related activities of those in the individual's immediate social graph.

■ LIKING: MICROACTS OF APPRECIATION YIELD MACRO IMPACTS

"Like" is basically similar, in principle, to the "favorites" feature found in many popular communities, such as Twitter, which essentially served as an in-network bookmarking system. This small but important feature nonetheless has the ability to reinforce relationships between friends and followers and those who produce, interact with, and share content.

Made popular by services such as FriendFeed, and now Facebook, the idea of "liking" an update is much stronger than merely bookmarking or favoriting ("favoriting" is now a verb, too) updates from friends and contacts for later reference or sharing. Liking is the epitome of the relationship-based culture powering the authenticity, ethics, and reciprocal interactions on the Social Web. It's a powerful form of microrecognition, which serves as an approving, motivating, and uplifting nod from someone else.

Likes also set forth the potential for macro impact within social networks. The deed of liking an update resonates within and outside the social graph, as those who follow your activity will receive your signal in their respective timeline and it will serve as a potential trigger for them to view what it is that has caught your attention. If they in turn like the object, this further amplifies the source post by placing the trigger within the timelines of their friends and followers as well as their network of friends of friends (FoFs), precipitating action and additional views and likes.

As the Social Web and new services continue to migrate into and permeate everything we do online, we're faced with an increasingly thinning state of continuous partial attention[4] (CPA). It's affecting how and what we consume, when, and more importantly, how we react, participate, and share. That "something" is forever vying for our attention and relentlessly pushing us to do more with less, driven by the omnipresent fear of missing out on what's next.

Likes are incredibly powerful as they facilitate the sharing of "the love" in byte-sized actions that reverberate throughout social networks, resulting in a formidable network effect of movement or diversion. It is the digital curation of relevant content that binds us contextually. Liking sets the stage to not only introduce new content to new people, but also to facilitate the forging of new friendships in the process.

Chapter 11

The New Media University

Social Media 402

Collectively, we contribute to the wisdom or irrelevance of the crowds and citizen journalists that rule the Social Web. The brilliance of social media is that at any point in time, we can gauge the sentiments and impressions, perceive the states of affairs and potential or existing hot spots, glean insights, and trendcast opportunities to diagnose, discover, and determine the fate of our brand. This real-time digital sampling is infinite in its benefits and promise.

Let it guide you.

Be thoughtful.

Make me care.

Inspire me to follow you.

Help me learn.

Earn my respect and trust.

■ ESTABLISHING A SYNDICATION NETWORK

The fundamentals and associated benefits of a syndication network serve as the mechanics of SMO. In addition, a well-established and thoughtfully constructed syndication network can not only improve SEO and SMO, but also enhance the consumption diets of those who choose to follow your activities. Similar to the social dashboard we discuss in Chapter 6, a syndication network operates on the premise that people don't find and follow objects and the individuals who interest them in the same ways. It's our job to serve as a bridge between the interesting content we create and those who are seeking it—in the networks where they're actively searching for meaningful content.

While directly participating in the social networks of significance (a topic we discuss further in our review of "The Conversation Prism" in Chapter 18), the mere act of producing a pulse in outside networks is beneficial in establishing a community around a pure informational source.

Remember, in this section, we're not discussing the actions necessary to effectively cultivate a community through direct participation. Here, the social object becomes the participant and the greater visibility it receives through predefined distribution increases the potential for discovery, appreciation, and redistribution.

Thus the dawn of syndication and aggregation is upon us.

Syndication symbolizes our ability to upload one object and have it simultaneously appear across multiple networks.

■ SYNDICATING SOCIAL OBJECTS: AN ILLUSTRATION

Aggregation refers to the content consumption patterns of those seeking content in one place, and therefore we can create branded activity streams that channel our distributed content into one timeline (see Figure 11.1).

■ CHANNELING ILLUSTRATION: AN ACTIVITY STREAM

Building a framework that unites the distributed objects published in disparate networks is a primary goal of our social aggregation strategy

Figure 11.1 Syndicating Social Objects

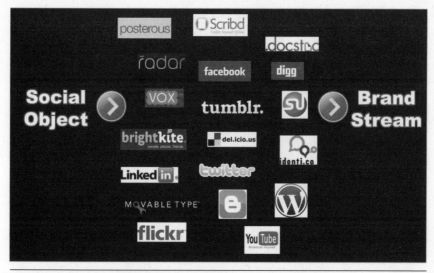

Figure 11.2   Aggregating Social Objects

(see Figure 11.2). In parallel, ensuring that individual social objects are beamed to other networks to balance our content marketing program is a chief objective of a social syndication strategy.

Aggregation + Syndication = Extended presence for scattered social objects and improved organic SMO and SEO

Everything starts with building a framework that extends from one source to other predefined profiles that accept outside feeds. We then build varying levels of activity feeds in designated networks to activate the content fire-hose for those consumers who prefer following full data streams.

The idea of the abstraction of content in aggregate or syndicate can be perceived as oxymoronic at times. When we talk about publishing one post across multiple networks simultaneously, we are syndicating that content. If we pull our diverse content from the multiple networks where they're hosted into one place, we're aggregating data. The confusion emerges when we realize that certain networks are both aggregating and possibly syndicating content simultaneously.

I know, this seems a bit overcomplicated, so let's step back for a second to look at syndication and aggregation from a byte-sized perspective to further examine these concepts.

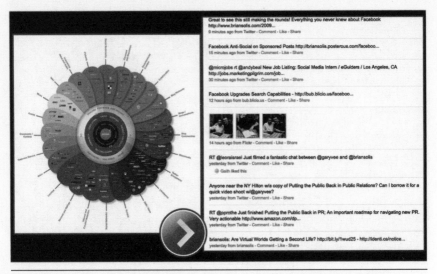

Figure 11.3   Channeling Social Objects into One Aggregated Stream

■ AGGREGATION: ASSEMBLING THE PIECES

Aggregation networks—also referred to as brand streams, lifestreams, activity feeds, or activity streams—collect the various feeds you specify and channel everything into a single branded presence (see Figure 11.3). These specialized services are hosted within dedicated social networks and allow followers to subscribe to your complete content stream for viewing, commenting, and sharing. Examples of aggregation networks include Plaxo Pulse, Tumblr, SocialThing, Lifestream.fm, Chi.mp, Profilactic, and FriendFeed (before the Facebook acquisition).

Essentially, we create a profile and presence in one or more of these networks. We then define which services we wish to funnel into these profiles, such as blog posts, Twitter updates, Flickr pictures, YouTube videos, documents from Scribd, and so forth. These services offer built-in features for automating and simplifying the process for adding a wide variety of feeds and presenting them in an easy-to-follow, aesthetically pleasing data river.

■ EXAMPLE OF ACTIVITY STREAM

Lifestream or activity feed systems also offer in-network response mechanisms, similar to blog posts, Twitter, and Facebook, for followers

Great to see this still making the rounds! Everything you never knew about Facebook
http://www.briansolis.com/2009...
9 minutes ago from Twitter - Comment - Like - Share

Facebook Anti-Social on Sponsored Posts http://briansolis.posterous.com/faceboo...
15 minutes ago from Twitter - Comment - Like - Share

@microjobs rt @andybeal New Job Listing: Social Media Intern / eGuiders / Los Angeles, CA
http://jobs.marketingpilgrim.com/job...
30 minutes ago from Twitter - Comment - Like - Share

Facebook Upgrades Search Capabilities - http://bub.blicio.us/faceboo...
12 hours ago from bub.blicio.us - Comment - Like - Share

14 hours ago from Flickr - Comment - Like - Share

RT @leoraisrael Just filmed a fantastic chat between @garyvee and @briansolis
yesterday from Twitter - Comment - Like - Share
  ⊚ Gaith liked this

Anyone near the NY Hilton w/a copy of Putting the Public Back in Public Relations? Can I borrow it for a
quick video shoot w/@garyvee?
yesterday from Twitter - Comment - Like - Share

RT @pprothe Just finished Putting the Public Back in PR; An important roadmap for navigating new PR.
Very actionable http://www.amazon.com/dp...
yesterday from Twitter - Comment - Like - Share

briansolis: Are Virtual Worlds Getting a Second Life? http://bit.ly/1wud25 - http://identi.ca/notice...
yesterday from briansolis - Comment - Like - Share

Figure 11.4   Social News Feed

to respond to your updates through comments, repost in their feed,
bookmark, or send to content-voting communities such as Digg or
StumbleUpon (see Figure 11.4).

Naturally, syndicating your content in these activity streams further enhances organic SEO and Web visibility around important
keywords.

■ IN-NETWORK AGGREGATION

Initially, social networks were islands: The content that was uploaded
within each network was exclusive to it. Over time, network architects

realized that the more people shared, the more conversations would ensue. Thus, social networks opened up the ability to import outside feeds into their profiles to increase in-network interaction—similar to activity streams—capturing and holding the attention of users in one network.

Facebook, for example, offers the ability to pull feeds from almost any network into your news feed through its "settings" option. It provides a seamless process for choosing which streams you wish to "pull" and, in turn, publish in your Facebook News Feed to thus be potentially discovered by those friends who choose to receive your updates in their timeline. As you publish new content from each respective network, the objects are automatically syndicated to and aggregated in Facebook. It's now very common to host multiple responses and simultaneous conversations wherever the content appears. For example, a blog post can entertain dialogue at the host site, but now that it also appeared in your news feed (which is visible by friends and followers) reactions are likely to occur within Facebook concurrently (see Figure 11.5).

Twitter is also a channel for creating and circulating original content (tweets), as well as an activity feed for sharing aggregated social objects from other social networks directly in your Twitter stream. Those who follow you on Twitter can receive your tweets plus the other social objects from unconnected networks in their timeline. If

Figure 11.5 Facebook Social News Feed

Funneling Distributed Social Objects into One Aggregated Stream

Twitter

New guest post on PR 2.0 by @cheeky_geeky Making Whuffie With Julia Allison http://bit.ly/6jwNu
9 minutes ago from web

A quick video interview with @karaswisher & me re: Putting the Public Back in Public Relations on @wsj – http://is.gd/2f8yV
about 17 hours ago from web

Reading Girls in Tech "Journalism 2.0" Panel: Speak Loudly and Carry a Big Stick by @karaswisher http://is.gd/2fAbG
about 18 hours ago from web

http://twitpic.com/dramn – Just received my copy of Pro Tips by@Rafe & @itdatabase. Rafe, will u sign my copy?
about 19 hours ago from TwitPic

Pictures from the #girlsintech event w/ @karaswisher http://is.gd/2fkG0
about 22 hours ago from web

Pictures from the #vemma + @techset blogger lounge at #ase09 in NY – http://is.gd/2fkEL @chrisbrogan @stephagresta @1938media
about 22 hours ago from web

Figure 11.6   Twitter Social News Feed

your target consumer base is highly active in Twitter, this will prove as a highly valuable system for channeling additional content in and around your tweets. Therefore, Twitter, like Facebook, is both an aggregation tool and/or a fundamental component of a broader syndication channel.

If you so choose, your tweets, as well as updates from other dedicated content networks, can also broadcast to other networks, including Facebook, as part of your syndication strategy, which we'll discuss next (see Figure 11.6).

■ SYNDICATION: WEBCASTING SOCIAL OBJECTS

To illustrate the potential for the syndication network, let's examine the prospective audiences for a standard blog post. With syndication tools, we can sync the availability of a blog post from the host site and have it automatically repost in additional networks such as Facebook, Twitter, Ning, and Tumblr, among many other networks of choice—thus extending and amplifying its visibility considerably. Likewise, we can publish a video on YouTube, an image on Flickr, or post a tweet, and have this particular object propagate immediately to all of our predefined channels.

■ AUTOPOSTS AND SYNDICATION

Those people who choose to follow your brand in any or all of these communities can receive the full portrait of the brand persona through strategically crafted and curated media. That's the point of all of this, I suppose. We are what we produce and visible where we publish.

Tumblr is an ideal microblog for publishing long- or (preferably) short-form original material. It also facilitates the aggregation of syndicated content into one channel. Contrarily, Posterous represents a new genre of intelligent microblog that also helps producers easily create short-form original posts. But instead of channeling syndicated content, it encourages publishers to autopost content sourced from Posterous Web-wide to blogs, Twitter, Flickr, Facebook, Tumblr, and so forth. It also offers a unique syndication option in which you can easily dictate which posts are sent to which outside networks. It's essentially up to you whether you send updates to all or a combination of networks as dictated by the nature of the content and the communities you host within each.

There are many other tools that enable seamless syndicated publishing of social objects to outside networks, while certain communities offer this functionality inherently.

To channel objects to other networks that don't already offer the ability to pull feeds from other sources, "feedcasting" tools are readily available. For example, automating the syndication of a blog post to say, Twitter, TwitterFeed, or Feednest can connect the post as it is published directly to Twitter in the form of a tweet with an integrated link back to the source post. Setting up similar feeds, social objects published on other networks can also automatically simulcast to Twitter and/or other networks of your choosing.

Other services such as Ping.fm offer a discrete solution for publishing one update across prearranged, multiple services from Twitter to Facebook to BrightKite to Tumblr (and many others).

It is vital that you establish a viable, functional, and streamlined social architecture that complements the activity of other individuals and groups within the company, as well as the social presences they create and promote.

■ DON'T CROSS THE STREAMS

As we weave together our syndication and aggregation networks, we must remain acutely aware of each channel and where it sends or receives objects to ensure that we "don't cross the streams." This is especially true for larger organizations with multiple marketing, PR, and service departments. The likelihood for overlapping feeds is compounded not only by the size but also the mastery and savvy of those responsible for producing content, and further complicated by the reality that within most businesses, the opportunity will exist for multiple branded accounts within each social network.

Let's walk through an example of a tangled feed. If you automate the publishing of a blogpost to Twitter and have your Tumblr account set to receive either the blog post or the Twitter feed, and Twitter is automatically fed to Facebook, you've seamlessly broadcasted one post to three networks without any potential issues of crossing the streams. However, this one sentence shows that the intersection of content can potentially occur.

Let's say we publish a blog post and it's sent to Twitter and Tumblr, and ultimately Facebook. We have to ensure that Tumblr isn't set up to receive duplicate feeds from the blog or Twitter. Likewise, we also need to ensure that the Facebook settings are instructed to receive only one of those signals. Otherwise, it's quite feasible to have the blog post fed to Twitter and Tumblr, while Tumblr might also publish both the post and the tweet about the post, and then, in Facebook, we could view the post, the tweet about the post, the Tumblr post about the post, and the Tumblr post with the aggregated tweet from the post.

The Conversation Prism (Chapter 18) will serve as your central source for revelation and direction in the intersections of posts.

■ DESTINATION UNKNOWN: DEFINING THE JOURNEY THROUGH YOUR EXPERIENCE

Through the creation and distribution of online videos, blog posts, tweets, images, status updates, or a combination thereof, social objects rife with thoughtful and helpful content and intentions become an effective form of unmarketing through education, entertainment, and engagement. If we're creating content in disparate networks, we are indeed reaching people where they seek content, in the formats they prefer. But for those who choose to visit our site after viewing the media we publish in their respective network, we must ask ourselves—where are we sending these prospects and what is the impression they form or action they take once they get there?

By way of illustration, if a customer, influencer, or peer viewed a video on YouTube or picture series on Flickr, stumbled across a story on Digg, became of member of our Facebook group, or favorited one of our tweets or status updates, what is it the next action that we're defining? How do we connect them to other relevant information, content, and satisfaction? Does our website, as it stands, suffice for those who choose to click-through to the homepage or designated product pages?

Did you just hear those brakes screeching?

It's an all-too-common occurrence that, rather than socialize the experience from introduction to action, we send prospects to a static dead end at our website.

Participating and engaging is only part of the process. Defining the experience and guiding those whom you reach to a destination that invites further interaction and steers, enhances, and reinforces perceptions and impressions balances and strengthens the branded chain of events. (See Figure 11.7.) It is also an opportunity to capture user information and promote commerce.

As we syndicate our story and value proposition, we must funnel attention to its designated channel of relevance—a dedicated hub that serves as a visual menu for people seeking to connect, learn, communicate, share, and procure content or products and services. Today, when we participate and engage in the Social Web, we directly and indirectly drive consumers to review our profile page to learn more about us. From there, it's usually unclear where they go unless we establish a click path. But most of the time, we send them to our home page or we send them into the ether, and none of it is guided, strategic,

Figure 11.7   Defining the Experience

or tactical. Referring people to a traditional landing or home page in the Social Web is not only immeasurable, it's ineffective.

At the beginning of any social media initiative, we must establish an endgame—what is it that we are hoping to accomplish and how are we going to measure it?

The first step in answering this question is to realize that social media is not relegated solely to the creation, production, and distribution of social objects.

There's no shortage of businesses, and, more specifically, the individuals who represent them, seeking insights, answers, and directions to simplify, organize, and elucidate the intimidating and confusing set of available options. The Web has both simplified and complicated the process of decision-making. In unison, we mistakenly take comfort in the assumption that our customers and influencers already view us as a source of guidance and wisdom. However, it's not enough to create content. As you know, anyone with an opinion, a keyboard, camera, or microphone, fueled by the desire to freely and perpetually share, can do so at will nowadays. The question is, how do you as an authentic marketer, business leader, and service professional convince prospects that you're believable, qualified, and ready to lead?

Our job is to build the bridges that connect what we represent to those whom we can soundly advise, tethered by the answers, information, and exchanges that fortify each passage.

Once we understand how to build the bridges that connect knowledge and aspiration, we ultimately become accomplished and experienced social architects.

As we're learning, however, the bridges we build between people and social objects and the experiences they encounter along the way are fragmentary if not steered, strategically presented, and governed. These bridges need to lead to destinations that not only provide information, but also lead the followers to resolution. Therefore, social engagement is routed through the roads, highways, off-ramps, and ports of call that are devised and constructed by thoughtful and well-prepared social engineers.

It is this social engineering that enables the fabrication and interconnection of experiences and perception.

Partnering with the Web team is paramount, and not optional. In order to guide people to action, we have to engineer and build a complete and cohesive experience that connects social networks and social objects to our overall brand, its defining tenets, and its community.

But, what about the corporate website?

What about the company's commerce site and associated search and reviews engine?

Figure 11.8   Brand Identity Crisis

How about the hosting of conversations directly on the company site in addition to conducting dispersed social interactions across the Web?

What about building cohesion between our brand and the objects and networks where it's syndicated?

The experience must be complete and dynamic from the point of introduction to the point of action, tied together by the ideas and intentions we wish to convey and instill. Regardless of social or broadcast or static presences, we must always purport, represent, embody, and personify a harmony of oneness. (See Figure 11.8.)

We are one . . .

But the paradox of oneness in social media is that we relinquish control of the brand and the message—either unknowingly or willfully or both, without regard for the inevitable disconnection of the brand and the dissociation of its attributes. Contrary to popular belief, a brand is not completely crowd-sourced, nor should it be.

In a report published on ClickZ in July 2009,[1] Bill McCloskey, in partnership with StrongMail, observed the e-mail marketing campaigns of top brands and how they integrated social presences into the corporate fold. The data he analyzed revealed that top brands were reviving e-mail campaigns with the inclusion of links to social profiles, specifically Facebook, Twitter, and also MySpace.

In the ClickZ article, McCloskey reported that top brands such as Nike, Intel, The Gap, Pepsi, Sony, HP, Home Depot, Lane Bryant,

Circuit City, Saks Fifth Avenue, Polo Ralph Lauren, Lands' End, and J.C. Penney included social media within e-mail marketing messages. Since 2007, the number of e-mail campaigns that contained links to Facebook and Twitter dramatically increased, becoming the two most prominent links integrated in all e-mail marketing initiatives in 2009. For example, in 2008 McCloskey tracked 215 campaigns with a Twitter link and 729 programs promoting Facebook. In 2008, the number grew by 1,081 percent to 2,540 campaigns spotlighting Twitter profiles and 1,635 percent to 12,650 featuring Facebook. Midway through 2009, the numbers are progressively growing, but still astonishing nonetheless. As of June, the number of campaigns that included a link to the branded Twitter account grew to 41,399, with 41,052 for Facebook. The report was published partially through July 2009 and by the 27th of the month, McCloskey noted 9,063 campaigns including Facebook links and 10,277 e-mail initiatives with links to branded Twitter accounts.

Not only are these numbers off the charts in terms of year over year growth, companies referring e-mail recipients to Twitter profiles surpassed Facebook pages—yet both continued to grow remarkably. In another study released in July 2009, Burson-Marsteller[2] also validated that brands were opting for the promotion of Twitter over Facebook and corporate blogs. In fact, the numbers documented in a study of Fortune 100 companies showed that 54 percent of companies maintained a presence on Twitter, with only 29 percent on Facebook. Thirty-two percent of those reviewed published a corporate blog. In aggregate, the numbers painted a picture of opportunity. Twenty-one percent of those companies studied relied on one channel (Twitter, Facebook, or blogs), 22 percent were active on two channels, 17 percent maintained presences across all three, and a surprising 40 percent of Fortune 100 companies had yet to embrace any of the three.

As an interesting aside, Burson-Marsteller found that of the Fortune 100 companies using Twitter, the top usage scenarios included company news, customer service, marketing promotions, and employee recruitment.

We need a hub that's consistent with the experiences consumers expect inside and outside our mission control.

■ ■ ■

H&R Block's Digits site (http://digits.hrblock.com) is an H&R-branded community that offers tax and personal financial resources through Q&As, forums, videos, podcasts, blogs, and more. The site provides a wealth of information from H&R experts to help people navigate the murky waters of mortgage refinancing, economic stimulus benefits, and tax preparation and deductions. Digits also provides a host of widgets, such as Economic Stimulus FAQs and Tax Answers, to further spread the company's resources across blogs and social sites.

The previous example represents destinations that extend and focus the company's corporate message at the market or product level, while still building equity for the brand overall. If we evaluate the typical sales process that customers experience, we can intertwine a messaging platform that's consistent across social networks and objects:

1. Need/want/desire is recognized
2. Search for information
3. Evaluate options
4. The action of purchase
5. After-purchase evaluation

Adding to the list of attributes that are fundamental drivers for creating effective online presences and corresponding communities, we should also include those seeking:

1. Recognition
2. Affinity/association
3. Purpose
4. Insight
5. Entertainment
6. Rewards
7. Empowerment
8. Resolution
9. Access
10. Exclusive content

Addressing each of these points with content, design, structure, and click-paths will inspire new, enriched, and socially effective experience-driven programs not unlike what we might expect to see in a standard experiential marketing initiative. For those not familiar with experiential marketing, it is the art of creating an experience where the result is an emotional connection to a person, brand, product, or idea.[3] In social media, people engage others directly and indirectly through conversations and conversational objects.

At the very least, the marketing, communications, services, and sales teams representing social and traditional must collaborate on the redesign of all online entities, especially the corporate focal point—that is, the main website.

You must ensure that the landing/home pages feature social objects, opportunities for interaction, spotlighting of customers and visitors, and also a directory of external social presences and aggregated content from each, within one location. Also, be respectful of the thinning attention span of those who have consciously and intentionally clicked through to your site. Grab and hold their attention and walk them through their paths of choice, making it simple and rewarding to take action, but define that action before you attempt to channel it.

Define the experience you wish to impart and transfer.

More specifically, when you are actively participating in the Social Web and when you are establishing the profiles, pages, and communities in each respective social network, ensure that you point them to pre-determined destinations within the corporate site or to a hub where action can be captured.

This is how we focus attention, trigger activity, and measure ROI.

■ BRAMBLE BERRY: A CASE STUDY

Soap-making supplier Bramble Berry (www.brambleberry.com) brings a taste of both e-commerce and social features to its home page. From the start, it's instantly apparent what the company does and how to find and purchase needed supplies and products. And from a social standpoint, the home page offers a more personal connection with the company, as well as affording visitors plenty of opportunities to interact. Visitors can instantly check out Bramble Berry videos on YouTube and Vimeo, see their presence on Facebook, and follow their tweets. And there's always a real customer story featured as "Soaping Success Stories," a sidebar that also encourages customers to write in with their own Bramble Berry success stories.

But even more important, Bramble Berry has made sure to fill its sites and social presences with helpful tips and other resources for the soap-making hobbyist and professional. For example, the Soap Queen Blog and Soap Queen TV (both featured very prominently on the website) offer new recipes, video tutorials, and business tips. And there are links to other soap-making resources on the Web. As a result, Bramble Berry becomes a go-to site for soap makers.

Chapter 12

The New Media University

Social Media 403

We travel through many places in our expedition toward social media adeptness, and most of it is unfamiliar territory—from digital anthropology and psychology to active listening and linguistics to experiential marketing and engagement rooted in empathy to social architecture and engineering and everything else that emerges in between. But this is why these times are so inspiring, exciting, and promising.

We're about to review a topic that is instrumental in defining the face, voice, and personality of a brand in socialized media and the ideas and lessons that materialize will most likely impact your next steps.

■ ESTABLISHING AN ONLINE PRESENCE AND DEFINING THE BRAND PERSONA

In the era of the Social Web, we are all brand advocates and managers—whether we know it or not.

While I spend a significant portion of my time sharing the importance of listening and observing to noteworthy conversations and the enveloping cultures that define relevant online communities, when it comes to participation and engagement, identity and branded personalities are often an afterthought.

The challenge, however, isn't necessarily how to convince management of the need to outwardly engage online. The real obstacle is defining and reinforcing the brand personality as it either existed prior to social media and/or how it should display and present to those across the Social Web. This is only complicated by the addition of human personalities into the equation, as they may or may not embody and personify the brand essence and, consequently, they can dilute the brand in every update and interaction.

Many just jump in and then get caught up in the treadmill of listening, learning, responding, and listening again, without ever stopping to ask:

What is it that we want to accomplish?

How do we wish to be viewed?

How are we contributing to the depiction of the brand?

What do we stand for?

What are our core values?

Where do we stand in these social networks, as it relates to the culture of each, and where do I as a spokesperson fit into the mix?

How does my personal brand affect the company brand and vice versa?

■ ONLINE PROFILES SPEAK VOLUMES ABOUT YOU AND YOUR BRAND

Yes, for many, everything starts with the username and the profile you create within the specific social networks of influence.

These data fields, while simple in their design and intent, can potentially speak volumes for the brand when the brand spokesperson isn't there to speak on its behalf. At a minimum, profiles and bios verbally and visually serve as brand beacons to position and reinforce the company, brand, value proposition, and mission, and elucidate our role as a curator, trust agent, connector, and problem solver.

Visually, profiles provide limited or boundless canvases for painting the picture that introduces, portrays, and symbolizes our brand. Less is more in social networks and therefore we should seek influence and direction from the school of minimalism, a movement in various forms of art and design where the work is stripped down to its most fundamental attributes and features.[1]

Usernames are also an important factor in establishing online identities and the presentiment established upon encountering the online persona—prior to official engagement. This is pivotal as our usernames can benefit from a consistent presence across the Web—for the company and products, as well as the people representing them. To clarify, there are several username strategies to evaluate and plan: the company, the products, and the personal brands who personify them in respective social networks.

■ MULTIPLE PERSONALITY DISORDER

The inevitability of a brand identity crisis is caused by the proliferation and saturation of online presences untethered from a centralized strategy. Essentially, chaos and anarchy are inevitable as companies, spokespersons, and worse, unauthorized spokespeople swarm the Social Web and involuntarily contribute to multiple personality disorder.

But before we design backgrounds, define usernames, create profile pages, and populate information fields, we first have to take a step back to assess the state of the brand, its eventual direction, and its future goals. We begin with an identity assessment and planning strategy to create a center of gravity and parallel orbits around the brand axis we represent and also distribute to orbiting brand satellites in the social mediaverse.

Our profile should reflect our corporate soul and personality. It is our job to introduce the elements, essence, and purpose that attract the individuals seeking alliance and rapport with others possessing similar attributes.

Many companies view the tactical process of establishing online profiles as a simple "check" on the to-do list, when in fact, this is the proverbial book cover on which we're judged.

Without going through a dedicated and renewed branding exercise at the beginning of the social process, we inadvertently invest in multiple, differing personalities of not only each respective social profile, but also the people who interact on behalf of the company. Even something as seemingly harmless as not maintaining a consistent username or profile across social networks contributes to brand disarray.

Before jumping in, establish objectives, procedures, and a plan for social branding, perception management, and customer relations.

■ MULTIPLE PERSONALITY ORDER

One of the more important conversations that will earn prominence now and over time is whether or not a professional should participate in the Social Web as him or herself, or as a branded representative of the business that they represent.

There isn't a right or wrong answer to this. But, however you engage, it must be practiced in a genuine, participatory, helpful, and endearing fashion. It's not unheard of to build two online personas: one personal and the other professional. And it is this strategy that I strongly urge you and your marketing, PR, product, HR, and service teams to consider.

Dell and Zappos for example, created branded user accounts for each individual. For example, at Dell, we see names such as Richard@Dell and Lionel@Dell. At Zappos, we see a pattern based on FIRSTNAME_Zappos. In addition, Zappos boasts more than 250 Zappos-branded employee accounts. They are careful, as anyone on the Social Web should be, with what and how they share. Their activity must collectively build relationships while also boosting the brand and, in most cases, these accounts are used exclusively for work or professional interaction, while a separate, personal account is maintained to publish personal content.

At the point of introduction of any brand in the Social Web is the "brand you." Ideally, your character and behavior are in alignment with that of the brand you represent. In many ways, this is a role you play and that role is defined differently than the personality you exude in your personal life.

The question to ask yourself is: Who do you want to be, as defined by different groups of people with whom you wish to connect over time? For example, you obviously connect differently to friends and family than to peers. You share content accordingly. Contemporaneously, you will produce content and interact differently among professional contacts when you're on duty for work. In your "day job," you may share special offers, interesting observations about market trends, updates about new products and services, or details regarding an upcoming event.

While "being human" is consistent throughout the cycle, you are indubitably a different person to different people in different circumstances. You further fortify these dedicated personas irregularly, making it difficult to establish meaningful connections among your multiple online personalities. In some cases, these ties overlap, but most of the time, they are divergent in nature, intentions, and outcome. To put it bluntly, I really may not care about one or the other, based on the essence of our connection.

All of this is about bringing it together, even if they're maintained separately. In other words, it's far more effective and beneficial to you and the brand(s) you represent to maintain multiple accounts, at the very least, one for each professional and business persona online.

Case in point: Richard Brewer-Hay, online media maven for eBay, maintains dual personalities on Twitter. For friends, family, and peers, he maintains @ESBAle, an account dedicated to Elizabeth Street Brewery, a name that affectionately refers to the residence of his family in San Francisco, which is designated as a "pub by the people for the people." This is where you get to know the person behind the persona. Simultaneously, Brewer-Hay also manages the @ebayinkblog account to share updates, news, observations, and conversations related to eBay, a company that in and of itself hosts many accounts dedicated to varying divisions, each communicating exclusive content, dialogue, and notifications.

PitchEngine, a social media release and social media newsroom generator (and a company of which I'm a stakeholder) maintained its presence on Twitter as @pitchengine. The company's CEO, Jason Kintzler, managed the account, attempting to strike a balance between professional (PitchEngine) and personal (Jason) updates as he operated under the assumption that in order to humanize the brand, you have to act and communicate as a human being. As time passed, Kintzler struggled to draw the lines between his personal and professional personas. The community also showed signs of splintering through its public responses. Kintzler ultimately split his online persona, dedicating @pitchengine to corporate-related interaction and @jasonkinztler to share personal and professional thoughts, updates, and observations.

As individuals embrace social media, in due course, they will find themselves at the inevitable crossroads of choosing an equitable personal versus professional branding strategy that's scalable, enduring, and portable. Ultimately, this discussion precipitates the necessary and fundamental obligation and requirement to establish the online brand personality, attitude, spirit, and behavioral traits that will synthesize and bolster all concerned brands now and henceforward.

■ DISCOVERY AND ACTUALIZATION

In order to get us started, I borrowed from the school of personal development to help us uncover the attributes that are beneficial to the professional, personal, and corporate brands we represent. I included an early version of a Brand Reflection Cycle (Figure 12.1) to assist in the exploration and navigation of brand discovery, definition, and direction. Copy it, recreate it, change it. Whatever you do, make sure to use it or some variation of the cycle in order to assess and dictate the state and bearing of the brand (and the personal brands supporting it).

This process is not unlike the identity circles used in methods for reflecting on inner qualities in order to assess strengths,

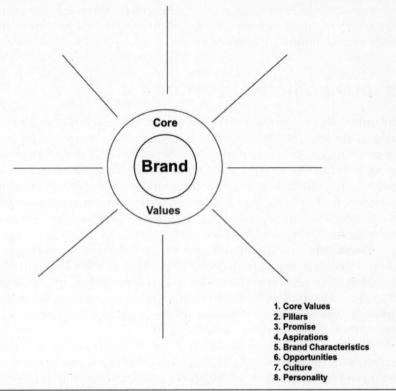

Figure 12.1   Brand Reflection Cycle: Establishing Online Identity and Persona through Introspection

recognize weaknesses, and identify growth qualities as a means of promoting self-awareness and efficacy and building collaboration in team dynamics. It's how we recognize where we are, where we need to be, and how to cultivate focused, interactive, and flourishing communities.

Everything begins with an assessment of the brand's journey through the past, to where it is today, and, in the fullness of time, where it will reside in the future. A brand continually evolves and its past, present, and future are defined not only by the characteristics we place around this chart; they're also established and fortified through the words and actions that emanate during engagement, thus contributing to the overall interpretation and impression post-rendezvous. In any exchange, we must account for twists in the message based on the individual encounter and the reality of what we say and how it's perceived through the filters and biases that establish individual character and identity.

Storytelling: Remember, in every experience, there are always three sides to storytelling—what's said, what's heard, and the pure state of the story in and of itself, in between.

■ SHAPING THE BRAND PERSONA

In order to initiate the process of brand identification and personality definition, we must establish a body and a supporting process of governance. This board, should it prove beneficial, will also be instrumental to the development of social media guidelines, training, governance, and ideation. Depending on the infrastructure of your organization, it may or may not be necessary to invite representatives from executive management, sales, product development, customer service, marketing, and/or public relations.

Those departments should interact on behalf of the brand in the interactive Web and participate at some level in the definition of the brand as it relates to specific classes of customers, peers, and prospects. This is to safeguard against the common fallacies that assume that one audience exists purely for the consumption of our corporate messages and therefore responds to each directive.

The Brand Reflection Cycle will uncover a series of important revelations that illuminate the brand, its personalities, and its characteristics, in addition to those of the individuals representing it online—as it stood yesterday, as it stands today, and what it will represent tomorrow.

You can access it online, or recreate it, but at the very least, run through each of the following reflection cycles and fill in the blanks, as a team, and finalize the top traits to serve as a blueprint for building the brand persona.

■ THE CENTER OF GRAVITY: CORE VALUES

The audience, surrounding environment, and the circumstances in which we are summoned define our disposition and character. Ergo, the process of corporate soul-searching may generate varying brand attributes. We need at the very beginning to establish a common center of gravity to support the orbiting characteristics that can interplay seamlessly in different situations and under a variety of conditions.

This hub is defined by our core values, and they must be consistent and prominent in defining our brand persona in the Social Web. Exploring and documenting the core values is central to substantiating our stature, intentions, purpose, and associations, as reinforced by our actions and words. They serve as the framework and pattern for our culture and ensuing communities. The goal at this stage is to identify and define our core values, as well as relate each of them to behaviors. Try to strive beyond "genericism," that is, those bland qualities that could define any and every company. Instead, choose to dig deep and determine what your brand stands for, and why customers and prospects should care.

■ BRAND PILLARS

Pillars are the support objects that serve as the foundation to sustain and fortify the brand. These qualities help us stipulate the essential properties that govern perception and regulate resonance—in a variety of conditions and affairs. In many respects, it is these pillars that influence every aspect of the social identity cycle—now and in the future.

It is during this stage where we establish the principal, central themes, and hallmarks.

What is unique to our brand that people need to know as it exists today?

■ BRAND CHARACTERISTICS

Defining the brand characteristics will help us establish the traits we wish to associate with the brand through our involvement. It, of course, leverages and includes the qualities and characteristics that signify and define the brand today. Consequently, these properties should adapt to the nuances and expectations of the individuals who populate the online communities we aspire to join and inspire.

What is it that we aim to portray?

What are the words customers and peers use to describe us?

What primary characteristics describe our competition?

What are the terms that designate our desired depiction?

In societal domains, they may differ from our presumptions and assumptions.

■ PROMISE

The promise of any brand is not necessarily analogous to its aspirations—however, it is this pledge that paves the way to its meaning and direction.

The brand promise should answer a simple, yet momentous question: What is our mission?

While searching for the answer, we will discover our ambitions and commitments and rally a team of leaders into agreement and eventually into the forging of a corporate guarantee.

This response will serve as the backbone of the brand ethos as well the communications doctrine that affects all outbound marketing, service, and sales materials—essentially, this process defines the mission statement.

■ BRAND ASPIRATIONS

No brand is inanimate. The characteristics defined in the process of social personification require purpose and vision in order to maintain relevance. The attributes we define today must continually evolve along with the evolution of online media. Reaction is not our stimulus. The objective of defining brand aspirations helps us establish a goal that symbolizes those attributes we hope to one day embody. Branding is an unending story, documented and narrated through progression and maturation.

We are continually redefining what our brand symbolizes in each network and in each instance, while aspiring to typify promise, community, exemplification, and guidance.

■ OPPORTUNITIES

Part of the process of merging brand attributes and personality characteristics is the unplanned reward of exposing hidden and unnoticed opportunities for direction and enlightenment.

As we fill out the "Brand Reflection Cycle," we identify the attributes that are missing based on the conversations we monitor in each respective network where we intend to make an impact. These conversational trends affect us, as they should, and require us to adapt, based on the possibilities that recurrently appear. Note, I'm not purporting the behavior of simply "moving and reacting," and thus becoming a brand that exudes an opportunistic presence. I envision an organization that can acknowledge and accept growth opportunities and maintain the desire and ambition to transform into a more customer- and market-focused partner wherever it is warranted and expected. These attributes are communicated through the brand presence and personality in every social transaction and interaction.

■ CULTURE

The term *culture* can refer to many different facets of anthropology, knowledge and learning, sociology, organizational and human psychology, and ethics—with each carrying its own definition. When establishing a brand persona for the Social Web, we can focus on the interpretation of culture as the beliefs, social forms, and material traits of a particular group. Culture also represents the shared attitudes, values, goals, and practices that characterize an organization (see Merriam Webster's definition[2]).

Using the "Brand Reflection Cycle" chart (Figure 12.1), your brand team must search the corporate soul to document and associate the words and personality attributes that help define, strengthen, and protect the brand, and earn the respect, confidence, and loyalty of those who join the brand's culture.

■ PERSONALITY

If we haven't determined so by this point, it is absolutely crucial to contemplate, review, and designate the elements that we wish to illustrate and represent. It is a combination of these traits that forms our unmistakable brand personality.

While filling out the "Brand Reflection Cycle," we explore, identify, embrace, and manifest the personality and temperament of our brand and how we wish to portray it within each social object, community, and network.

Through this process, we reveal the threads that weave the brand to key characteristics, to best match them to the personalities within our organization. This marriage of brand personality to individual dispositions pivots on how we merge into one persona that symbolizes and personifies the brand as we've designed and nurtured it.

Chapter 13

The New Media University

MBA Program—First Year

In the spirit of the New Media University metaphor, we've now graduated and are pursuing advanced learning, the same way we would seek to earn an MBA in continuing education.

■ FROM INTROVERSION TO EXTROVERSION

As you may or may not know, I'm a big believer in, and also forever a student of, the "social" aspects of new media. I've dedicated a significant amount of time to studying the sociology behind the technology, as well as the implications of technology in society and how we interact with one another, knowingly and unintentionally. Indeed, I believe the implications are much bigger than we think or initially imagine. In many cases, the promise and potential of online sociology are still greatly underestimated.

The staggering adoption numbers accumulated and widely circulated around the Social Web both document and bring to light a veritable quantum shift in how we communicate, behave, and socialize. We are vociferously and decisively empowering a new genre of digital extroverts, encouraged and reaffirmed by what I playfully refer to as "The Verizon Network"—the armada of virtual friends and peers who journey with us as we traverse online and offline. Perhaps this is more accurately defined as a personal support system or quite possibly a socialized ego-system that champions free thought and speech, while instilling confidence and self-esteem with every comment, retweet, reaction, and connection we earn.

This observation is much more profound and significant than we may initially expect. And its implications for the future of media and marketing are not yet understood. As we examine the social landscape and our place within it, acknowledging this transformation and cultural evolution will only promote meaningful, respectful, and accurate interactive communications and service programs and processes.

■ THE NOW WEB: NOW IS INDEED GONE

We are witnessing a shift in power. Once tightly controlled by publishers, broadcasters, and corporations, the power to publish and connect messages and stories to people was considered a luxury only a generation ago—a privilege many of us never would have experienced without the introduction of social platforms, distribution networks, and supporting communities. Technology is a change agent, and the capabilities and accompanying benefits that it offers are liberating our channels of influence.

The simultaneous advantage and disadvantage of new media is exemplified in its expansiveness, inertia, and volume.

Twitter, Facebook News Feeds, life and activity streams, and other microcommunities that define the real-time Web (or the "now Web") are concurrently captivating and distracting our focus. But, while many argue that they're decreasing productivity, they're also engaging a more active and enlightened community of media-literate socialites.

Twitter is the culprit and is proudly holding the smoking gun. When the ability to search the billions of Tweets that were flying across our screens materialized, we were bestowed with a gift of instant insight and revelation.

This is the dawn of the real-time Web, and it's further feeding our insatiable hunger for information as it's published.

When it comes to searches, the most notable comparison between traditional and real-time discovery is represented in the difference between human memory and consciousness. The experience of searching for relevant information is personified in the context of what you're doing and not necessarily that of what you're typing into the search box. As Edo Segal, investor and founder of Relegance, says: "The Internet is more biology than technology."

The patterns for real-time search offer an augmented reality, mapping who we are on the Internet. The constructs of what, where, how, and to whom we communicate and share information are converging through an aggregated view of related activity and a syndicated architecture designed to extend and amplify our voice. What we're learning through Twitter Search is that people want access to the immediacy of conversations tied to keywords, regardless of the authority, page rank, and SEO.

It's the difference between finding the right content on the Web and finding the right content, right now, across the Web and social media.

As Gerry Campbell, CEO of Collecta, a real-time search engine puts it, "I want to know what people are saying about my topic, right now. The minute you put rankings and filters on search, it stops representing real-time. Every minute, stories are told on the Web. Yet in traditional search, most are usually ranked out of the results and therefore, people don't get a chance to see them."

In 2008, I introduced the Conversation Prism with Jesse Thomas to map the social landscape as a way of gaining *real* insights into the conversations transpiring across social networks, where and when they occurred. The dream was, of course, to have a search window into the Social Web and the social graph, in real time. Specialized tools such as Collecta, OneRiot, Topsy, and PeopleBrowsr are peeling back the layers of society, focusing our attention to enhance and amplify listening, and plugging us directly into the conversations that shape impressions and perceptions. We'll discuss these search tools in a later chapter on listening and monitoring.

While searching the Conversation Prism in real time is not yet fully realized, it is imminent and it is powerful.

Real-time search of the now Web reveals a river, while traditional search architectures discover oceans.

■ THE RISE OF THE STATUSPHERE

In 2009, Twitter stole the spotlight with millions of passionate users not only promoting Twitter, but also ushering in a new generation of real-time, searchable conversations. Twitter is one of many social networks that provide a platform to do so, usually prompted by a question for you to answer in your intentionally limited short post or update.

I call this new form of updating and posting "the Statusphere,"[1] a play on other descriptors of social media such as the blogsphere, Twitterverse, and socialmediasphere. The *statusphere* is what defines and shapes the *egosystem*.

To define it more precisely, the statusphere is any network where your post is intended to answer questions related to activity or thoughts. The idea is simple: Provide a quick update in a short form and click "update." This short-form response is much easier to produce than a blog post, podcast, webcast, or video, which may require long and involved production cycles.

At the moment, Twitter, Facebook, and other microcommunities define the statusphere and are driving action and determining the direction and course of individual attention.

The statusphere is particularly important for brands, since publishers and consumers are losing the luxury of infinite awareness and thus channeling and upgrading their information sources—meaning that they are narrowing their focus onto only those voices and peers who share their interests, passions, and insights. Consequently, we are now forging networks within networks, based on contextual alliances.

We can now readily identify and connect directly to existing contacts and also forge new friendships to create a series of interconnected contextual networks within broader networks. This sets the stage for the emergence and exercise of a sweeping friends of friends (FoFs) effect that propagates pertinent information across multiple social graphs.

This is especially salient for businesses seeking to tap into targeted micronetworks rich with incessant and material updates to learn and also contribute to the streams of rapid-fire content.

It's in the way that you use it.

Yes, the statusphere is brimming with unimportant chatter, but it is also overflowing with highly curated and valuable information, important questions and answers, influential opinions and observations, breaking news, trending activities, feedback, and personal insight, all of which would otherwise go unnoticed in the volume of online chatter.

Producing and posting updates that people find invigorating, insightful, entertaining, and enriching is how you build a meaningful foundation for which people follow, admire, and trust you. You are a beacon for all that moves you.

■ THE WIRE: WHEN EVERYDAY PEOPLE BREAK NEWS

While we may argue over the degree of intelligence behind the wisdom of the crowds, the ability to swiftly spark word of mouth to propel information across the Web is incontestable.

Twitter, Facebook, and other micro and macro social networks are defeating even the most nimble news agencies and bureaus, and they are shaping our appetites for information.

Without having to do anything other than open the window to your social graph of choice, you have immediate access to information, as it happens, curated by your friends and contacts, even before the traditional media has time to report it. Think about it. Over the last three years, we have had access to the following information in real time, as told by people, who report live from the center of activity:

➤ News of earthquakes and other natural disasters.

➤ The passing of celebrities.

➤ An airplane making an emergency landing in the Hudson River.

➤ The election in Iran.

➤ Terrorist bombings.

➤ Sports scores and updates.

➤ Earnings reports and stocks.

➤ Gossip.

Now and in the future, information will find *you*. And it will be spread through the vision and words of our peers and other citizen reporters who are compelled to leverage their networks of influence to unite people, if for but a moment, around information that captures the heart, mind, and soul.

The real-time Web also serves as a telltale source for trends and represents a leading indicator for any topic related to your interests or business.

The era of "now" is fueling new media. The pursuit of "now" is conditioning us to expect information as it happens, whether it's accurate or developing.

The question is: How will this latest chapter of community-powered news and information production, distribution, and consumption affect your ability to connect with your audiences?

As "now" media continues to mature, its impact is clear and incontestable. The opportunity for social media and its inherent benefits lies in our ability to build a two-way information bridge between the point of our content introduction, alternative sources for information, and the people looking for insight and direction. To build a community, we have to be an active participant in it.

As Paul Saffo, a forecaster and essayist exploring long-term technological change and its practical impact on business and society observed, "News doesn't break, it tweets."

Today's news and trends no longer break through traditional news sources, voices, or wires; they're captured through the camera lenses, mobile phones, and laptops of people who serve as both witnesses and reporters.

The question governing micronetworks, such as What are you doing now or what's happening now? begets questions that lead to answers that gain in significance and relevance.

■ THE ATTENTION RUBICON

We live in an increasingly thinning state of focus resulting from the overwhelming volume of information flying at us simultaneously within our networks of interest. It's affecting how and what we consume, when, and, more importantly, how we react, participate, and share. It's the quest for an unquenchable thirst for something we cannot yet define. And that "something" is forever vying for our attention and relentlessly pushing us to do more with less, driven by the omnipresent fear of potentially missing what's next.

For those attempting to capture attention, this section will reveal the state of awareness in order to eventually produce a more concentrated and substantive signal that effectively rises above the noise.

Attention is a precious commodity. And if you subscribe to the theory of Attention Economics, we're indeed living in an era on the verge of attention scarcity and bankruptcy.

Attention economics suggests that human attention is a scarce commodity and attempts to resolve and streamline the management of information and its associated challenges through the application of economic theory.[2]

Linda Stone, a widely recognized visionary thinker and thought leader, observes that attention is "the most powerful tool of the human spirit. We can enhance or augment our attention with practices like meditation and exercise, diffuse it with technologies like e-mail and Blackberries, or alter it with pharmaceuticals. In the end, though, we are fully responsible for how we choose to use this extraordinary tool."[3]

The Social Web and new services that continue the migration and permeation into everything we do online, are proving that attention is, as expected, not scalable. However, the rate of information that flows to and past us only continues to escalate.

As documented in an August 2009 article in the *Wall Street Journal* written by John Freeman,

> *In the past two decades, we have witnessed one of the greatest breakdowns of the barrier between our work and personal lives since the notion of leisure time emerged in Victorian Britain as a result of the Industrial Age. It has put us under great physical and mental strain, altering our brain chemistry and daily needs. It has isolated us from the people with whom we live, siphoning us away from real-world places where we gather. It has encouraged flotillas of unnecessary jabbering, making it difficult to tell signal from noise. It has made it more difficult to read slowly and enjoy it, hastening the already declining rates of literacy. It has made it harder to listen and mean it, to be idle and not fidget. This is not a sustainable way to live. This lifestyle of being constantly on causes emotional and physical burnout, workplace meltdowns, and unhappiness.*[4]

He then asks the reader, "How many of our most joyful memories have been created in front of a screen?"

Freeman's assertions are accurate and I don't disagree with him. However, his proposal for change, while wonderful and commendable, is idealistic, unachievable, and presumptuous.

Freeman believes,

> *If we are to step off this hurtling machine, we must reassert principles that have been lost in the blur. It is time to launch a manifesto for a slow communication movement, a push back against the machines and the forces that encourage us to remain connected to them. Many of the values of the Internet are social improvements—it can be a great platform for solidarity, it rewards curiosity, it enables convenience. This is not the manifesto of a Luddite, this is a human manifesto. If the technology is to be used for the betterment of human life, we must reassert that the Internet and its virtual information space is not a world unto itself but a supplement to our existing world, where the following three statements are self-evident.*

His three statements are as follows:

1. Speed matters.
2. The physical world matters.
3. Context matters.

I mentioned that I find his views and ambitions idealistic and pre-sumptuous. After all, his essay is adapted from his book, *The Tyranny of E-mail: A Manifesto for Slow.*

E-mail is losing territory to social networks as you read this book. Slow is gone, never to return.

See, as content publishers, we must understand the psychology and sociology governing the socialization of online information. Those contributing to the "egosystem" are not yet ready to step off the treadmill per se. We're individually and actively investing in our intelligence and social capital as much as we're defining the new boundaries for discovering and sharing material information.

Instead of inhibiting the pace and breadth of information flow, we must channel relevant details and data.

It's part technology and part science and conditioning of the mind.

This is what I refer to as "The Attention Rubicon."

A rubicon is defined as a limit that, when passed or exceeded, per-mits of no return and typically results in irrevocable commitment.[5] We have hit an information crossroads and many of us are unknow-ingly contributing to the Attention Rubicon as we increasingly con-sume, and interact with information, social objects, and the people who actively participate in the attention economy.

The Attention Rubicon is the acceptance that our appetite for information has passed the point of no return. Therefore, we must concentrate our energies on innovation and inventiveness, techno-logically and psychologically, to effectively process and parse data and, in turn, shift its momentum behind our online persona to earn equity online and offline. Embracing this Attention Rubicon and in-vesting in our ability to learn, share, and contribute is how we will thrive in today's attention economy.

Linda Stone offers a solution to this dilemma. She refers to it as Continuous Partial Attention and defines it this way:

Continuous partial attention describes how many of us use our attention today. It is different from multi-tasking. The two are dif-ferentiated by the impulse that motivates them. When we multi-task, we are motivated by a desire to be more productive and more efficient. We're often doing things that are automatic, that require very little cognitive processing. We give the same priority to much of what we do when we multi-task—we file and copy papers, talk on the phone, eat lunch—we get as many things done at one time as we possibly can in order to make more time for ourselves and in order to be more efficient and more productive.

To pay continuous partial attention is to pay partial attention—CONTINUOUSLY. It is motivated by a desire to be a LIVE node on the network. Another way of saying this is that we want to connect and be connected. We want to effectively scan for opportunity and optimize for the best opportunities, activities, and contacts, in any given moment. To be busy, to be connected, is to be alive, to be recognized, and to matter.

We pay continuous partial attention in an effort NOT TO MISS ANYTHING. It is an always-on, anywhere, anytime, any place behavior that involves an artificial sense of constant crisis. We are always in high alert when we pay continuous partial attention. This artificial sense of constant crisis is more typical of continuous partial attention than it is of multi-tasking.

Whatever we call it, we are in truth learning to publish, process, and react to content in "Twitter time." This new genre of rapid-fire interaction is further distributing the proverbial conversation and is evolving online interaction beyond the host site through syndication to other relevant networks and communities.

■ CHANNELING OUR FOCUS:
THE ATTENTION DASHBOARD

Attention is engaged at the point of introduction, and for many of us, we're presented with worthwhile content outside of our RSS readers or favorite bookmarks. Retweets (RT) and favorites in Twitter, Likes and comments in Facebook, posting shortened links that connect friends and followers back to the source post, have changed our behavior and empowered our role in defining the evolution of the connectivity and dissemination of information.

We are in control of what we read and learn, and responsible for what we share.

As technology matures and transforms, our sources for discovering and consuming information also continue to evolve. With the pervasiveness and pace of information published and distributed through the activity streams we follow, our attention spans are overloaded and scattered.

Our intentions are limited by available time, responsibilities, distractions, and the volume of data that flows through our data streams.

Our RSS readers are neglected.

The individual updates that stream through our social networks are largely unnoticed.

Responses to the content we create or comment upon are often missed and overlooked.

Our bookmarks are languishing.

Conversations and social objects are distributed beyond our reach and they are tugging at our attention and focus.

In 2009, the introduction of tools and services that funneled information into one aggregated stream caused the proliferation of desktops and mobile devices, while many consumers relegated their attention to one, maybe two, dedicated streams on Twitter.com or Facebook.com.

These tools essentially channeled updates from one or multiple networks into one easy-to-read activity stream, allowing individuals to stay up-to-date on information and trends, clickthrough to shared content, respond directly in the timeline, and also read and send private messages to their contacts. Tools such as TweetDeck, People-Browsr, Seesmic, Co-Tweet, and HootSuite, among others, thus served as the attention dashboards for individuals active in social media.

I introduced the concept of attention dashboards in 2008 in reference to Twitter and Facebook specifically, as they served as the window to the social world. I suggested that these windows were open for the majority of the day and provided the ability for us to stay connected and keep our ears to the ground, while maintaining productivity and attention focused on other responsibilities. As such, these news feeds and timelines serve as our centralized attention dashboards and determine what we read, what we say, and who responds, simply by the information that continually flows through it. We're engaged at the point and place of introduction and bound by context and time.

■ ■ ■

Businesses must tap into the statusphere and these attention dashboards in order to earn awareness and, more importantly, build relationships with those who share affinities for the information, products, and services they represent. As we're learning, noticeable content sparks curiosity and dictates our next move and subsequently the next moves and reactions of friends and friends of friends (FoFs). The most effective and successful initiatives require a personalized engagement strategy, in order to consistently vie for consideration. The laws of attraction and relationships management will support your efforts when you create compelling content and transparently connect it to the people whom you believe will benefit.

It's now our job to identify and recognize those influencers, trust agents, and tastemakers in order to establish an effective contextual network. With each new connection, businesses can appear in multiple, dispersed dashboards and timelines to syndicate content across the social graph and related social networks. Worthy social objects, combined with evangelism and clever promotion, will earn visibility and expanded syndication through retweets (RT), link shares, Diggs, Stumbles, bookmarks, tweetbacks, Likes, and other forms of social recognition. With each new instance of sharing, content reverberates through extended social graphs.

The ability to provoke a response through the attention dashboard requires creativity, relevance, and a natural understanding of the nuances that designate triggers, interests, biases, and channels of influence. This insight is only discernible through the active observation and participation in the communities, and furthermore, with individuals whom you wish to engage and galvanize.

■ THE SOCIAL EFFECT: THE FUTURE OF COMMUNITY-GENERATED BRANDING AND WORD OF MOUTH MARKETING

The responsibility is yours to create a dedicated tribe that supports, shares, and responds to your professional and personal interaction in both the statusphere and throughout the predefined channels we've established to steer experiences. It's the only way to build a valuable and portable community around you and what you represent.

■ ■ ■

The challenge, however, is first getting noticed and then successively energizing the migration of social objects and stories to individual attention dashboards across the respective social graphs in order to trigger a broader reaction that reverberates throughout the Social Web. In the process, we gain awareness and recognition, reinforced by our following actions and words to effectively recruit peers, empower champions, and establish dedicated tribes.

The ability to engage someone directly in the attention dashboard, incite a response, and hopefully have them share their experience with their network is what I termed *the social effect*, a modern adaptation of the network effect, driven by word of mouth.

To better define the network effect, it is the phenomenon that occurs when one user of a good or service affects the adoption and subsequent use of the product by other people.[6] In other words, the network effect dictates that a service becomes more valuable as more people use it, leading to an ever-increasing number of users. The most commonly used example of the network effect is the telephone. A more modern example would most definitely include the Internet.

And just to stay on the social highway, we couldn't ignore Twitter, Facebook, or YouTube. While word of mouth is often influential in the beginning—for example, you may use something because someone you know uses it—eventually the masses will adopt a product or service because *everyone* uses it.[7]

The social effect is rooted in similar theory. It is the social effect that determines actual reach, resonance, and the course for social objects and relevant dialogue. The analysis and reverse engineering of the social effect visualizes and uncovers behavior, paths, interaction, conversations, sentiment, and click patterns.

Connections with friends, followers, and their respective FoFs are constantly shifting and never duplicated in exactly in the same way. The conversations one maintains online produces a resulting expansion and contraction of the network at a particular point in time based on the topics of discussion. I refer to the state of the social graph characterized by time, discussion, and connections as the relevant net and, as we've discussed earlier, it is linked and represented by context.

The social effect, its reach and resonance, are defined by a series of gauges, measurements, and scales governed by the study of the elements and conditions that contribute to the ability to disrupt or distract activity in your favor (see Figure 13.1).

Disruption point: The place and moment when a social object is introduced into the attention dashboard. This is the point that I believe determines the potential extent and reach of a social object based on a series of factors that are either completely or partially in alignment, or, in some cases, completely misaligned.

Figure 13.1   Microdisruption Theory and the Social Effect

The microdisruption theory therefore suggests that we study sharing and consuming behaviors within our relevant communities in order to establish criteria and conditions associated with successful viewing and sharing activities. We thus deduce the following social barometers: attention aperture, time, networks, and backchannels.

Attention aperture: We are susceptible to diversion at specific and also random intervals during our daily routine. The state and direction of an individual's focus represented by the prospect, probability, and receptiveness to outside distraction based on conditions and surrounding circumstances defines the opening of the attention aperture. Identifying our influential tastemakers, trust agents, and authorities, and also observing when they most often share content or objects produced from others, will help us define windows of opportunity to garner attention and mindshare.

Time: Time is a major factor in determining interaction and sharing levels when new updates, tweets, uploads, or blog posts are introduced into the timeline. Updates published in the early morning on a Monday will garner greater attention than a midday post on Wednesday. Time therefore suggests that we monitor activity immediately after each post to track responses, shares, and views to discover the time portals for introducing new content when our communities are most receptive. Try experimenting with the sharing of a series of intelligent, free URL shorteners such as bit.ly. You can immediately track the associated traffic and referring sources for each distinct URL you create, in order to gauge immediacy in views, response, and momentum. This, however, provides only a cursory analysis and deeper study in the form of Web analytics and conversation monitoring and sentiment assessment is required to document and eventually shape social activity.

Networks: Networks represent the social graph and the potential for extending the migration of an object or conversation from the disruption point (when we introduce the object into the timeline) to the individual social graphs that span multiple networks. For example, if we introduce the object in Twitter, through our own syndication channel, we have the ability to potentially reach multiple individuals in various networks simultaneously. They can then share, respond, and react to the content within each respective network, thus triggering a social effect across multiple networks in unison.

Backchannel: The backchannel is among the most influential and effective means for propelling social objects and sparking conversations within each social network. The backchannel is defined as the conversations that occur outside of the public eye—private messages on Facebook, DMs on Twitter, traditional e-mails, etc. This is where we introduce new content to influencers with whom we've already established relationships. It is through these direct connections that we can orchestrate the wide and expansive reach of content and objects. As these planned updates debut in the public timelines, connected friends and followers step in to further embrace and share the content as it stems from a trusted source.

Encompassing, understanding, and mastering disruption theory and the social effect unveil the most important factors in determining the thread and viral opportunity for potential conversations and content sharing. A true social graph and the relationships that define it, which are constantly in flux, is measurable only as snapshots tied to subjects frozen in time. Microdisruption theory visualizes the true opportunity for resonance and the potential course and reach for the ensuing social effect that connects people and content across social graphs.

Remember, the secret to attracting comments, likes, or stimulating retweets is not governed by a formula, but instead by the intent, quality, relevance, and nature of sharing something worthy of response, along with the establishment of a trusting inner circle.

Chapter 14

The New Media University

MBA Program—Second Year

Scholastic institutions all over the world are preparing tomorrow's workforce for jobs, challenges, and market conditions that don't yet exist. This book and others, as well as blogs, micromedia channels, social networks, and the voices that power them, will collectively pave the way for all of us to learn and adapt to the perpetually evolving landscapes of media, business, and influence.

In the previous chapter, or, in keeping with our metaphor, in the first year of your MBA program, we studied the rise of the statusphere, the focus of awareness on attention dashboards, the thinning of attention span, and the competition for being a leading source of intellectual stimulation. We also discussed the fabric of the social effect and the influential factors that propel social objects across social graphs, thus making them legitimately viral.

I alluded to filtering earlier, and this is where we continue our higher learning. We'll then follow up with a study of how people currently populate the social landscape, in order to shape and fine-tune our social initiatives.

■ IMPROVING THE SIGNAL-TO-NOISE RATIO

Social media, for the most part, has thrived on the excitement of users when they find themselves being a part of a new (r)evolution that is defined through participation, consumption, sharing, and contribution. However, as we're experiencing this (r)evolution, our threshold for information processing, the disruption point, is lowering, and simultaneously, our attention aperture is closing. Part of this is due to what's referred to as social network fatigue (SNF), blended with hints of information overload.

Social network fatigue is not well defined, beyond its label. It refers to the phenomenon of user exhaustion, caused by recreating social network profiles in every new, hot, or popular network that appears on the social radar screen. SNF also stems from burnout associated with the emotional, intellectual, and time commitments required to stay connected to peers in one or many social networks concurrently.

As a brand manager and ambassador, your endurance must be greater than others of your tribe and correlated factions (also referred to as nicheworks or niche networks, those subcommunities within larger communities). The future of communications, human interaction, and media consumption and production lies in our ability to focus and filter. Many new products have recently launched that employ advanced semantic and artificial intelligence algorithms that filter RSS feeds and updates in your attention dashboard as well as search results, based on a myriad of factors—depending on the technology and the solution. In 2008 to 2009, many semantic applications and semantic social networks were discussed, developed, and deployed.

Let's back up a bit to review the definition of semantic in order to understand its pertinence to the future of marketing, media, and communication. For example, when you insert a query into a search engine, the technology behind the scenes matches your criteria to content on the Web. While the results are sometimes exact, most of what you receive is irrelevant and useless. This is because search engines don't necessarily understand what you're asking at a human level.

Customers and peers experience the same problem and that is why we have to understand and manage active and intelligent SEO, SMO, and, eventually, semantic programs.

More specifically, the semantic Web is technology that connects data to personal preferences and intentions through discovery, automation, integration, and reuse across various applications.[1] The Altova company website article "What Is the Semantic Web?" states the following:

> Currently the focus of a W3C working group, the Semantic Web vision was conceived by Tim Berners-Lee, the inventor of the World Wide Web. The World Wide Web changed the way we communicate, the way we do business, the way we seek information and entertainment—the very way most of us live our daily lives. Calling it the next step in Web evolution, Berners-Lee defines the Semantic Web as "a Web of data that can be processed directly and indirectly by machines."[2]

Through semantic technology, machines can be taught to understand language similar to how people process information. A semantic Web search engine would be able to distinguish between John F. Kennedy the airport and John F. Kennedy the person, or have the ability to tailor search results for your next vacation based on your interests and behavior, instead of serving up an overload of all activities and details related to the destination.

■ UPGRADING EXPERIENCES AND INTERACTION THROUGH TOMORROW'S TECHNOLOGY, TODAY

The processes and supporting systems for engaging, helping, guiding, and shaping communities are driven by sociology and connected through technology. Technology will evolve, adapt, and pioneer new applications that help us in our mission to serve communities, and also increase presence, brand awareness, and resonance, and, of course, grow and cultivate our businesses.

Less dependent on the wisdom of the crowds and human meta-tagging, these technologies filter content in your streams, feed readers and networks to automatically tier the content that will most likely align with your interests, and moreover, your interests *at the moment*. Amazon recommendations are an early form of this technology. However, Amazon originally was tied to the correlation of products based on the purchase and wish list behavior of existing customers. New recommendation technology will match your interests as defined by your activities and also factor in the related behavior of your trusted networks.

Over the last two years, I focused heavily on the positioning and launching of several semantic- and recommendations-focused technology companies, including AdaptiveBlue, mSpoke, Trusted Opinion, My6Sense, and FlyChat, among many, many others. What each shared was the ability to more effectively, directly, and efficiently help you find content and information by doing the legwork for you behind the scenes, instantly.

AdaptiveBlue (Glue) is a browser plugin that automatically helps you find books, music, and movies through your friends' choices as you browse popular sites.

mSpoke provides intelligence behind online activity, most specifically adding machine-learning technology to observe what each user actually reads, and using that knowledge to choose the most relevant content on the Web. The company also created a service platform to help businesses optimize their content and objects for machine learning.

Trusted Opinion fuses a semantic social network with new recommendation technology that provides referrals for movies, music, and restaurants based on your reviews and consumption behavior as it relates to your inner circle of "trusted" contacts, including their first-level network of people who share similar tastes—not just people who are friends of friends.

My6Sense debuted a Web and mobile application that channels your social streams and news feeds through a "digital intuition" layer that matches interests through behavior and alliances and presents only the updates and information that you would want to see.

FlyChat is a mobile app that created a social graph based on context by sharing your updates with other users of the app who shared similar interests. Each time you publish new social objects, they're delivered to others who also publish homogeneous content, thus expanding your social graph contextually.

Each one of these examples demonstrates how you must now think about the evolution of technology and how communities interact with one another, as well as with the social objects that capture their attention.

And we can't totally rule out the wisdom of the crowds in the future aggregations of recommendations and influence.

We don't necessarily need to socialize in order to effectively serve content to and connect with our communities. If you think about it, prior to the socialization of media, surfing the Web was a lonely experience. And in many cases, it continues to be mostly an isolated process when it comes to reading, shopping, and general browsing, despite the swelling adoption rates for social networks, tools, and services. Surfing without socializing isn't necessarily antisocial, it simply represents the reality of how we as consumers use the Web when we're not producing or responding to content.

Mob mentality or crowd rule helps online businesses, publishers, marketers, and content producers apply collective intelligence to the process of streamlining the results that emerge within an in-site search. However, it could also be used to effectively connect brands to people and people to peers, all based on the human elements and interests that bind us together.

An easy way to explain this concept is to draw the comparison to ant life, not that I'm making a correlation to human behavior and ants per se—although, actually, maybe we should for the sake of this discussion. By employing the theory of swarm intelligence, we can learn more than we imagine. Swarm intelligence introduces the idea that ant colonies, for example, can serve as an inspiration to solve complex human problems. At the very least, it can help us apply new thinking to organizing information and connections online based on the activity of linking, directions, and abandonment.

Deborah Gordon, a biologist at Stanford University who has spent decades studying harvester ants in the Arizona desert, summed up the concept this way: "Ants aren't smart. Ant colonies are."

Site owners can leverage the wisdom of those people who define their communities to precisely forecast meaningful results related to almost any search. And the collective wisdom only increases with every search and subsequent series of clicks.

With every search (whether or not it successfully generated accurate results or led to visited pages or purchases or to abandoned transactions), and with every click, we're presented with insight into how to organize and present data to visitors to complete the consumer's experience, based on expectations. This everyday behavior reflects the impartial, honest, and current sentiment, assumptions, and outlook of the colony.[3]

The study of collective intelligence harnesses the wisdom of the crowds without requiring a significant effort on behalf of the consumer or visitor.

Much in the same way that ants leave behind a chemical trail when seeking and then returning to the nest with food, as individuals we provide real-time feedback with every action and reaction we perform online—most of the time however, it's ignored and unharnessed.

The study of these emerging technologies serves as investments in today's real estate market and also tomorrow's bridges and roads, which will more effectively link everything together. Think of it as a social version of the principles and rewards associated with the perennially popular game, Monopoly.

■ WEB SQUARED AUGMENTS OUR REALITY OF WEB 2.0 AND SOCIAL MEDIA

If you haven't yet heard about *augmented reality* or *Web squared*, allow me to make a quick introduction.

This is the next iteration of the Web and also desktop and mobile applications, and is indicative of the future hybrid Web and device experience. And no, it's not called "Web 3.0."

Augmented reality[4] joins the likes of the semantic Web, geolocation, and artificial intelligence (AI), among many other emerging technologies, in what the father of Web 2.0, Tim O'Reilly, refers to as *Web squared*.

Web 2.0 earned momentum over the years, going back to 2003, which seems almost like an eternity in Internet years. Web squared refines Web 2.0.

Tim O'Reilly and John Battelle, the originators of the Web 2.0 conference whose names became synonymous with the rebirth of the Web after the dot-com crash, heralded the new era of the next Web in a recently published white paper, "Web Squared: Web 2.0 Five Years On."[5]

As O'Reilly and Battelle originally observed, Web 2.0 is all about harnessing collective intelligence. But when asked about what was next, the duo shared their thoughts: "Ever since we first introduced the term 'Web 2.0,' people have been asking, 'What's next?' Assuming that Web 2.0 was meant to be a kind of software version number (rather than a statement about the second coming of the Web after the dot-com bust), we're constantly asked about 'Web 3.0.' Is it the semantic Web? The sentient Web? Is it the Social Web? The mobile Web? Is it some form of virtual reality? It is all of those, and more."

The Web has come a long way from its origin of serving and connecting static Web pages around the world. The Web continues to also evolve beyond its 2.0 evolution, in which websites become platforms and systems for harnessing collective intelligence or "crowdsourcing."

Fundamentally, Web squared is based on the premise that the collective intelligence that spawned and developed as a result of innovation during this period of Web 2.0 has more to offer than only data sourced from crowds. O'Reilly and Battelle refer to the definition of intelligence to demonstrate their premise: "But is this really what we mean by collective intelligence? Isn't one definition of intelligence, after all, that characteristic that allows an organism to learn from and respond to its environment?"

They presage the next iteration of the Web with a question: "The question before us is this: Is the Web getting smarter as it grows up?"

The answer is not only a resounding *yes*, but that the Web is already growing up right before our eyes. The *information shadow* and the *Internet of things* are enabling the Web to become smarter, faster, more personalized, and mobile.

Dion Hinchcliffe, the publisher of *Social Computing Journal*, paraphrased Winston Churchill in his assessment of Web 2.0 and Web squared: "Now this is not the end ... but it is, perhaps, the end of the beginning."[6]

Hinchliffe's interpretation of Web squared clarifies the future of the Internet for us to conceptualize how we will adapt our presences and create new platforms, networks, and objects to thrive in the next iteration of the Web.

> *Web Squared articulates a broader fusion between the world-at-large, the Web, and the people connected to it. It's a more extreme view of Web 2.0 while at the same time hinting that while social computing has been a major transformative force recently in the consumer world and beyond, the relentless growth of devices, network connectivity, and sensors into our lives across our homes, workplaces, and external environment, is casting a growing "information shadow" that is increasingly hard to ignore.*

As you can see, Dion also clearly delineates the stages that define Web 1.0, Web 2.0, and Web Squared (see Figure 14.1).

And in the convoy of new technologies and platforms that define Web squared, we've witnessed and discussed semantic, filtering, and collective intelligence technologies. Now we're also observing the fusion of mobile and social characteristics, and the convergence of Web and reality—documented and defined as augmented reality.

Augmented reality (AR) refers to the live direct or indirect view of a real-world environment where elements are supplemented with, or *augmented* by, computer-generated imagery. The augmentation is

	Web 1.0 ➡	Web 2.0 ➕	Web Squared
Value Source	Network Center	Edge of Network	Edge of World
Feedback Loop Latency	Months/Weeks	Days/Minutes	Real-Time
Interaction Model	Request/Response	Rich User Experience	Autonomic
Key Strategic Asset	Products	Hard-To-Recreate Data	Data Ecosystems
Data Generation	Publishing	User Generated Content	Information Shadows
Virtuous Growth Cycle	"Going Viral"	Network Effects	Generative Processes
Data Structure	Schema/Taxonomy	Folksonomy	Implied Metadata
Allocation of Resources	Competition	Participation	Open Supply Chains
Richest Data Source	Publishers	People	Environment

Figure 14.1

Source: Dion Hinchcliffe, 2009 (http://hinchcliffeandcompany.com).

conventionally in real-time and harmoniously displayed through meaningful context with environmental elements.

In 2009, we witnessed the release of new augmented reality applications for mobile platforms that paved the way for innovation and mainstream adoption and usage of immersive engagement.

Yelp's Monocle reveals businesses within our vicinity simply by holding up an iPhone 3GS and pointing it in any direction.

The Metro Paris Subway application visually points us in the right direction as we progress toward the station of our choosing. As we migrate closer to or further away from the different stations, the objects respectively increase and decrease in screen presence, mimicking real-life perspective (see Figure 14.2).

Google's Street View provides consumers with the ability to search businesses and locations, but the results also now fuse the real-world view with an online link to learn more about each result.

The London Bus example, similar to the Metro Paris Subway app, helps us find routes and combines what we see through the lens of the camera with the digital visualizations that are placed on top of real-world elements.

This particular application also inspired what could be seen as the future usage scenarios for businesses and brands, especially those who are local and regional.

Figure 14.2   What does this mean for you?

Essentially, in an early example, we envisioned "virtual" billboards that can emerge when viewing your surroundings through the lens of your mobile device.

As a user, augmented reality apps merge the virtual with reality—or combine the augmented data and objects with real-life experiences. As a content producer, you now have the ability to bring your content to life—and this is incredibly powerful and transformative.

Part

III

Brand Representative versus the Brand You

Chapter

15

Fusing the "Me" in Social Media and the "We" in the Social Web

The evolution of media and communications is perpetual and time-less.

Once we put these lessons and insights into practice we truly graduate into apprentices of new media.

But before we do so, there's an important element in the social-ization of media that can't go undisclosed: the socialization of media starts with you and me. Let's spend one chapter together exploring and unraveling the potential "butterfly effect."

The butterfly effect is an example made popular in the 1980s and taken from chaos theory that describes how the fluttering of a butterfly's wings may be the initial cause that sets off events that result in a large storm. In reference to the Social Web, it is a potentially chaotic effect created by something seemingly insignificant, whereby a small change in one part of a complex system can have a large effect somewhere else.[1] That "somewhere" else could have devastating effects on you and/or the brand you represent.

It sounds alarming, but this is not science fiction, nor is it yet another essay on "The Top 10 Secrets of Social Media." I need your attention as we move forward together, as our journey is only just beginning.

■ CASTING A DIGITAL SHADOW: YOUR REPUTATION PRECEDES YOU

You will be googled. . . .

This couldn't be any truer. This might make you smirk, but go google yourself.

View the results as if through the eyes of a stranger, a business prospect, a recruiter, an HR professional, your current or future boss—I'm leaving out BFFs and family, as it skews your perspective. We need an unbiased encounter with the results that return.

But also pay attention to what you don't see. Pay attention to how these results portray who you are and what you represent today and also discern how these pieces of the puzzle establish your potential for accomplishing your short- and long-term goals.

Truthfully, stop and think a bit about what it is you stand for, believe in, and aspire to become. And consider whether or not the search results in Google, Twitter search, Search.PeopleBrowsr.com, or Collecta reinforce your intentions or paint an unexpected and possibly surprising picture.

Everything starts with you. Your actions and words online are indeed extensions to how people interpret, perceive, and react to the brand you represent. At the same time, you also represent your personal brand—the digital identity that's established through the collection of digital shadows you cast across the Web.

Our contributions to the Web are indexed and archived for years to come. When we Tweet, upload videos and pictures, post on blogs and comments, and update our status on social networks, we cast a digital shadow that parallels our activities and mimics our convictions

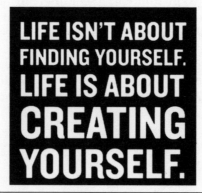

Figure 15.1

Source: George Bernard Shaw.

in real life. This digital shadow is cast across the Web only to be reassembled through the search pursuits of others—whether they're prospective partners, employers, employees, customers, influencers, or stakeholders.

■ A RUDE AWAKENING

Individuals who are currently employed are also at risk of losing their jobs based on their behavior on social networks and what they choose to share online.

British Airways staff created a Web-wide uproar when they called passengers "smelly and annoying" and Virgin Atlantic fired 13 employees for complaining about passengers on Facebook.

And there's certainly no shortage of firings due to posts on MySpace.

Two employees of Houston's Restaurant were canned[2] when managers received access to information in a private MySpace group that divulged derogatory statements about managers, customers, and also private information about upcoming product knowledge tests.

The two filed suit, claiming invasion of privacy. Hillstone Restaurant Group, which owns the Houston's chain, defended its decision with a statement to CNN: "This is not a case about 'cyber-snooping,' the First Amendment, or privacy. It's about two staff members who were let go for unprofessional conduct, including disparaging comments about our guests, and sharing a product knowledge test before it was administered. This misconduct was voluntarily brought to light by a member of the online group."

While we enjoy freedom of speech, we must still be mindful of what we publish and share . . . even if it's in a seemingly private and protected environment.

■ DEFINING YOUR ONLINE PERSONA

The social economy is defined by the exchange of ideas and information online and in the real world, and is indexed by the dividends earned through new opportunities and alliances. Relationships are the new currency of the social economy as they fuel and extend interaction, insight, and loyalty, and in turn, contribute to the social capital of the individuals who actively invest in their personal branding portfolio.

We are now defined by the size of our social graph. Size isn't the only thing that matters, however. This is always an intriguing comment to make, of course, but in all seriousness, our experiences and resulting circumstances, possibilities, and options are defined by how we uniquely engage and participate throughout the Social Web. To put it another way, our interactions and contributions earn keys that unlock the doors to future opportunities.

In the workforce and in our personal lives, the things we share online define who we are—it's a fortunate or unfortunate reality (depending on how you look at it). Social profiles in Facebook and MySpace aren't protected in a secret society that only the cool people can find and share. These profiles are showing up in search engines, and what's in them can tell us everything about how you view yourself and therefore how you may wish others to view you. It's not only your profiles in the social networks where you participate, it's what you say and share everywhere, from blog posts and comments to wall posts, the music you listen to and the widgets you embed, as well as your status updates and even product or service reviews.

This is your digital identity and your real reputation and it's yours to define and nurture.

It's important to proactively weigh, factor, and contribute to the impression you want others to have when they stumble upon or intentionally find your profile(s). This is the first step in defining and shaping your online brand.

■ SOCIAL NETWORKS

Many of us aren't masters of Web design and, therefore, the idea of creating our own entity on the Web is untenable and perhaps even unnecessary. Social networks provide an easy-to-use, fully searchable, and discoverable platform for us to create, define, and fortify our identity.

The most popular social networks, such as MySpace, Facebook, Bebo, and LinkedIn offer users the full ability to customize and personalize their pages and, in the process, represent the ability to consciously paint a more accurate self-portrait.

Social networks are indeed a hub for your digital identity and activity, connecting the disparate pieces of your persona from across the distributed Web and portraying a more crafted, organized, and representative digital resume and knowledge portfolio.

There are social networks for almost everything you can and can't imagine. Join those networks that are instrumental in associating your brand with the industry, ideas, content, and people that further its reach and resonance. And in each case, craft a consistent profile that conveys what it is you stand for and the value you bring to the table. Yes, it's cumbersome and time-consuming, but it's the only way to ensure the integrity of the specific and unique attributes that define your brand and reputation.

By the way, a simple but often-overlooked tip is to start with professional quality portraits. No, I'm not referring to a department store studio. Your picture says more than you know.

■ NEWSFEEDS AND LIFESTREAMS

Obviously you have passions, experiences, and aspirations. Share the content that reinforces these strategic attributes through the tools that keep you connected to the communities that are important to you. Social networks feature the ability to showcase your activity in various networks, packaged neatly in the form of embeddable applications. For example, if you're active on Twitter, Flickr, YouTube, upcoming.org, blogs, and so on, many of these services offer applications or widgets or feeds that can be installed directly onto your profile. They display your latest contributions and events and, more importantly, compartmentalize your content into a presentable focal point for the brand "you."

Applications aren't the only way to filter this content into your profile. Practically every social service produces an RSS feed that can be imported into personal newsfeeds. And, in the land of social networks, these feeds are evolving into lifestreams and activity feeds that channel external and in-network proceedings into one, easy-to-follow flow.

The practice of channeling the most representative and complimentary pieces into one complete puzzle is known as curation. The practice of curation is the most effective policy for presenting and communicating a well-crafted personal brand. It requires the identification, collection, and contributions of meaningful and topical content that, when aggregated, creates a more holistic and powerful depiction of any brand or idea.

Social network profiles and associated newsfeeds aren't the only tools available to curate and present strategic content. Tools dedicated to the art of streaming are gaining in popularity. Similar to the newsfeeds within social networks, these dedicated communities provide the ability for users to also aggregate their activity into one river of relevance. They collect the feeds and updates from the services you choose to include and merge them into a personal or brand stream.

Here is a text-based example of John Smith's lifestream:

"Conversations taking place in social networks help to define one's online brand"—via Twitter XX date, XX time (link)

Uploaded a new photo album entitled, "diagram of my social map"—via Flickr XX date, XX time (link)

Wrote on Jane Doe's wall, "Excellent post today on conversations across the distributed Web. I agree. Have you experimented with reputation management tools such as Echo?—via Facebook XX date, XX time (link)

Published a blog post, "Using social networks and online content to create and reinforce your online brand"—via ACME: The Brand You Blog XX date, XX time (link)

Robert Johnson commented on "Using social networks and online content to create and reinforce your online brand," "John, nice post. I learned a lot, thanks!"—via Tumblr XX date, XX time (link)

Bookmarked "Online brands and the art of aggregating ideas into a collective and cohesive flow"—via delicious XX date, XX time (link)

■ BLOGS

Lifestreams and social networks aren't the only tools to help aggregate and centralize your digital identity or collectively assemble the bits and pieces that, when combined, help to define your identity and reputation. Blogs are perhaps still the most effective platform for sharing your observations, thoughts, ideas, expertise, and vision on the subjects you're most passionate about—as they provide context around your ideas, expertise, persona, and interests.

Unlike micromedia tools, such as Twitter, Plurk, Identi.ca, and FriendFeed, as well as social network profile pages where brevity is promoted and rewarded, blog posts inherently boast the ability to share expanded content, text, video, audio, images, tags, links, to more effectively and deeply express, explain, and support the ideas and context related to any given topic.

Blogs with an almost undeviating mission of focusing on key topics boast an expansive library of keywords that can intentionally or unintentionally contribute to a valuable search engine optimization (SEO) infrastructure that ranks your brand and ideas higher in search results for related topic searches. And, as your content library grows and expands, your blog's page-ranking authority escalates along with it. Higher page ranking combined with keyword density (the concentration of keywords related to your expertise) equates to the greater authority you're given in search engine ranking pages (SERPs).

Remember, blogs are indexed in traditional and blog search engines, and with a focused emphasis on SEO and page ranking, your blog will almost always consistently rank higher in search results over any other form of social content you contribute or publish, especially as more people link back to your posts.

■ REPUTATION AND EXPERTISE AGGREGATION SERVICES

A necessary set of online services are permeating the Social Web to help track and aggregate the activity of individuals, improve the caliber of feedback and comments, and, in the process, create a concentrated portfolio of published content and commentary. Echo, Disqus, and Intense Debate are systems that run inside blog comments sections, forums, and websites, and make the process of content creation and the ensuing conversations more interactive and lively. BackType also provides a search window into the millions of comments that populate the blogosphere. Now, the commentary that shapes the conversations affected by the content introduced in a blog post becomes part of the bigger conversation online.

Conversations are now in fact distributed. A blog post can syndicate to multiple networks simultaneously and spawn commentary and host dispersed conversations in multiple networks. On the other side, whether you're the blogger or the commenter, your contributions can have a reverberating effect now as tools such as those described above are making blogging relevant again by aggregating the commentary related to the source post and funneling them into an organized flow in the blog comments section.

Similar to the activity streams we reviewed earlier, intelligent commenting systems can pinpoint commentary related to the post and reel it in to centralize webwide conversations in one place. Now, for example, a blog post will not only feature direct comments, but also the related Tweets, updates from the statusphere, and also other blogs and social networks, in one place. Replies to the respective individual discussions that pipe in from other networks will in turn broadcast back to the originating source. These tools make the world of online conversations a much smaller, more connected, and useful paradigm once again.

This is where you come in . . . comments are trackable and central to defining your online reputation.

For example, these systems offer readers the ability to not only comment on a post, but also aggregate or organize individual comments and activity history into one digital commenting portfolio that provides interested visitors with an amalgamated representation of your views and aptitude.

These services aggregate the distributed thoughts and dispersed identity beacons of individuals into one representative profile. As active participants in the Social Web, we comment on relevant articles in addition to publishing our own thoughts on our blogs. With one click, anyone can view a history of our posts and comments, in one place, tied to a profile that we define.

■ YOUR BRAND VERSUS THE BRANDS YOU REPRESENT

Whether we believe it or not, everyone within an organization is at some level responsible for public relations (but not publicity, media relations, analyst relations, or investor relations). Everything we do, online and offline, builds the public perception of not only our personal brand, but also that of the organization we represent. They must be symbiotic. And while many insist that a brand must "be human," it must not act or interact as one—or at least not just any human. Remember, we're defining and contributing to the personality of the brand we represent, as well as our own.

As an active participant in social media and also a professional working in any capacity within a company, eventually an important and cognizant decision will determine your outward presence and whether or not your personal brand and your corporate responsibilities intersect, compete, or clash.

As many businesses are realizing, there is not only the possibility, but, in many cases, the requirement to participate and engage with customers, peers, influencers, and prospects in their respective communities. New roles and responsibilities for outbound communications and service emerge for all employees.

■ MANAGING YOUR ONLINE REPUTATION

Everything starts with listening and observing where, how, and why these conversations are taking place and the tone and nature of the dialogue.

As part of the marketing process, companies employ (or should incorporate) an online reputation management (ORM) program.

Typically, ORM focuses on company and product name(s), executives, and/or brands, and each of these services automate the process of searching and present the results in a manageable, easy-to-navigate dashboard. The differences between each lie under the hood, where the individual algorithms distinguish each service in how they discover, track, and present data. And none of these services are all-inclusive. There is still a manual element involved, requiring you to search specific communities directly.

ORM isn't limited only to businesses. In the era of digital reputations, individuals can also benefit from the process of monitoring the conversations related to their personal brand.

Real-time search engines such as Collecta and OneRiot and Google Alerts, which scours News.Google.com, Blogsearch.google .com, and other Media properties, are among the most effective, free services available for tracking keywords and presenting them to you as they appear online. They give you, as the primary stakeholder, the opportunity to participate and respond immediately, as you should, in order to protect the integrity of your brands as well as the ability to continually cultivate your community.

Emerging and socialized media will only continue to provide us with the opportunity to build and grow our personal brands and establish a position of authority based on our expertise. The more attention we devote to listening, participating, and contributing to related conversations over time, as well as allowing them to permeate our personal defense systems, the more our reputation matures and expands. Feedback and criticism can offer value, even if they're incorrect in their assumptions and reactions. Each response offers value in the form of how an individual perceives you and your convictions.

You are your best investment and you'll earn the rewards and relationships you deserve.

■ WE ARE ALL BRAND MANAGERS

Effectively organizing, curating, showcasing, and managing a strategically posed online personal, professional, and corporate brand is critical to how our peers, those we already know and the others we have yet to meet, perceive us in the real world.

Again, the comments we leave, the posts we publish, the pictures and videos we upload, the statuses we broadcast in social networks and streams, collectively contribute to disparate digital recreations of how people perceive us—as an individual, representative of a company, and/or the corporate brand we manage. While we can't control the filters that control how people ultimately assemble these pieces and assess our personality, reputation, value proposition, and expertise, we can shape and steer perception by sharing tactical and complementary content that contributes to the brand we wish to portray and represent.

We are all, at some level, becoming brand managers.

We are in control of the digital shadow that materializes when the spotlight is cast upon our persona.

Take this opportunity to showcase your accomplishments, strengths, interests, goals, skills, and talents. Reinforce what it is you stand for as well as what moves you. In many ways your profiles and the material you share online contribute to a digital resume, whether you wish to present your CV or not. It's there, right now, representing you, without your direction.

Decide what person or group you're trying to impress with your social profiles and updates, and realize that the answer may change over time. First think about what it is you're sharing, and why, before you upload it to the public Web.

With social media comes great responsibility. . . .

What do your profile, activity, and search results say about you?

Chapter

16

Learning and Experimentation Lead to Experience

In new media, we're frequently challenged to venture outside our lair of solace, and the more we live outside it, the more we begin to actually redefine our center of judgment, transforming how we interpret, process, and act based on how new information reaches us.

Curiosity and experience can reveal new, more effective, and more efficient ways to get from here to the ever-elusive "there," all while venturing into the unknown. It's what we implement that converts theory into practice, and practice into education and innovation.

Caution, however, isn't something we ought to carelessly throw to the wind. Within social networks and the blogosphere, the rules of engagement are currently in the process of being defined, through its careful development, real-world testing, and continual modification. There's much to learn, but we can't grasp or master anything by sitting idly and watching the world pass us by. Nor can we jump in with both feet and engage without observing how we effectively contribute value and earn the relationships that spark communities, associations, and ultimately action and/or commerce.

■ BECOMING THE EXPERT

You've already acquired a great deal of knowledge about your industry, through seminars and conferences, blogs, articles, and newsletters.

This is your moment, and it starts with becoming the type of person you would want to listen to, watch, read, and otherwise seek guidance from. You are empowered to lead the way and test and employ the lessons and insight you absorb in order to apply experiences that parlay into your reality, your world.

Many are faced with the reality of having to successfully justify, initiate, and implement their education and vision. We are basically attempting to chart the specific steps necessary to accomplish new and great things while tying strategies and tactics to real-world business value, not because we have to, but because we can.

Sure, those responsible for green-lighting a new pilot, campaign, or program may or may not be qualified to do so. They may, instead, stand in the way, in a desperate bid for job security, and attempt to direct a social media project into oblivion, tangle innovation with a Web of process requirements and aging infrastructure, or, even worse, denounce new ideas.

Okay, so then what?

Thankfully, there are also gatekeepers who are never content with the status quo and recognize opportunity and their chance to not only adapt and evolve along with their customers and influencers, but also help lead them to answers and insight to make more informed decisions.

We're all learning. However, history, experience, and intuition will help save us from learning and progressing through friction, public chastising, loss of revenue and brand stature, or perpetual mistakes.

We are the champions.... We are the experts.

■ YOU'RE THE REAL THING

While many individuals can demonstrate the benefits of and processes for building and managing personal brands online, only those who have faced business-specific challenges, tested numerous initiatives, experienced buy and sell cycles, and lived through successes and failures related to their markets are eligible to become bona fide experts. The rest of us are still learning together, forever students of emerging media.

It's not about the tools.

It's not about the ability to build profile pages within specific social networks.

It's not about creating a blog and populating it with content.

And, it's definitely not about creating and polluting the Web with irrelevant social objects.

This is about social architecture, engineering, and the empathy required to build bridges between your company, its brand, and its audiences, customers, and peers. It's also about contributing value to the communities in which you wish to participate.

Want to master Twitter? Don't jump to purchase a book on Twitter. It's less important to know the history of Twitter or how to "tweet" and more important to use Twitter as an extension of who you are, what you stand for, and the value that you can add to the community.

The same is true for Facebook and LinkedIn, for that matter. At the end of the day, they're channels—albeit rich channels—for listening, learning, and participating. Understanding the unique culture of each social network as it relates to your business and the corresponding behaviors that define the subgroups of niche networks is critical to establishing, implementing, and managing successful programs.

Tools are just that: tools. They will help you reach people. They'll adapt. They'll change. They'll emerge and merge. And many will simply vanish.

Think about it for a moment.

Your focus, no matter which tools you use, must be on assessing weaknesses and opportunities, defining goals and objectives, auditing the landscape and competitive activity, listening to where and how the community is speaking, and identifying expressed concerns and challenges. We must take steps to create a governing and measurable strategy in order to justify, refine, and improve our activity.

■ WHEN POV BECOMES A POINT OF VALIDATION

In order to appeal to customers, peers, and other influencers, we need to embrace their point of view, which provides insight into their frame of mind. Doing so will lay the foundation that will allow us to learn from an educated position. From there, our experience and training builds upon itself in line with our markets.

We're usually missing the "day in the life of" viewpoint and the "why should I listen to you" perspective in our strategy and execution, yet it's supposed to serve as the core of anything and everything we do and should be doing.

In my experience, we tend to broadcast, even when we are listening. We tend to communicate without regard for the bigger picture as it relates to participating parties, even if we're engaging.

The experience that's earned through the process of establishing and promoting a personal brand and building prominence, cultivating an active and vibrant community, earning trust and loyalty on behalf of a company brand, and inspiring measurable action and transactions, is immeasurable.

You represent the future of your brand's connections, and resonance within emerging media. Don't get distracted. Get to work.

■ LET'S TALK ABOUT MEANINGFUL EXCHANGES

Any anthropologist or sociologist will tell you that before attempting to join any society, we must conduct initial fieldwork to observe and document the culture, behaviors, communication styles, customs, and traditions of its citizens. And before we can determine which networks we prioritize, we have to first "listen" to the conversations across multiple social networks to identify and distinguish relevant interaction from worthless chatter.

Use the Conversation Prism (see Chapter 18) to establish a Conversation Index.

Transformation begins with observation.

We need to spend more time listening and less time broadcasting or talking "at" people.

We must realize that there are benefits to monitoring, observing, listening, communicating, and connecting.

Earning the attention of peers as part of an integrated B2B, B2C, or D2C (Direct to Customer) communications program necessitates a level of mastery that shares roots and certain tactical attributes with personal branding, but requires supplemental skills and talents that inspire and fuel relevant techniques and strategic vigilance, which ultimately beget presence and mindshare.

■ WHO OWNS SOCIAL MEDIA?

It is essential to figure out who's in charge of the conversations around your industry. Is it advertising, PR, marketing communications, or customer service? It's all of the above!

How do you integrate social media into the marketing fold without either being laughed at or, even worse, fired? Perhaps CEOs, directors, and investors will read this and force the change from the top downward. But in most cases, change will be driven from the bottom upward, and also will be influenced by middle management. As social media becomes accepted and practiced industry-wide, change will also stem from outside pressure.

The easy answer is that no one owns the conversation and that each division and each person representing the company, inward and outward, will be responsible for contributing to it.

Conversations will always map directly to specific departments within a company, thus requiring participation from everyone, including service and support, PR, marketing communications, executives, product development, finance/investor (if applicable), and so forth.

The best companies will release their control associated with the gatekeeping of the brand and messages in social realms and trust their employees and customers to carry forward. Don't get me wrong, traditional marketing can still run as it has; it simply now needs a more complementary role with all the new media activities. There also needs to be a more cognizant process for understanding the people who comprise the markets you're trying to reach

■ GETTING DOWN TO BUSINESS

The primary metric for business success is measured in profitability and market share, not friends and followers. It is quantified in predefined and desired actions, not conversations. It is metered in presence and not chatter. The path to direct success is impeded by the tollgates that are manned by customers and influencers who govern passage and direction.

While basic communications and personal skills factor into user engagement, they are technically responsible for defining perception, reach, and persona.

While many preach the importance of personality and voice and the humanization of the corporate brand in social networks, there's something to be said for mystique and there's definitely something to be said for behavior.

Being "yourself" or simply being present isn't enough, and many times it can also take away from the persona that symbolizes the company and its products. We examined the need to define and personify the personality of the brand earlier.

Would Apple maintain its magic if hired everyday social media experts were actively engaging with people on Twitter? Would Steve Jobs preserve his charisma if we as the public could freely access him through social networks? Or would these prestigious brands lose their luster and charisma?

But think about it. Would simply having access to the company wherever, whenever, through the voices and personalities of John or Jane Doe change your perceptions of Apple or Mr. Jobs?

I remind you of this here because you are the first line of defense and offense.

In social media, the brands of participants will forever be at odds with the brands they represent. Who we are as an individual and who we are as a representative of a company aren't always in harmony or unison. However, there is an attainable balance and it's this balance that inflates and steers the impression of all brands involved on both sides of the conversation—as it relates to the calculated brand personality.

While we profess to inject a human element into the image of those companies as a way of making them approachable and compassionate, we must assess our intended role and the advantages of engagement in the communities we wish to reach before our inaugural utterance or declaration. Then, and only then, can we plot our bearing and trajectory.

It's a matter of "being human" versus "humanizing the story," and there is a stark difference between them.

Humanizing the brand is necessary if, and only if, a human voice will reduce or eliminate potential friction between the customer and the company. Otherwise, social strategies must personify the greater purpose, significance, and symbolization of the brand, and reinforce those traits through everything we contribute. We do so by also humanizing our existing and potential customers, gaining empathy and sincerity in the process. But we must do so at a profound measure, through not only a deep-rooted comprehension of human nature and connections as it relates to our individual personality, but also an entrenched comprehension of perception management, brand shaping and reinforcement, and active counseling and guidance that leaves those you encounter more informed, aware, and fulfilled. We're instilling the attributes that engender awareness, enthusiasm, and loyalty.

We look to you to act as the gatekeeper who protects the brand while serving the interests of those you're chartered to reach.

The shift from specialist to authority is driven specifically by experience and the activities that define your social portfolio. As a business professional seeking guidance, direction, and insight, become the person you're trying to reach by using the voice of the persona you wish to convey and fortify.

This is connectivity through inspiration. In the process, we become the very social media experts we sought to employ.

Be bullish.

Stand up and assume command.

You are the voice, spirit, and mind of the brand and the people and culture that define it.

Part

IV

We Are the Champions

Chapter 17

Defining the Rules of Engagement

To prevent information leaks and other liabilities, companies are drafting guidelines for social media interaction. A rule of thumb: Don't be stupid.

— *BUSINESSWEEK*[1]

With access to social tools, we are more influential than we realize, and that works both for and against us.

Before we create and implement outbound social media programs, we must first educate employees on the benefits and hazards associated with social media and the workplace. However, this should not include banning access to these networks. We'll discuss that topic more thoroughly a bit later.

We previously reviewed the circumstances and consequences surrounding the personal use of social media when it links or refers to employers, employees, coworkers, competitors, and affected brands in general. Without realizing the impact of a single update, employees are jeopardizing brand stature, reputation, and competitive edge. Without thinking, employees are sharing candid and damaging thoughts and updates—intentionally and unintentionally—that possess an uncanny ability to surface when least expected and be discovered by people who were never supposed to see them in the first place.

And, perhaps accidentally, employees are sharing company secrets and information that should never see the light of day, and are doing so simply because they have access to the tools that personally connect them to their friends, family, and peers.

Yet, heeding *BusinessWeek*'s advice is easier said than done. One might believe that common sense is pervasive and prevailing;

however, I believe that "common sense" is mostly uncommon. In a new media world where many of us are literally learning as we go, commonsensical behavior usually acquiesces to a more likely set of circumstances that resembles common nonsense, rather than sense and sensibility. Therefore, we need to proactively avert crises before they arise.

■ INSIDE THE OUTSIDE: ASSESSING THREATS AND OPPORTUNITIES

Businesses are scrambling to understand the technologies and platforms associated with social computing and how to integrate them into the existing network of vetted and proven applications and systems running behind the firewall. More so, information technology (IT), human resources, and executive management are also struggling with the impact of social networks on the culture and productivity within the company, as well as the resulting shifts in internal behavior.

Traditionally, new technology and policies were introduced to organizations in a top-down process, once they were formally evaluated and ratified by IT and management. If new technologies, services, and applications were introduced by employees or outside influences, IT was responsible for assessing the benefits and risks, from the perspective of improving and streamlining workflow and processes, and possibly cutting expenses.

Social computing has created a backdoor for many of these services that also introduces potential dangers to the existing infrastructure and to the systematic routines and channels for ensuring productivity. For the first time, new technologies are permeating the enterprise and business infrastructures from the bottom upward. And these technologies precipitate change, carrying the ability to significantly transform business processes and revolutionize marketing, sales, service, production incentives, and many other disciplines and divisions in the process.

Some companies view social networks and blogging platforms such as Facebook and Twitter as a threat to productivity, network security, and company intelligence. They are therefore prohibiting access to these networks from within the firewall. Many studies have already concluded that there are indeed productivity decreases when employees have unregulated access to personal communications tools and distractions. While formerly traced to smoke breaks, coffee breaks, and water cooler chats, distractions began to include telephones and cell phones, instant messaging, and now social networks. Concurrently, many cases have already been documented where personal systems and corporate networks were compromised due to scams, worms, viruses, and Trojan horses shared through social media. However, this is hardly new; malicious software has long permeated the firewall through e-mail and Web browsing.

Other businesses and organizations are going so far as to ban usage of these networks as a representative of the company inside and outside of the work perimeter, regardless of whether it's done on or off the clock.

In August 2009, the United States Marines banned the use of Twitter, MySpace, Facebook, and other social networks for a period of one year, citing the risks to both personnel and network security.

The Marine Corps order attempted to explain the rationale:

> *These Internet sites in general are a proven haven for malicious actors and content and are particularly high risk due to information exposure, user generated content and targeting by adversaries. . . . The very nature of SNS [social network sites] creates a larger attack and exploitation window, exposes unnecessary information to adversaries and provides an easy conduit for information leakage that puts OPSEC [operational security], COMSEC [communications security], and personnel . . . at an elevated risk of compromise.*[2]

When news of this order initially surfaced, journalists and social media experts reacted in disbelief and displeasure. However, understanding their concerns allows us to assess possibilities whereas to deploy and guide usage as it relates to the business and mission of the armed forces, and any civilian organization for that matter.

On the other hand, prior to the ordinance issued by the Marines, the Army ordered bases to allow access to social networks after a year-long banishment.

The Army public affairs managers shared the operations order publicly to clarify intentions and justify the command:

> *. . . the intent of senior Army leaders to leverage social media as a medium to allow soldiers to "tell the Army story" and to facilitate the dissemination of strategic, unclassified information. Therefore, the social media sites available from the Army homepage will be made accessible from all campus area networks. Additionally, all Web-based email will be made accessible.*[3]

In an interview with *Wired's* Danger Room, Price Floyd, the Pentagon's newly appointed social media czar, shared his views of and vision for social media:[4]

> *OPSEC is paramount. We will have procedures in place.... What we can't do is let security concerns trump doing business. We have to do business.... We need to be everywhere men and women in uniform are and the public is. If that's MySpace and YouTube, that's where we need to be, too.*

As such, the Pentagon ordered a review of social networks in the second half of 2009 to craft policies that dictate usage scenarios and goals for services such as Twitter, MySpace, and Facebook.

Officials acknowledged the potential influence within the military and also in the greater population for these networks. As a result, they developed rules that would allow the military to take advantage of the expedient communications inherent within social networking without exposing sensitive information, jeopardizing personnel, or placing computer networks at risk.

A number of top commanders and officers already maintain public profiles on social networks.

Admiral Michael G. Mullen,[5] chairman of the Joint Chiefs of Staff, and Army General Ray Odierno,[6] the top commander in Iraq, maintain Facebook profiles. Mullen also actively tweets.

Responding to questions on Twitter as to whether or not Mullen would continue to participate during times when the security, threats, and benefits of social networks are questioned, Mullen wrote, "Obviously we need to find the right balance between security and transparency. We are working on that. But am I still going to tweet? You bet."

In an interview with the *Los Angeles Times*, Navy Captain John Kirby, a spokesman for Mullen, acknowledged that the chairman had already seen the importance of using social media to communicate with the public. He stated,

> *The genie is out of the bottle. There is just such a power in it, we have to find a way to achieve this balance. No one wants to provide information to potential enemies, but this is a dialogue that we cannot afford not to be a part of.*[7]

Top generals are also are taking the initiative to reach troops and other constituents through personal blogs. For example, Major General Michael Oates,[8] a two-star general overseeing 19,000 U.S. soldiers in southern and central Iraq, maintains a blog and hosts chats to communicate within and to those defining the chain of command, as well as maintaining dialogues with troops that are scattered across Iraq.

So why am I sharing examples of social media bans and active communications in the military?

The answer is as simple as it is profound. If the U.S. military is actively seeking guidelines for defining, regulating, and promoting the use of social media to improve communications and influence constituents, then it's safe to assume that your organization should follow suit.

Everything starts with assessment and the implementation of structure, followed by management and responsibility.

■ POLICIES AND GUIDELINES

Best Buy initially broke ground with its Blue Shirt Network, which fueled and fostered conversation, interaction, and content to improve employee communication and team spirit. The company also catalyzed customer support and participation when it introduced IdeaXchange, a dedicated feedback community designed to solicit feedback in order to make Best Buy a better place to shop.

Among many other accomplishments, Best Buy again pioneered a new and controversial social program with the introduction of its @Twelpforce account on Twitter. The account is simple in design but radical in concept, deployment, and implications. Arguably one of the most outlandish social media mavens of its time, Best Buy leveraged the reach of mainstream traditional media in the form of television commercials to generate awareness and attention for a specific new media initiative.

Twelpforce tapped the wisdom of its own crowds to assemble and deploy an armada of service professionals to help answer questions posed by existing and prospective customers on Twitter, and also to proactively share insights from their personal/professional accounts on the @twelpforce account directly (see Figure 17.1).

Without direction, training, and a supporting infrastructure, this program would most likely have imploded. However, Best Buy provided a set of guidelines and instructions to guide participants in the program to help them assist customers and ultimately engender goodwill and inspire action in the process.

Risky?

Yes.

Creative?

Yes.

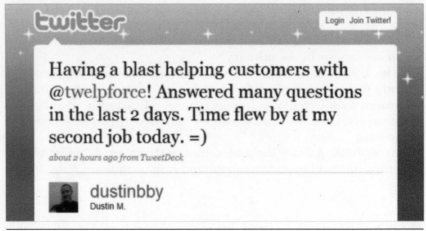

Figure 17.1

Another example of overusing "tw" in a name?
Yes.
Effective?
Yes!
An excerpt from Best Buy Connect,[9] an internal network that serves as the voice of the Best Buy employee, offers guidance to participants of the @Twelpforce program:

The promise we're making starting in July is that you'll know all that we know as fast as we know it. That's an enormous promise. That means that customers will be able to ask us about the decisions they're trying to make, the products they're using, and look for the customer support that only we can give. And with Twitter, we can do that fast, with lots of opinions so they can make a decision after weighing all the input. It also lets others learn from it as they see our conversations unfold.

When you start, remember that the tone is important. Above all, the tone of the conversation has to be authentic and honest. Be conversational. Be yourself. Show respect. Expect respect. The goal is to help. If you don't know the answer tell them you'll find out. Then find out and let them know.

To help you establish programs and policies, I've included the complete set of instructions, as I feel that they are indicative of a solid foundation for implementing and sharing guidelines.

Approach

Tell them you're from Best Buy—part of the Twelpforce. Be engaged, know what's going on out there but don't intrude or invade. If someone is talking about how they're looking for a product that we may sell, don't swoop in and tell them they'd be better off buying it from us. If they're looking for help, or opinions, they'll ask.

Don't talk about private company stuff even in direct messages. Don't ask for personal customer information even in direct message. Offer an e-mail via direct message instead.

Connect people to outside sources or other Best Buy people when appropriate. Don't directly refer them to other customers on Twitter or elsewhere. If your answer requires more than 140 characters, create a blog on your local store page and refer customers to it. Or look in the Best Buy Community Support Forums—there's tons of great questions and answers there.

Above all, if you don't know or if you're not sure, ask. Always respond quickly and follow up quickly. Apologize for delays or misunderstandings.

What Do You Have To Do?

You don't need any special skills—you just have to be curious, proactive, and helpful—much of the same stuff you do everyday.

The best thing you can do to start is to listen to what people are saying and asking on Twitter. Go to http://search.twitter.com and search for things you're interested in. Search for your favorite brand, your favorite category, for Best Buy. Find out what questions and problems people have. And figure out a way to help them. It all starts with a simple post.

Customer:

yoshimac: need to buy a new tv for bedroom so i can watch what i want no desprate housewifes blaaaaaaaaaaaaaaa

You:

@yoshimac If you need some help figuring what to get, let me know. I work at Best Buy in the Home Theater Dept and could give you some opinions. If not, thats cool too.

What if someone else already answered their question? Have a different opinion? Let them know what you think. The goal of Twelpforce is to share our knowledge and give people the information they need to make a decision. When I look for a new home in a new city, I don't just ask one person, I get opinions from as many trusted sources as I can and then after weighing the input, I make a decision. But remember—if you engage, show respect. Expect respect. The goal is to help. Not to be creepy.

Other Tools For Searching For Twitter Questions Or
Customer Problems

Search @twelpforce on http://search.twitter.com after July 19th. Customers will be directed via the media support to ask questions directed at @twelpforce.

1. Twitter Search: It's the most basic and most obvious, but this tool now allows for RSS feeds as well as filtering based on language.

2. http:spy.appspot.com spy can listen in on the social media conversations you're interested in. What do you want to listen for?

3. http://www.monitter.com: It's a twitter monitor, it lets you "monitter" the twitter world for a set of keywords and watch what people are saying.

4. http://tweetbeep.com: Free Twitter alerts by e-mail.

5. Twist: Free site for Twitter visualizations over time.

6. Twitter Browser: Free application to view whom is connected to whom. Good for relational analysis and velocity of a users network.

7. Tweetstats: If you want to research a specific user, you can see how often they post, when they post, and who they retweet (i.e., who influences them) and plan accordingly.

Assumptions have no business in business—especially when influential voices can sway the crowd for or against you.

Policies and guidelines must be clear and explicit in intentions and implementation and leave nothing to chance. Training is absolutely required as I can assure you that no matter what people say or believe, no one knows everything there is to know about emerging media and human behavior.

To help those who are unfamiliar with style guides, document or capture and convey the brand essence and how to accurately display it in various forms of media. Usage scenarios, approved artwork, type treatments, and approved language should all be included.

These style guides serve as the sheet music to ensure that we as employees and brand representatives are singing the same song, in key, in unison, and beautifully.

Every company should create and distribute a style guide or handbook of guidelines, not only for social media, but specifically for each social network in which the company currently engages or expects to engage, as well as policies and instructions for discrete programs and campaigns.

When I wrote the guidelines for Facebook use for a Fortune 500 company, it was 25 pages long. I'll update the guidelines and share them on the website dedicated to this book so that you can have it as a free example of the level of detail required to address most unspoken questions and concerns that arise as employees participate online.

While you may offer a "quick-start" guide to help you and your team kick-start programs, true success is defined by understanding, reinforced by practice. Therefore we cannot overlook the need for a detailed instruction manual complete with best practices, scenarios, objectives, metrics, rewards, and associated consequences.

■ EXAMPLE GUIDELINES AND POLICIES

Here are some additional examples to glean inspiration and direction. Please keep in mind, however, that these examples are representative of "what is" and not always "what should be." As you read these, remember the lessons, stories, and advice that I've shared with you thus far. Source these for inspiration only, and create a social style guide that is representative of *your* world and the questions, concerns, capabilities, and opportunities that are present for your business.[10]

➤ Intel Social Media Guidelines[11]

These are the official guidelines for social media at Intel. If you're an Intel employee or contractor creating or contributing to blogs, wikis, social networks, virtual worlds, or any other kind of social media both on and off intel.com—these guidelines are for you. We expect all who participate in social media on behalf

(continued)

of Intel to be trained, to understand and to follow these guidelines. Failure to do so could put your future participation at risk. These guidelines will continually evolve as new technologies and social networking tools emerge—so check back once in awhile to make sure you're up to date.

When You Engage

Emerging platforms for online collaboration are fundamentally changing the way we work, offering new ways to engage with customers, colleagues, and the world at large. It's a new model for interaction and we believe social computing can help you to build stronger, more successful business relationships. And it's a way for you to take part in global conversations related to the work we are doing at Intel and the things we care about.

If you participate in social media, please follow these guiding principles:

➤ Stick to your area of expertise and provide unique, individual perspectives on what's going on at Intel and in the world.

➤ Post meaningful, respectful comments—in other words, no spam and no remarks that are off-topic or offensive.

➤ Always pause and think before posting. That said, reply to comments in a timely manner, when a response is appropriate.

➤ Respect proprietary information and content, and confidentiality.

➤ When disagreeing with others' opinions, keep it appropriate and polite.

➤ Know and follow the Intel Code of Conduct and the Intel Privacy Policy

Rules of Engagement

Be transparent. Your honesty—or dishonesty—will be quickly noticed in the social media environment. If you are blogging about your work at Intel, use your real name, identify that you work for Intel, and be clear about your role. If you have a vested interest in something you are discussing, be the first to point it out.

Be judicious. Make sure your efforts to be transparent don't violate Intel's privacy, confidentiality, and legal guidelines for external commercial speech. Ask permission to publish or report on conversations that are meant to be private or internal to Intel. All statements must be true and not misleading and all claims must be substantiated and approved. Product benchmarks must be approved for external posting by the appropriate product benchmarking team. Please never comment on anything related to legal matters, litigation, or any parties we are in litigation with without the appropriate approval. If you want to write about the competition, make sure you know what you are talking about and that you have the appropriate permission. Also be smart about protecting yourself, your privacy, and Intel Confidential information. What you publish is widely accessible and will be around for a long time, so consider the content carefully.

Write what you know. Make sure you write and post about your areas of expertise, especially as related to Intel and our technology. If you are writing about a topic that Intel is involved with but you are not the Intel expert on the topic, you should make this clear to your readers. And write in the first person. If you publish to a website outside Intel, please use a disclaimer, something like this: "The postings on this site are my own and don't necessarily represent Intel's positions, strategies, or opinions." Also, please respect brand, trademark, copyright, fair use, trade secrets (including our processes and methodologies), confidentiality, and financial disclosure laws. If you have any questions about these, see your Intel legal representative. Remember, you may be personally responsible for your content.

Perception is reality. In online social networks, the lines between public and private, personal and professional are blurred. Just by identifying yourself as an Intel employee, you are creating perceptions about your expertise and about Intel by our shareholders, customers, and the general public—and perceptions about you by your colleagues and managers. Do us all proud. Be sure that all content associated with you is consistent with your work and with Intel's values and professional standards.

It's a conversation. Talk to your readers like you would talk to real people in professional situations. In other words, avoid

(continued)

overly pedantic or "composed" language. Don't be afraid to bring in your own personality and say what's on your mind. Consider content that's open-ended and invites response. Encourage comments. You can also broaden the conversation by citing others who are blogging about the same topic and allowing your content to be shared or syndicated.

Are you adding value? There are millions of words out there. The best way to get yours read is to write things that people will value. Social communication from Intel should help our customers, partners, and co-workers. It should be thought-provoking and build a sense of community. If it helps people improve knowledge or skills, build their businesses, do their jobs, solve problems, or understand Intel better—then it's adding value.

Your responsibility. What you write is ultimately your responsibility. Participation in social computing on behalf of Intel is not a right but an opportunity, so please treat it seriously and with respect. If you want to participate on behalf of Intel, take the Digital IQ training and contact the Social Media Center of Excellence. Please know and follow the Intel Code of Conduct. Failure to abide by these guidelines and the Intel Code of Conduct could put your participation at risk. Contact social.media@intel.com for more information. Please also follow the terms and conditions for any third-party sites.

Create some excitement. As a business and as a corporate citizen, Intel is making important contributions to the world, to the future of technology, and to public dialogue on a broad range of issues. Our business activities are increasingly focused on high-value innovation. Let's share with the world the exciting things we're learning and doing—and open up the channels to learn from others.

Be a leader. There can be a fine line between healthy debate and incendiary reaction. Do not denigrate our competitors or Intel. Nor do you need to respond to every criticism or barb. Try to frame what you write to invite differing points of view without inflaming others. Some topics—like politics or religion—slide more easily into sensitive territory. So be careful and considerate. Once the words are out there, you can't really get them back. And once an inflammatory discussion gets going, it's hard to stop.

Did you screw up? If you make a mistake, admit it. Be upfront and be quick with your correction. If you're posting to a blog, you may choose to modify an earlier post—just make it clear that you have done so.

If it gives you pause, pause. If you're about to publish something that makes you even the slightest bit uncomfortable, don't shrug it off and hit "send." Take a minute to review these guidelines and try to figure out what's bothering you, then fix it. If you're still unsure, you might want to discuss it with your manager or legal representative. Ultimately, what you publish is yours—as is the responsibility. So be sure.

Moderation Guidelines

Moderation is the act of reviewing and approving content before it's published on the site. Intel does not endorse or take responsibility for content posted by third parties. It is preferred that all content be posted by registered users of a site in accordance with accepted terms and conditions and a code of conduct.

Intel Content: We do not moderate content we publish. This means we allow our blog authors to post directly without approval, as long as they have taken the required trainings.

Anonymous Content: Anonymous content is defined as content submitted as a comment, reply, or post to an Intel site where the user has not registered and is not logged in to the site. For anonymous content, we require moderation on all submissions. Authors of the originating content and space moderators are required to review the content for approval or deletion before the content can be published.

Registered Content: Registered content is content submitted as a comment, reply, or post to an Intel site where the user has registered and is logged in to the site. We do not require moderation of registered content before the content is published to the site. Registered content is directly published and content is moderated post-publishing.

Intel strives for a balanced online dialogue. When we do moderate content, we moderate using three guiding principles.

The Good, the Bad, but Not the Ugly. If the content is positive or negative and in context to the conversation, then we approve the content, regardless of whether it's favorable or unfavorable to Intel. However if the content is ugly, offensive, denigrating and completely out of context, then we reject the content.

➤ **IBM Social Computing Guidelines**[12]

Responsible Engagement In Innovation And Dialogue

Whether or not an IBMer chooses to create or participate in a blog, wiki, online social network or any other form of online publishing or discussion is his or her own decision. However, emerging online collaboration platforms are fundamentally changing the way IBMers work and engage with each other, clients, and partners.

IBM is increasingly exploring how online discourse through social computing can empower IBMers as global professionals, innovators, and citizens. These individual interactions represent a new model: not mass communications, but masses of communicators.

Therefore, it is very much in IBM's interest—and, we believe, in each IBMer's own—to be aware of and participate in this sphere of information, interaction, and idea exchange:

To learn: As an innovation-based company, we believe in the importance of open exchange and learning—between IBM and its clients, and among the many constituents of our emerging business and societal ecosystem. The rapidly growing phenomenon of user-generated Web content—blogging, Social Web applications and networking—are emerging important arenas for that kind of engagement and learning.

To contribute: IBM—as a business, as an innovator, and as a corporate citizen—makes important contributions to the world, to the future of business and technology, and to public dialogue on a broad range of societal issues. As our business activities increasingly focus on the provision of transformational insight and high-value innovation—whether to business clients or those in the public, educational, or health sectors—it becomes increasingly important for IBM and IBMers to share with the world the exciting things we're learning and doing, and to learn from others.

In 1997, IBM recommended that its employees get out onto the Internet—at a time when many companies were seeking to restrict their employees' Internet access. In 2005, the company made a strategic decision to embrace the blogosphere and to encourage IBMers to participate. We continue to advocate IBMers' responsible involvement today in this rapidly growing space of relationship, learning, and collaboration.

IBM Social Computing Guidelines:
Executive Summary

1. Know and follow IBM's Business Conduct Guidelines.[13]

2. IBMers are personally responsible for the content they publish on blogs, wikis, or any other form of user-generated media. Be mindful that what you publish will be public for a long time—protect your privacy.

3. Identify yourself—name and, when relevant, role at IBM—when you discuss IBM or IBM-related matters. And write in the first person. You must make it clear that you are speaking for yourself and not on behalf of IBM.

4. If you publish content to any website outside of IBM and it has something to do with work you do or subjects associated with IBM, use a disclaimer such as this: "The postings on this site are my own and don't necessarily represent IBM's positions, strategies, or opinions."

5. Respect copyright, fair use, and financial disclosure laws.

6. Don't provide IBM's or another's confidential or other proprietary information. Ask permission to publish or report on conversations that are meant to be private or internal to IBM.

7. Don't cite or reference clients, partners, or suppliers without their approval. When you do make a reference, where possible link back to the source.

8. Respect your audience. Don't use ethnic slurs, personal insults, obscenity, or engage in any conduct that would not be acceptable in IBM's workplace. You should also show proper consideration for others' privacy and for topics that may be considered objectionable or inflammatory—such as politics and religion.

9. Find out who else is blogging or publishing on the topic, and cite them.

10. Be aware of your association with IBM in online social networks. If you identify yourself as an IBMer, ensure your profile and related content is consistent with how you wish to present yourself with colleagues and clients.

(continued)

11. Don't pick fights, be the first to correct your own mistakes, and don't alter previous posts without indicating that you have done so.

12. Try to add value. Provide worthwhile information and perspective. IBM's brand is best represented by its people and what you publish may reflect on IBM's brand.

You can read a more detailed discussion of IBM's Social Computing Guidelines on the website created for this book.

■ TOP 10 GUIDELINES FOR SOCIAL MEDIA PARTICIPATION

My good friend Todd Defren, president of SHIFT Communications, assembled a Top 10 Guidelines for Social Media Participation and offered it up for public dissemination and motivation.

TOP 10 GUIDELINES FOR SOCIAL MEDIA PARTICIPATION AT (COMPANY)

These guidelines apply to (COMPANY) employees or contractors who create or contribute to blogs, wikis, social networks, virtual worlds, or any other kind of social media. Whether you log into Twitter, Yelp, Wikipedia, MySpace, or Facebook pages, or comment on online media stories—these guidelines are for you.

While all (COMPANY) employees are welcome to participate in social media, we expect everyone who participates in online commentary to understand and to follow these simple but important guidelines. These rules might sound strict and contain a bit of legal-sounding jargon but please keep in mind that our overall goal is simple: to participate online in a respectful, relevant way that protects our reputation and of course follows the letter and spirit of the law.

1. Be transparent and state that you work at (COMPANY). Your honesty will be noted in the social media environment. If you are writing about (COMPANY) or a

competitor, use your real name, identify that you work for (COMPANY), and be clear about your role. If you have a vested interest in what you are discussing, be the first to say so.

2. Never represent yourself or (COMPANY) in a false or misleading way. All statements must be true and not misleading; all claims must be substantiated.

3. Post meaningful, respectful comments—in other words, please, no spam and no remarks that are off-topic or offensive.

4. Use common sense and common courtesy: for example, it's best to ask permission to publish or report on conversations that are meant to be private or internal to (COMPANY). Make sure your efforts to be transparent don't violate (COMPANY)'s privacy, confidentiality, and legal guidelines for external commercial speech.

5. Stick to your area of expertise and do feel free to provide unique, individual perspectives on non-confidential activities at (COMPANY).

6. When disagreeing with others' opinions, keep it appropriate and polite. If you find yourself in a situation online that looks as if it's becoming antagonistic, do not get overly defensive and do not disengage from the conversation abruptly: feel free to ask the PR Director for advice and/or to disengage from the dialogue in a polite manner that reflects well on (COMPANY).

7. If you want to write about the competition, make sure you behave diplomatically, have the facts straight and that you have the appropriate permissions.

8. Please never comment on anything related to legal matters, litigation, or any parties (COMPANY) may be in litigation with.

9. Never participate in social media when the topic being discussed may be considered a crisis situation. Even anonymous comments may be traced back to your or (COMPANY)'s IP address. Refer all social media activity around crisis topics to PR and/or Legal Affairs Director.

(continued)

> **10.** Be smart about protecting yourself, your privacy, and (COMPANY)'s confidential information. What you publish is widely accessible and will be around for a long time, so consider the content carefully. Google has a long memory.
>
> **NOTE:** Mainstream media inquiries must be referred to the Director of Public Relations.

I've shared with you some of the most comprehensive examples available, and as you can see, they share many common attributes:

➤ Ensure a consistent, personable, and brand-enhancing tone or voice.

➤ Add value to each engagement—contribute to a stature and legacy.

➤ Respect those with whom you're engaging and also respect the forum in which you participate.

➤ Ensure that you honor copyrights and practice and promote fair use of applicable content.

➤ Protect confidential and proprietary information.

➤ Be transparent and be human (well, be believable and helpful).

➤ Represent what you should represent.

➤ Know and operate within the defined boundaries.

➤ Know when to fold 'em and don't engage trolls or fall into conversational traps.

➤ Keep things conversational as it applies to portraying and reinforcing the personality and value of your brand and the brand you represent.

➤ Stay on message, on point, and on track with the goals of your role and its impact on the real-world business to which you contribute.

➤ Don't trash the competition—not directly, anyway.

➤ Apologize when necessary.

➤ Be accountable for your actions and offer no excuses.

➤ Know who you're talking to and what they're seeking.

➤ Disclose relationships, representations, affiliations, and intentions.

➤ Practice self-restraint; some things are not worth sharing.

Stop reading this book and establish or champion the development of personal guidelines in reference to the business and brand right now.

■ THE LOUISIANA PURCHASE AND THE GREAT BRAND LAND GRAB

Okay, so you put down the book or your electronic reader to set guidelines for employee usage, right? Great. Glad to have you back. Let's continue.

Much like the early days of the Web, which eventually contributed to the chaos and madness of the dot-com era and its eventual financial fall, the Social Web is providing a veritable land grab for social real estate at a fraction of the price that it will be worth to you tomorrow.

As in anything new and exciting, there's usually a rush to action. But for some reason, in social media the rush to relevance seemed subdued—at least initially. It was understandable, however. After all, depending on the organization, skepticism, procrastination, and/or lethargy were at play.

Part of the rules of engagement require that we establish a consistent presence across the social networks where we need to maintain a presence as well as plan for those where we might one day need to engage or simply protect our brand assets.

These usernames, pages, and profiles are instrumental in how we portray our brand and brand story as well as interconnect our greater social construct that links visitors to the predefined channels and pages that deliver our intended experience and help them obtain their desired results.

➤ In every network, the brand and product name should be identical.

➤ The profile pages must reflect the aesthetics, information, and personality as determined by the social style guide in the spirit of the network they appear.

➤ Define the clickpaths to help visitors navigate your information network.

It should go without saying, but as you may or may not know, the landscape for social networks is vast and may be beyond our initial reach. However, excuses, ignorance, and ambivalence aside, we are responsible for attaining and managing our personal and professional brands, as well as those we represent, even if it simply implies that we secure the domain or username—including its derivatives, both positive and negative. For example, companyx, productx, companyxsucks, or companyxmustdie.

Create a standard naming convention that is simple, uncomplicated, concise (friendly to microblogs and other forms of micromedia), and easy to both remember and also to input on mobile devices. In addition, create a naming formula that is friendly and identifiable by the outside world. Too many organizations that I have worked with over the years forget that people outside of the organization may not understand the significance of a unique department or division. Others attempt to inject more information than is necessary, embellished by quotes, underlines, and other symbols. This only leads to brand dilution and confusion.

This is true online as well. In 2008, FairWinds Partners[14] released a study that documented the power of Internet gripe sites. The *Wall Street Journal* explored the topic with an in-depth article, "How to Handle 'IHateYourCompany.com,'"[15] which reviewed what some companies are doing, or not doing, to protect their brands online.

In its study, FairWinds researched the Web to identify gripe sites specifically containing "sucks.com." The study uncovered over 20,000 domains with only 2,000 ending in the phrase "stinks.com." Of the major companies surveyed, only 35 percent owned the domain name for their brand followed by the word "sucks."

But domain names are only one of the many opportunities for customers to share their discontent, and in the emerging era of the two-way Web, communications, customer service, and brand and reputation management teams must not only collaborate to actively survey the landscape to detect and diagnose negative experiences, but also proactively plan for it. And part of that process is securing and establishing a uniform brand name in addition to its positive or negative variations and adaptations.

Service providers such as Knowem.com can not only scour the entire Web for available and taken usernames in social networks for you, but also acquire them and cost-effectively create profiles based on a template you create. One of the greatest value propositions of this service and others like it is that it also will automatically create profiles in emerging networks to prevent opportunists and angry customers from squatting on desired usernames. And if the username is unavailable (read "squatted"), Knowem provides helpful steps to retrieve domain ownership.

For example, when I worked with Anheuser-Busch, we initially discovered that the names associated with the premier corporate and product brands were already taken in key social networks, which required us to manually contact each network to transfer ownership back, even if we weren't planning on deploying a strategy within each network immediately or in the near future.

■ RULES OF ENGAGEMENT

As the Social Web continues to emerge, establishing not only policies and guidelines but also defining the "rules of engagement" will help shape proactive and reactive dialogues to benefit the business, brand, customer, peers, and prospects. This is not the same as implementing and managing rules of conduct. Assessing the common traits found in the guidelines referred to previously, here is a suggested list of Rules of Engagement with which to compose your "sheet music."

➤ Unveil the communities of influence and discover their choices, challenges, impressions, and wants.

➤ Participate where your presence is advantageous and mandatory; don't just participate anywhere and everywhere.

➤ Consistently create, contribute to, and reinforce service and value.

➤ Concentrate participation where it will offer the greatest rewards for both sides.

➤ Assess pain points, frustrations, and also expressions of contentment to establish emotional connections.

➤ Determine the brand identity, character, and personality you wish to portray—and match it to the individual persona who's in front of it when online.

➤ Adapt predefined personalities with the voice of the community in which you engage.

➤ Observe the behavioral cultures within each network and adjust your outreach accordingly.

➤ Become a true participant in each community you wish to galvanize.

➤ Don't speak at audiences through messages.

➤ Dig deeper to connect what transpires in the Social Web to your business objectives.

➤ Learn from each engagement.

➤ Ensure that any external activities are supported by a comprehensive infrastructure to address situations and adapt to market conditions and demands.

➤ Establish a point of contact who is ultimately responsible for identifying, trafficking, or responding to all things that can affect brand perception.

➤ Act, don't just listen and placate—do something.

➤ Earn connections through collaboration.

➤ Empower advocacy.

➤ Embody the attributes you wish to portray and instill.

➤ Don't get lost in conversation or translation; ensure your involvement strategically maps to objectives specifically created for the Social Web.

➤ Establish and nurture beneficial relationships online and in the real world as long as public perception and action is important to your business.

➤ "Un-" campaign programs and ensure they're part of a day-to-day cause.

➤ "Unmarket" by offering solutions and becoming a resource to your communities.

➤ Give back, reciprocate, acknowledge, add value, and contribute where it makes sense.

■ INTEL'S DIGITAL IQ PROGRAM

While guidelines are critical, they are only as effective as the training and implementation of that insight into day-to-day, real-world practice.

I serve as an advisor to Intel as part of the company's Intel Insider program, along with Frank Gruber, Tom Foremski, J. D. Lasica, Cathy Brooks, and other incredible people. I have enjoyed the opportunity to help instill these messages with the already visionary and forward-thinking people defining Intel's marketing, communications, and service teams. Ken Kaplan is responsible for the implementation of this educational program as driven from the PR team. But its reach is company-wide, and thus carries a global impact.

I have also had the benefit of working with Bryan Rhodes on educational and organizational transformation projects (this will be discussed in more depth later) and I believe that Rhodes's work and the corresponding new media educational programs that Intel has implemented and fostered should serve as the standard for all organizations.

Rhodes serves as the Curriculum Architect and Senior Digital Strategist for the Intel Social Media Center of Excellence and chairs the Digital IQ program for all employees who already or who will participate in new media on behalf of the company—for internal and external communications.

The goals of the Digital IQ program complement the company's shift of marketing investments from traditional to new media by increasing employee capabilities. The topics shared as part of this program provide insight into sales and marketing techniques, online retailing and reselling, and media, as well as search, analytics, and metrics. In all, Rhodes and his team have compiled a curriculum of over 55 courses complete with videos, supplementary materials, and a test at the end of each course (see Figure 17.2 for a list of some of the courses).

The aim of Digital IQ is to:

➤ Create a vast Intel digital force.

➤ Unlock digital genius.

DIGIQ216	Twitter Like You Mean It: The Right Way to Tweet Your Brand	Launch
DIGIQ217	Online Marketing Without Breaking the Bank New!	Launch
DIGIQ219	Importance of Brand Identity in Social Media	Launch
DIGIQ221	Timeless Marketing Practices in Digital Times	Launch
DIGIQ301.1	The Power of Search - Advanced	Launch
DIGIQ301.2	The Power of Search - Intro	Launch
DIGIQ304.1	Influencing WOM for Your Company	Launch
DIGIQ304.2	WOM: The Anatomy of Buzz	Launch
DIGIQ304.3	DWOM: Digital Word of Mouth Marketing Basics	Launch
DIGIQ305	Digital PR	Launch
DIGIQ306	Social Media Measurement	Launch
DIGIQ307	Advanced Search Engine Optimization	Launch
DIGIQ308	Digital Natives: Marketing to Youth Around the World	Launch
DIGIQ309.1	Case Study: China Social Media	Launch
DIGIQ309.2	Case Study: APAC Social Media Landscape New!	Launch
DIGIQ309.3	Case Study: EMEA Social Media Landscape	Launch
DIGIQ309.4	Case Study: IJKK Social Media Landscape	Launch
DIGIQ310	Mobile Marketing: The Wide Reach of the Small Screen	Launch
DIGIQ311	Marketing on Small Screen Mobile Devices	Launch
DIGIQ312	Introduction to Omniture Site Catalyst	Launch
DIGIQ313	Viral Marketing	Launch
DIGIQ314	End to End Marketing Online: A Fundamental Shift	Launch

Figure 17.2 Digital IQ Program Guide

➤ Capture digital sales and marketing best known methods.

➤ And, the application of this knowledge on the job.

As such, Intel has instituted four role-based training levels:

1. Level IV is created for the digital marketing specialist, where the results of the program are intended to enhance and guide the creation of improved, relevant, and compelling content and social objects.

2. Level III is programmed for integrated marketing, communications managers, and internal bloggers, providing them with the tools, guidelines, lessons, and directions for integrating and distributing insight and information.

3. Level II serves as the blueprint for helping Field Account Managers sell effectively, using social tools, networks, and services to reach their customers and prospects.

4. Level I is designed for "the rest of us," to help employees understand the landscape and promise of new media and how it impacts their job and career, today and tomorrow.

The Digital IQ program mirrors university models in that its employees register for required courses as well as electives to earn a diploma, which serves as a certification to participate at the corresponding level and new media role on behalf of Intel.

To complete each level, participants are required to attend and pass as many as five courses to earn the corresponding certification. Each year, employees must complete courses in the continuing education program for recertification.

Perhaps the most common response to Intel's groundbreaking program is one of appreciation, followed quickly by skepticism about the ability to fund, design, and institute such a program within your organization.

If the potential perils aren't enough to convey the need to do so, and induce a sense of urgency, think about Intel's results.

By the middle of 2009, Intel's then 10-month-old program had served over 18,500 courses and delivered a total of 16,000 training hours. Over 68 percent of participants found it immediately applicable to their job, with even more attesting to the potential of their careers as they evolve. Funding for the program was overwhelmingly approved due to the buzz, improved morale, and company-wide engagement.

There is no choice. Employees must learn the art and science of content creation and distribution, one-on-one interaction, and community development in order to lead conversations and the tribes that form around your brand, culture, and ideologies.

■ WITH SOCIAL MEDIA COMES GREAT RESPONSIBILITY

Please remember these words. . . .

Perhaps the biggest mistakes committed by businesses, personalities, and brands in social media occur when people jump into social networks blindly without establishing guidelines, a plan of action, a sense of what people are seeking and how and why they communicate, an understanding of where people are congregating, a definition of what they represent and how they will personify the brand online, and the goals, objectives, and metrics associated with participation.

Everything starts with education and the institution of policies to protect individuals and brands.

In addition to setting the guidelines and regulations for how and when employees should and shouldn't engage online when it relates to the company, we must now teach our spokespersons, ambassadors, and advocates how to leverage the immediacy, extent, and potential of these powerful social tools. Our communities will follow by example.

Holding informal and infrequent workshops and/or publishing internal guidelines for self-consumption and interpretation is not nearly enough to satisfy the substantial requirements for an in-depth comprehension of the scenarios, circumstances, objectives, hazards, and nuances associated with engagement, influence, and community building.

This is more than publishing and it's far more important than empowering employees with the ability to chat online.

It's our responsibility to contribute to the increase of a significant, tuned, and strategic signal, with a high ratio to noise. I assure you that in doing so, you will earn a place among the elite in the ranks of social, new, and emerging media practices within your organization.

■ ■ ■

We are vested in the brands we represent—especially if we're on the front lines of emerging media. We must instill and balance our interests and passions for our personal and represented brands in everything we do online. It not only complements and invests in the cohesion and presence of the brands involved, but also champions advocacy and community, because enthusiasm, energy, spirit, and fervor are contagious, inspirational, and addictive.

Chapter 18

The Conversation Prism

How to Listen

Active listening and the resulting, informed engagement plants the seeds that flourish into meaningful conversations and relationships. Implementing engagement guidelines and best practices for personal and professional "brands" before and after any official social media program is introduced is a prerequisite for every business—that's the bottom line. But how do we know where to engage once these guidelines and directives are in place?

After all, we reviewed so many examples and will discuss many more over time, but how do we know what's right for us? Could practicing social media really be as easy as following the conversational template that seems so pervasive in marketing, communications, and customer service landscapes today?

While the tools businesses use may appear to weave a common thread, their implementation and, in turn, their usage are anything but ordinary.

Every company is responsible for charting its own course in the interactive Web and as such, each brand creates its own social DNA that's distinctive in personality and uniquely reflected in the conversations and people who define and populate our online and offline landscapes.

The process of charting engagement strategies and routing our navigation and bearing ensures that we stay on course now and in the time to come.

■ I'M YOUR CUSTOMER . . . REMEMBER ME?

Be careful. You just might reinvent the wheel.

The wheel, after all, is an almost perfect example for reducing friction while we progress, but to reinvent it is to go over ground that has been thoroughly explored. However, the phrase itself is flawed. Many aspects of business require reinvention. Evolution is only as strong as its base. Let's take customer service as an example.

For many years, businesses sought to reduce costs at the expense of customers by outsourcing support services to either domestic agencies or offshore organizations. Businesses also introduced automated front-ends to call centers, to practically eliminate any level of human or official employee interaction. While companies saved money, they intentionally created chasms between brand and consumer, diminishing opportunities for advocacy and referrals. Increasing profitability is smart business, but at some point "smart" decisions did not take into consideration the value of customers and the power of word of mouth. Offshoring a critical business function that reduces negativity in company or product experiences and/or solves problems is both a function of service and also one of strategic marketing. Placing this function in the hands of teams who may or may not understand the dynamics of the business environment and the true pains and challenges of customers can engender animosity rather than instill happiness and satisfaction. It's nearly impossible to serve as a brand evangelist or champion if you're not vested nor rewarded to do so. Customers can sense whether a representative is speaking from experience or reading from a script.

In 2008, the *Wall Street Journal* published a research survey authored by Jonathan Whitaker, assistant professor of management at the University of Richmond's Robins School of Business; M. S. Krishnan, professor of business information technology at the University of Michigan's Ross School of Business; and Claes Fornell, a professor of marketing at the University of Michigan's Ross School of Business.[1] The study analyzed offshoring and outsourcing activities of 150 North American companies and business units from 1998 and 2006. The results were not a surprise. According to the findings, outsourcing support and service caused a significantly negative impact on customer satisfaction. And, when customer satisfaction degrades, it carries with it a financial impact that can affect sales and/or share value.

Whether intentional or not, poor customer service can also affect the psychological experience of customers, introducing feelings of insignificance and a sense of being unappreciated. We've heard it many times, yet we are now just starting to acknowledge and respect its meaning and implications: "A happy customer tells several friends and an unhappy customer tells many more."

The democratization of content publishing has only made this aphorism more applicable.

Psychological research indicates that positive reinforcement is most effective when introduced immediately after a negative experience, to affect conditioning.[2]

Bruce L. Katcher, Ph.D.,[3] an industrial/organizational psychologist with more than twenty years experience in conducting customized employee opinion and customer satisfaction surveys for organizations, observed that the average business never hears from 96 percent of unhappy customers. And, for every complaint received, there are 26 customers with problems, 6 of which are considered serious. An average customer with a problem tells 9 to 10 other people, and 13 percent tell 20 or more.[4]

If we don't know that we're missing these opportunities, then we set the stage for a dramatic showdown that will almost always play out on a public stage.

Time to reinvent the wheel? Reinvention is already underway and it is driven by consumers offering and seeking answers, insight, and direction online, right now.

It's time for companies to reassess current practices and processes to proactively find and address issues with a human and empathetic voice. The role of engagement belongs with those who can effectively and genuinely represent the brand, its intentions, promise, and persona, in a social ecosystem.

■ THE VALUE CYCLE: YOU, ME, AND MUTUAL VALUE

Before we are marketers, communicators, service agents, product architects, and human relations advisors, we are consumers. We purchase products. We share our experiences. We recommend and also complain about brands practically every day. Yet when we approach consumers as a company representative, we tend to forget the dynamics of relationship building and consumer behavior. We stop thinking like consumers and start acting like employees.

In the interactive Web, people aren't lured into relationships simply because you cast the bait to reel them into a conversation.

Sincerity extends beyond the mere act of creating a profile on Twitter or forming a fan page on Facebook or a group in LinkedIn. Transparency carries a dual definition, see-through and genuine, with each separated by intent and action. Relationships are measured by the values, actions, and sentiments that others take away from each conversation. To talk "at" or respond automatically without merit, intelligence, or quality is to grossly underestimate the people you're hoping to befriend and influence. It's the difference between a community and a halfway house; one will flourish, while the other will shelter transients, never growing into a thriving citizenry.

Identifying connected communities and observing the themes and culture of each provides entrée into the personification necessary to foster a genuine and equal ecosystem for dialogue.

It's about bringing information and solutions to people where they congregate before attempting to host their attention on our terms.

The art of conversations is mastered through the practice of both hearing *and* listening.

I hear you.

I'm listening to you.

I understand.

Action.

Identify opportunities to engage, but more importantly, experience the nature, dynamic, ambience, and emotion of the dialogue in order to sincerely and intelligently empathize and converse as a peer. Customers have been neglected long enough, don't you think?

■ THE CONVERSATION PRISM

Navigation is only as effective as the map we use to plot our course. As social media represented an uncharted world, the industry required a social cartographer in order to safely navigate its passages and accurately map the thousands of online continents, countries, and islands, and the rivers and oceans in between.

The map, as we would soon learn, exposed a vibrant and expansive new world that would only continue to magnify and improve with every new discovery.

In 2007, I initially sketched a proposed map for the social landscape that would later see a formal introduction, two iterative releases, and millions of views and downloads. It wouldn't have its official inauguration until mid-2008, and would never have earned intellectual consideration if it weren't for the design prowess of Jesse Thomas of JESS3.

We titled this cartographic visualization as "The Conversation Prism"—see www.theconversationprism.com. Version 1 of the social map officially debuted in August 2008 and provided the first comprehensive and structured view of the Social Web and the networks and communities that defined it at the time (see Figure 18.1).

What it also offered initially, besides an organized view of the new Web, was to demonstrate the sheer volume and magnitude of the Social Web's potential, activity, required commitment, and overall reach.

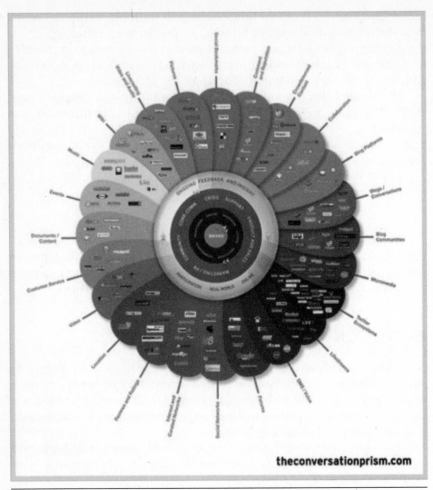

Figure 18.1 The Conversation Prism
Source: Brian Solis and JESS3.

In the processing of mapping and arranging "the conversation," I recognized that the act of categorizing social networks within a visually rich graphic would be temporary at best, demanding endless iterations in order to accurately document evolving and shifting online conversations as well as the communities that promote them.

In the two years since its official introduction, the speed by which the landscape evolved only hastened and therefore required active cartography in order to maintain relevance and structural integrity.

The goal was to observe, analyze, dissect, and present the dynamics of conversations, how and where they transpired. It was driven by necessity, based on my work with many emerging and established brands looking to engage or already participating in the Social Web. The companies I would counsel required tangible evidence to support the notions that online conversations and communities were thriving in less popular, but still relevant networks other than Facebook and Twitter. And, in many cases, after initial research, we would prove that the activity in these newly recognized networks would validate instinct and demonstrate volumes and velocity that far outperformed those of the mainstream networks originally targeted.

The social map presented an organized view of social networks and communities categorized by subject, intent, and capabilities. Like the social networks that were forcing revisions of the Conversation Prism with every merger, introduction, or disappearances, top-level classifications for sorting them also continually transformed. The prevailing methodology and framework for cataloging social properties was most effective when condensed and simplified:

➤ **Social bookmarks:** Sites and communities dedicated to allowing users to share, organize, and search relevant content from around the Web in one place.

➤ **Comment and reputation:** Networks and platforms that centralize the ability to assemble a view of an individual based on the conversational interaction in the Social Web (comments, ratings, etc.).

➤ **Wisdom of the crowds:** Participatory sites that benefit from the crowd-sourcing of content and intellect and in turn offer an aggregated, community-edited, and systematic index of relevant content.

➤ **Crowd-sourced news and content:** Networks that feature content and stories submitted by users, which are then open to voting and commenting.

➤ **Collaboration:** Networks and application platforms where invited or general visitors can collaborate on any given document or project.

➤ **Blog platforms:** Platforms that host the blogs or provide blog software for the creation and hosting of fully customized blogs elsewhere.

➤ **Blogs and conversations:** Search engines and networks that reveal activities occurring within the blogosphere.

➤ **Blog communities:** Communities dedicated to featuring blog content, conversations around blogs, and organizing blogs within an organized network/channel.

➤ **Micromedia:** Online communities that focus on brevity and short updates, including text, video, and audio.

➤ **DIY and customer social networks:** White label social network platforms that allow users to build their own custom, dedicated social network for hosting within a fixed community or on any website of their choosing.

➤ **Activity streams:** Networks that channel social objects and updates from around the Web into one personalized stream.

➤ **Mobile devices:** Services, social networks, and communities that connect people, things, and content through mobile devices.

➤ **Virtual worlds:** Online communities where users create avatars, virtual representations of themselves or favorite characters, and interact with one another within the constructs and missions of dedicated worlds.

➤ **Forums/groups:** Message boards, groups, and discussion forums dedicated to topics, themes, projects, and purposes—this category represents sites and networks that are among the earliest examples of socialized media that are still pervasive today.

➤ **Attention dashboards:** Desktop and mobile clients used to stay connected to those who define the social graph.

➤ **Social networks:** Networks that house our social graph and facilitate the ability to interact, share, respond, publish objects, and post updates in and around the activity of our contacts.

➤ **Nicheworks:** Social networks specifically dedicated to topics, activities, targets, and intention.

➤ **Reviews and ratings:** Sites that feature user-generated feedback, analysis, and experiences with products, brands, and services.

➤ **Location:** Social networks and communities that combine updates and posts while revolving around the physical location of the user and their contacts.

➤ **Video:** Sites that feature user-generated videos and host corresponding activity such as comments, ratings, and also the external embedding of videos in outside networks.

➤ **Customer service:** Communities that host user-generated or brand-hosted interactions that detail the experiences, challenges, problems, and recommendations for the improvement of products and services.

➤ **Content and documents:** Social networks that host interaction, embedding, as well as the connections between people and relevant content, such as docs, spreadsheets, and presentations that span a wide variety of subject matter.

➤ **Events:** Sites that feature events as the central point of conversations and activity.

➤ **Music:** Communities tethered by music and music-related dialogue and networking.

➤ **Wiki:** Hosted and white label wiki platforms for joining existing dialogue or creating new frameworks for collaborating on specific projects.

➤ **Livecasting:** Online networks that offer the ability to stream audio or video in real-time and host corresponding conversations and interaction during the broadcast.

➤ **Pictures:** Social networks where activity revolves around pictures as the social object.

➤ **Questions and answers:** Also fusing Web 1.0 and Web 2.0 sites, Q&A networks provide forums for asking and answering questions related to popular topics and companies, as well as highly specific subject matter.

■ THE ART AND SCIENCE OF LISTENING AND MONITORING

Using the Conversation Prism as our starting point for either venturing into the Social Web for the first time or changing our current course, we can effectively identify and assemble the coordinates necessary to create an accurate social map that's specific to our journey and destinations.

The Conversation Prism is not the only means to discover the social networks and critical conversations that are relevant to defining and positioning the sentiments, perceptions, and resonance of the brand in the Social Web. It is the cornerstone of the bigger discussion as to where, why, and how to engage. The purpose of the prism is to inspire action and research that leads to earned relevance.

The impetus behind the prism was derived from a consistent observation of top-down methodologies and practices of brands, professional and personal, employed to create a visibility on the Social Web. Simply stated, brands focused on building presences in the most popular communities without regard to relevance nor to how they would attract attention. Ultimately, it is the interactions with people within each network that will determine the success of the ensuing dialogues.

The Conversation Prism also introduced lessons much more profound than simply listening to conversations in social networks to document activity.

It suggested a reversal in the traditional top-down approach to publishing and distributing content and associated activities, instead inspiring a bottom-up strategy that promoted social research, mapping, and ethnography (the study and systematic recording of human cultures).[5]

For those so inclined, aware, and prepared, the process of listening encouraged and detailed in these pages also offers a window into the cultures and relative behaviors of the communities you're researching and observing.

This sociological fieldwork is not only obligatory, it changes everything. At a minimum, it provides the insight necessary to develop an enlightened and culturally aware social media program that sets the stage to potentially humanize the brand, foster relationships, engender emissaries to carry goodwill, and inspire action across the Social Web.

■ LISTENERS MAKE THE BEST CONVERSATIONALISTS

The Conversation Prism is a reference tool for marketing, communications, and service-focused organizations to start listening to the voices that define and steer your markets. Unlike a map for all things Web 2.0, it features only the networks where conversations occur.

Tools and networks will come and go. Popularity will shift across existing networks, up-and-coming social sites, and not-yet-introduced websites. If you're not everywhere, then you're addressing only a small portion of a highly vocal contingent that may or may not reflect the perspective of your larger community. And there are important conversations taking place without you right now.

The risk and reality is that your customers and influential trendsetters could be misinterpreting your value proposition without dispute. Concurrently, they're also subject to the influences of your direct and indirect competitors.

Listening, learning, and participating in a measurable and effective social program require you to look beyond the usual suspects. This is one of the reasons why being proactive and not necessarily driven by the corporate case study du jour can help you innovate and excel. Not doing so handicaps the overall reach and effectiveness of your marketing, communications, and service strategies.

In the current stage of social media, online conversations, along with real-world activity, cannot be ignored. Identifying these discussions is only the first step, however. It takes much more than simply running Yahoo! or Google searches, setting up Google Alerts, monitoring Twitter, or limiting your results to any one listening service to unearth relevant dialogue. Casting a wide net in order to identify where your communities are thriving is the only way to truly identify which networks are important to your brand and business. It requires a manual approach, which can later be automated—mostly. And, once you understand where these conversations are transpiring, you can observe the cultures, climate, and basis for the dialogue and activity to create an intelligent participation strategy while also defining and justifying the participation of affected divisions throughout the organization.

■ CHARTING A SOCIAL MAP

Champions are defined not only by their enthusiasm; they are memorialized by their ability to always go above and beyond the call of duty. But, as in anything we attempt in life and work, everything begins at the beginning.

Use the Conversation Prism as a perennial resource. It answers the very questions we wish to ask of others. With this as a guide, we're empowered with the tools, methodologies, and strategies that allow us to become the experts we sought to consult.

Here's a secret—although after I reveal it, you'll realize that it's not really a secret after all—yet nevertheless, it's something that is oft-overlooked and definitely underutilized. Every network contained within offers a search box, and those results are frequently absent from the monitoring services to which we subscribe and upon which we base much of our activity.

If you don't already have it, now's the time to create or access the list of keywords that are pivotal to your organization. This list should include brand, products, industry lingo and buzzwords, names of competitors and competitive products, and any subtle nuances specific to your world that we may miss here. But also, just for laughs (and for creating a sense of urgency), maintain a separate list of results for keywords associated with "name+sucks," or variations with the word "hate" in it. To expedite the process, try using Boolean search techniques that include:

➤ NOT: Brand X NOT Brand Y
➤ AND: Keyword X AND Keyword Y
➤ OR: Keyword X OR Keyword Y

Many database searches are based on the principles of Boolean logic, named in honor of the British-born mathematician George Boole, it refers to the logical relationship among search terms.[6]

We'll review the results and how to package them specifically for usage by you and your team in just a few pages, but allow me to pave the way a bit here.

In order to make the case for direction, focus, and applied resources, we are required to document important and relevant discussions by each network to form the foundation for what will ultimately serve as our brand-specific social map. A social map condenses the vastness of social networks presented in the Conversation Prism to visually communicate definitive communities where important dialogue is materializing as chronicled by your research and observation. Suddenly, the social world becomes a much smaller place and a case can be made for how and where to focus.

In the social economy and the imminent attention economy, relationships and influence are the new currencies.

■ CONVERSATION WORKFLOW

Conversations are increasingly distributed. This social distribution fragments our ability to connect with masses, but promotes a one-to-one approach that yields a one-to-many upside through the influence of social beacons.

Many companies who are actively engaging now are not actually reaching those social beacons through calculation and premeditation. They're either broadcasting to anyone or they're interacting with everyone. Reaching influential voices in social networks carries the ability to scale and extend your story across a multitude of social graphs.

The Conversation Prism offers instruction that details the initial steps to proactively survey the entire social landscape and pinpoint relevant dialogue, prioritize participation strategies and direction, garner sentiment and feedback, and document activity, volume, pitfalls, and also opportunities. The results populate a social map, yes, but also unearth a tremendous amount of answers to the questions you already had and didn't even know how to ask. Fundamentally, you're also able to design a detailed and precise conversational program as dictated by the words and actions of the people with whom we're trying to reach and connect. And, once we understand the implications and extent of activity and hotspots, we also can design an engagement hierarchy and organization chart that matches resources with current activity. This process offers initial insight to the manpower and corresponding budget required to participate at varying levels.

■ TAKING CENTER STAGE

At the center of the Conversation Prism, we visually document the conversational workflow to which we refer in the previous section in a hub-and-spoke model that garners insight and gleans value for the umbrella brand as well as the individual business units as it turns.

The designation and rotation of the concentric circles within the Conversation Prism assist in the conceptualization of the systematic processes and prompt the value-added engagement that rhythmically beats a drum for listening, publishing, and participation.

To understand how to listen and accumulate value by using the Conversation Prism, let's dissect the meaning of each ring.

■ LEVEL ONE: THE EPICENTER

As a brand manager, you'll find yourself at the center of the prism—whether you're observing, listening, or participating.

➤ Halo 1: The System

The next layer of circles is supported by the activities of learning and organizing engagement strategies.

1. **Observation:** Discovering the communities that are actively discussing your brand by using the search box within suspect and targeted social networks and communities.

2. **Listening:** Hearing the people, assessing volume, and documenting the underlying sentiment in order to accurately craft response and participation programs, by assigned company representatives with each community.

3. **Identification:** Recognizing and acknowledging the social beacons to potentially enlist as brand ambassadors, as well as the consumers who simply need a response or your attention.

4. **Internalization:** Not every bit of feedback will be beneficial to your organization, but you will recognize patterns or spots of brilliance that provide necessary insight to improve existing products and services over time. Remember that actions speak louder than words or intentions.

5. **Prioritization:** Assess and structure where and how your team should focus, who should respond, and how. Ensure that a conversation management system is in place, as it's easy to lose track of who responded to which person if documentation that captures and shares status, required follow-up, or results is decentralized or nonexistent.

6. **Routing:** Serving as an extension to number 5, a system must be in place whereby delegates are assigned by topic and expertise and accountable for engaging, documenting the interaction, and communicating the outcome, conclusions, and any valuable wisdom or recommendations to consider. We'll review the lessons shared here and also in number 5 in the Chapter 23 discussion on social CRM, or sCRM.

➤ Halo 2: The Workforce

Social media represents the intersection of all departments that interface with the public and requires that each define a supporting infrastructure that employs a socialized series of guidelines, assigned players, and response and management strategies. Inward focus now must include outward contribution. Ideally, each organization will appoint a community or listening manager to monitor and also assign and manage the responses of each department. Over time, this process will be seamlessly integrated within the company's CRM infrastructure and, where applicable, will help establish an SRM (social relationship management) system for those departments not yet acclimated to social media and the technologies that support its scale and efficiency.

It's easy to see how this could quickly become overwhelming and unmanageable. One of the most fascinating aspects of listening, however, is that conversations and activities always map to specific disciplines within the organization and therefore authorities should be appointed within each organization to provide a competent and helpful response or to steer conversations as necessary or defined. These divisions usually include:

1. Customer or product support

2. Product and sales

3. Marketing/PR

4. Community

5. Corporate communications

6. Crisis

7. Support

➤ **Halo 3: Actualization**

The outer ring completes the imagery of conversational workflow, but not the cycle itself. It is the representation of lessons we're learning through listening and participation that shape our future, from engagement to introspection to evolution. The process is powered by the continual rotation of listening, responding, and edification online and in the real world.

1. **Ongoing feedback and insight:** This is a necessary ingredient to build in portraying a socially aware and trusted brand. We must learn and demonstrate growth based on the feedback we receive. We must also continually share knowledge, provide resources, and communicate vision to earn trust, authority, and respect.

2. **Participation:** It's been said that participation is the new marketing. Perhaps it's better said that participation is a great well of knowledge that leads to more effective marketing *and* communications. The things we learn online practically serve as a free focus group and mechanism for embracing humility to genuinely inspire us to humanize our story. It's how we learn and improve.

3. **Online:** Effectively building online relations and relationships increases brand visibility and strengthens brand value within social networks. Embracing and empowering the community carries our brand personality across social graphs. Our engagement defines our status, stature, and capital within each network.

4. **Real world (or IRL, in real life):** The true metric for relationships is how well they carry from the Web to the real world. It's not about reaching customers using the latest shiny new object or jumping into the hottest new networks. It's about reaching stakeholders and influencers where they go to discover and share information and interact in ways that build meaningful relationships that have meaning and worth, both online and offline.

■ CHARTING THE COURSE

This social map demonstrates the scope of missed opportunities to the team and decision makers and also unveils new possibilities.

While we can't control how our messages are internalized, we can surely shape perception at the point of discourse.

Remember, it's not what you say about your brand that reverberates and resonates as much as it is what your audience hears, how they share the story, and how you weave that insight into future conversations.

The Conversation Prism is a representation of social media and will evolve as services and conversation channels emerge, fuse, and dissipate.

In the social economy, relationships are the new currency, and in Socialized Media, you will earn the relationships you deserve, in the individual communities where stakeholders and influencers assemble.

Transform the Conversation Prism into a brand prism specific to you.

■ ESTABLISHING A CONVERSATION INDEX

It's our job to identify the communities where our customers, peers, and influencers communicate with each other in a way that's transparent and frictionless. It's how we build relationships and how we establish our personal and corporate social capital while simultaneously increasing intellectual equity.

Social networks are magnets for marketers, but the people who define each online community are increasingly savvy about and leery of hollow attempts at connecting as a means to create or extend a channel for broadcasting messages in a one-to-many hyperbole assault.

True social marketing is not marketing at all. The new era of communications necessitates personalization through a genuine and humanized approach. It fuses marketing, service, sociology, psychology, creativity, soft-selling, and a dedicated practice of transparent relationship management. Human nature and the desire to connect, interact, and elevate is perpetual. It's our job to determine our role within the ecosystem.

■ THE COMMUNITY STARTS WITHIN

Before a company can collaborate with its extended community, businesses must first learn to collaborate internally. The greatest social network is the one that perpetuates and exemplifies the values, expertise, and capabilities of the organization.

We must operate as one or risk the appearance of operating alone.

➤ Step 1. Listening

The first step is to "listen," by searching keywords that populate and bind our marketplace and performing an initial audit within a given time frame. By assessing the volume, frequency, and tone of conversations throughout each network, we can establish the Conversation Index (CI), a benchmark to assess the state of our brand in the Social Web and also serve as a metric by which to compare our future activity to past presence and brand perception.

Establish a Time Line

We cannot measure what we do not know. We need a baseline that extends across the Social Web. This process begins with a social audit that reveals activity and the state of our brand and competition within each network. I recommend researching keywords, at least initially, for a fixed period of time, usually spanning 30 days. For example, begin and end the audit using the previous month or a month that was uneventful as the research window. In months where a noteworthy or significant milestone occurred—for example, a product release, earnings report, or a shift in executive management—the results may offer a false impression of an increase in activity.

Determine the Keywords

Prior to listening, formalize the initial keyword list for which to research. While it's important to create a comprehensive list, it's critical that we limit the short list to only a handful of terms in order to provide a top-level, organized review and analysis.

The Conversation Index is measured first for a baseline and then at regular intervals to draw comparisons and insight. The CI is also helpful to capture sentiment, reactions, visibility, action, and feedback surrounding specific events, leading up to, during, and following the landmark.

➤ Step 2. Documentation

Documenting the activity that you uncover is critical to establishing the Conversation Index. It is how you capture it for analysis and presentation that later determines relevance, direction, and strategy.

Many existing listening tools, such as BuzzGain, PeopleBrowsr, PR Newswire's Social Dashboard, Radian6, and so forth, offer a report template that captures activity and packages it in an easy-to-read format for analysis and presentation. I recommend that when you're initially listening to the Social Web, especially if you're following the principles and methodologies that define the Conversation Prism, that you do so manually.

It's time consuming.

It's potentially tedious.

Some of this research can be automated through other tools.

These points may be valid. However, the time and energy you save is directly linked to a loss of perspective, insight, and perception. The process of establishing the Conversation Index serves two purposes: documentation of activity and also the ability to garner empathy. No tool has proved that it can capture everything. In fact, in many cases, tools can miss a significant portion of result-altering data. And as you manually digest the updates you're recording, you can't help but sense the underlying meanings in what you're reading. When we discuss the need to humanize our brand, we do so through an earned sense of compassion, concern, and caring.

As listening produces results that are unique to each brand, this template provides a framework for you to further customize.

Use a spreadsheet that includes our criteria in order to effectively capture and export our findings into reports, charts, and presentations. Assuming that we run a search over a 30-day period, the elements necessary to define, identify, and capture the Conversation Index includes, at a minimum, the following columns:

Network: The social network where the conversation occurred.

Instance: The specific mention of the keyword and the supporting context.

Date: The specific date of the mention.

Sentiment: Hand-curated sentiment to assess whether the instance was negative, positive, or neutral.

Response candidacy: The assessment of whether or not the captured update required a response from a company representative and, if so, an additional column that suggests the division most appropriate for responding. In my research, I've noted that usually conversations can be handed over to PR, service, product development, marketing, and HR.

Reach: Depending on the network, this input varies. Reach refers to the potential degree an update can range. For example, if the incident was on Twitter, document the number of followers that particular individual is connected with. If the mention is in a blog post or blog comment, note how many visitors the particular destination receives on any given day (determined by Alexa or Compete.com). While it's not intended to provide a total representation of influence, authority, or definite impressions, this information does give us a sense of scope, scale, and potential impact.

Competitive mentions: While it's time consuming to research this activity on behalf of your brand, it may be unrealistic to do so when measuring the volume of your competitors. Simply running through each network and documenting total numbers of mentions may suffice in order to establish a sense of the general share of voice between your company and its competition in the Social Web.

➤ Step 3. Presentation

When documenting the results during the listening exercise, it's absolutely critical to capture persuasive and credible criteria in a way that's presentable and incontestable to decision makers. Exporting the numbers that dictate key findings as visual charts will establish a compelling case and benchmark for further endeavors into socialized engagement, as well as the ability to reference past status.

Packaging counts for everything as it visually demonstrates all that we've speculated and theorized. We either make or break our case with the information we've collected and the method for communicating our findings. Fundamentally, we must create a document or presentation that visualizes what we know and what decision makers and affected groups and individuals need to know. Ten categories to consider are:

1. **Timeframe.**
2. **Volume:** Total number of "conversations" captured.
3. **Active Networks:** Organize the most active networks of relevance based on quantity of collective activity, justified by numbers, sorted by activity (for example, Facebook 10 percent, Twitter 30 percent, Blogs/Blog Comments 30 percent, Forums/Groups 10 percent, YouTube 5 percent, Flickr 5 percent, Digg 5 percent, Delicious 5 percent).
4. **Sentiments:** For example: 25 percent positive, 25 percent negative, 50 percent neutral. Provide examples of sentiment in cases of positive and negative.
5. **Perception:** Provide a general summary of how a brand is perceived through text or graph and share a few examples of each to hammer the point home.
6. **Reach:** Total potential impressions (however, this is not representative of a true audience).
7. **Network reach:** Potential reach by network (for example, Facebook reach = 125,000, Twitter = 175,000, Blogs = 250,000, YouTube views = 75,000, Flickr views = 5,000).

8. **Responses required:** Quantity of missed opportunities for responses.

9. **Affected divisions:** Divisions tagged to respond based on missed opportunities (for example, Customer Service 35 percent, PR 20 percent, Marketing 15 percent, Product 15 percent, HR 5 percent, Sales 10 percent).

10. **Share of voice:** The share of conversations between your brand compared to that of your competition as established by the total quantity of mentions as well as the number of mentions by individual social network.

For extra credit, as you're reading through the instances that you're collecting, record trends that emerge and reappear related to potential topics, themes, areas for improvement, common questions, recommendations, and so forth. Provide these themes in an aggregate format that can be presented as a list or pie chart. For example, in the past 30 days we observed the following themes: new product, 20 percent; earnings, 25 percent; comparison to competitive product, 15 percent; questions about the future, 10 percent; missed opportunities, 10 percent; requests for response in social networks, 20 percent. We can also analyze data to anticipate trends and possible scenarios over the next 30, 60, or 90 days.

Among the potential trends we're observing, we're also subject to, and privy to, honest feedback and product/brand experiences that will reveal a sampling of consumer satisfaction and recommendations. The data that you will possess will serve as a leading indicator as to market position and will also divulge potential ideas and supporting rationale for improving or developing new products and services.

Monitoring reveals the Conversation Index, the state of conversations and the networks and people fueling the activity. This process also reveals potential calls to action that can be presented to demonstrate tangible next steps. Essentially all of the answers you need are contained within this research:

➤ Conversation state

➤ Active networks

➤ Brand awareness and resonance

➤ Business divisions and required resources

➤ Potential reach

➤ Framework for social media plan

➤ Rough estimates of required resources and costs

➤ Innovation

It is imperative that we fold in a response mechanism to our social network programs while moving forward. Monitoring offers intelligence. Activity, action, and response steer perspective and encourage a sense of community and advocacy.

➤ Step 4. Observation

Communities support each other. Citizens actively help others make decisions, offer suggestions and referrals, proactively share negative experiences, and repeatedly ask questions—with or without our participation.

As we are quickly learning, "management" and "relationships" are as distant from each other as their intentions.

Either way, we are missing opportunities right now.

Once our target networks are identified and our Conversation Index is documented, we must observe the conversational ecosystem within each network to understand the corresponding culture and behavioral dynamics. We may have the answers now, but the disconnect between execution and collaboration is represented by the cultures, behavior, and personalities that define the communities in which we will attempt to participate. And, they're different within each network.

We need to ask and answer several new questions. For example, How are people communicating within network A versus network B? How are subgroups interacting within each network? What does the back channel look like? Who are the power users within our segment and are they connected to each other, and if so, how? Are people publishing, responding, asking and answering questions? How are other brands interacting with their stakeholders and prospects, and how is the community responding?

This information can be captured by employing ethnography, a branch of anthropology that studies and describes modern human cultures (rather than human behavior or physical attributes).[7] The goal of ethnography is to provide cultural interpretation to define "webs of meaning," the cultural constructions of our communities of interest.[8] Through case reports or field studies, our role as pseudo ethnographers is to capture and communicate the definition and interworking of cultures through an emic[9] perspective, which we can refer to as an insider's point of view. It is this perspective that is missing from our listening and monitoring analysis and will serve us invaluably as we forge our engagement strategies and tactics.

As ethnography captures data that defines cultures within our relevant nets, we must also document behavior to effectively interact within each. Through observation, we can also characterize and personify the communities that are active and vibrant within our target markets. Interactive media unites people around topics and partisanship and therefore encourages an approach where we also organize our potential stakeholders and advocates by behavior, interests, and preference. Typically, brands have approached marketing and communications through the use of demographics to distinguish its audiences. Now we also embrace psychographics to better match the patterns of behavior and activity that are rife within the socialized Web that groups individuals not by age, gender, education, and so on, but by similarities, passions, and interests.

> **Demographics** *are defined as the statistical characteristics of human populations used to identify markets.*[10]

> **Psychographics** *are statistics that classify population groups according to psychological variables or trends.*[11]

The insight that we learn from listening and observing reveals dedicated and intermittent conversation ecosystems that spotlight real-world brand perception and the potential for evangelism, as well as crisis. It resets intentions, crystallizes engagement strategies, influences how we adapt our story to each community, humbles us, and introduces empathy into the process of connecting.

We learn, earn credibility, and procure strategic intelligence through immersion—before we have an official agenda.

To excel in social media, we have to embrace modesty and refrain from egoism. We must not only build roads that pave the way for outward engagement, but also build paths back to our organizations in order to hear, respond, and learn from our interactions. Negativity is onerous. Unwelcome feedback is grueling to swallow. Whether or not it's right or wrong, it's nevertheless real-world perception, and it impacts our bottom line.

We have to be open.

Let it touch us.

■ ADAPT

Reaction, change, and the practice of listening, hearing, and responding is the art and science of instilling trust and confidence that feed communities and determine the health and prosperity of brand resonance and social capital.

Allowing outside stimulus, instead of deflecting or disregarding it, is the art of embracing and embodying transparency and practicing genuine, unbiased engagement to facilitate meaningful relationships.

Otherwise, transparency and engagement are merely buzzwords in the quiver of marketing arrows.

Productive and mutually beneficial engagement is powered by effective listening and productive participation that results in measurable and favorable actions. It's not only measured by the Conversation Index, but also by the sales, referrals, relationships, and ensuing brand loyalties that escalate, and sometimes dip, in reaction to our contributions.

Influence is the ability to listen, learn, engage, and inspire measurable actions. It's also the observable progress people make as the result of engaging in a dialogue with us.

Observation will help you refine your program so that it's in cultural alignment as you immerse the brand within each community.

Adaptation will help you evolve and increase in relevance, both online and offline.

In the end, we are measured by our actions, and our words.

Chapter 19

Unveiling the New Influencers

■ WE ARE MEDIA

We, the people, demanded personalization in engagement, improved services that put the customer back into the spotlight, and acknowledgment that our feedback would incite a more value-added circle of overall communications and product adaptation. We have emerged influential and consequential to the bottom lines of businesses all over the world.

As consumers and publishers, we fervently stormed these new platforms and staged a social revolution that forced the attention of those who so readily dismissed us—silence was no longer golden.

Social networks and platforms have expanded the roles of customers and peers from consumer to authorities, ambassadors, and critics. Those who master their domains are developing persuasive and important communities around their areas of expertise, interests, and passions and now possess the prowess and authority to direct, instruct, and steer decision makers and referrers.

Aside from the discipline and behavior our profession dictates, we are far more than communicators, marketers, publishers, or chroniclers of life events. We are also knowledgeable people with ideas, opinions, observations, and frustrations that cannot be discounted and we bring these experiences to each conversation as knowledgeable consumers. But when it's time to reach our peers and colleagues, we seem to regress to message broadcasters and purveyors of disjointed and off-target information. In short, we lose sight of how what we represent truly impacts those whom we're trying to reach.

While we possess the ability to become the very people we wish to engender, we lose perspective in our methods and processes.

In the end, we earn the influence that our activities and shared experiences justify and warrant. Our presence and participation affect the decisions and impressions of those around us. We connect people to products and services and ultimately assist in the governance of future actions among those within our immediate social graph, as well as the graphs that link our friends, their friends, and so on.

Successful engagement is predicated by genuinely connecting with people.

■ BUILDING A BRIDGE BETWEEN BRANDS AND MARKETS

We're paying attention to A-list bloggers and tastemakers on social networks, from technology pundits to moms to lifestyle to politics and everything in between. But sometimes we overlook the magic middle, those bloggers and trust agents who actually inform and interact with prospective customers.

We're blindly jumping into social networks and engaging with the "avatars" tied to keywords instead of identifying, engaging, and recruiting those who can help us create valuable, thriving communities that support the exchange of pertinent information, knowledge, and direction. This is not about avatar relations, or keyword association and this is most certainly greater than ordinary media or blogger relations. This is the era of consumer engagement and empowerment.

Tastemakers and trendsetters are recognized as the new influencers, but their roles in affecting consumer behavior are not derivative of the Social Web. Simply said, these individuals have always existed, just as conversations have always prevailed. Neither originated because of social media. Instead, these market makers individually contribute to a more influential public and are now readily discoverable, courtesy of the search boxes and platforms that facilitate their recognition within the communities of consequence. Social networks, blogs, microblogs, and all other forms of people-powered networks provide a looking-glass into the interaction between consumers, as well as the ability to discern the level of authority each one possesses.

You've heard it time and time again: "People do business with people they like."

While that's true, they also spend money on products that help them do something that they couldn't do before, based on existing needs or frustrations with current experiences. Therefore, people are looking for answers, not necessarily friends. They're seeking societies where they can learn, share, and contribute. And they're using the tools, channels, and networks to connect with one another.

The lessons we learned in the last chapter teach us that listening and monitoring count for everything nowadays, and it's by far the easiest step in identifying, potentially embracing, and ultimately leading the transition from an introverted organization into an extroverted, community-focused human network.

It sets the foundation to not only listen and respond on the front lines, but also it necessitates the modification of the entire infrastructure to adapt to the real-world needs of customers, their peers, other influencers, and the insights and experiences they choose to share.

This is a privilege and an opportunity. We must remember this. . . .

It's the shift from top-down broadcasting to a more holistic methodology that embraces consumers directly with the tools and channels they use to communicate. The Conversation Prism is our blueprint. And effectively building a bridge between brand and markets requires the personification of the company and the ability to not only humanize its story, but also listen and respond to input through words and the adaptation of products and services.

Influential customers collectively create a network of information beacons that help others successfully navigate within their respective markets and industries. We're awakening to a new era of stature and authority that augments broadcast communications with the participatory groundswell of user-generated leverage and impact. In the world of social media, brands can also earn influence, using the same tools and networks that have empowered bloggers and tastemakers alike.

While D2C might imply business-to-consumer interaction, this model works equally well for business-to-business, nonprofit, government, verticals, education, and, essentially, any market or industry where individuals and influencers are interacting, seeking guidance, or affected by the information they discover online.

Now that we've used the Conversation Prism to identify influencers, we must actively monitor the dialogue and representative trends and invaluable feedback that enable us to establish a D2C program that tunes into inbound feedback, fosters relationships, creates a foundation for collaboration, inspires the creation of meaningful social objects, and establishes an internal ecosystem for adaptation and evolution. It's where we identify ongoing opportunities to add value.

■ ENGAGE WITH PURPOSE

As I've said before, conversation is simply conversation, regardless of the tools. The qualifications to maintain dialogue are trivial. The task of simply showing up to the table is honestly, child's play—the real question is about figuring out what we're trying to accomplish.

Those who pay attention to the dynamics, intricacies, and psyche of the words, tone, and nature of the dialogue can tell the differences between a simple response, reconciliation, and resolution.

When discussing social media and participatory protocol, let's no longer behave as though we were standing on top of a table during a cocktail party and obnoxiously yelling out messages at the crowd. This is the opposite of strategic social listening and engagement.

Actually monitoring, hearing, and internalizing the words of others inherently qualifies someone as worthy of engagement. Interaction, however, is measured by the exchanges that further the development and direction of the hosts of the original conversations as well as those who were peripherally observing and therefore affected. The process of identifying influencers and monitoring relevant conversations is only as valuable as the steps we take to inspire action.

Tastemakers and those who've earned the recognition of their peers are either dubious of corporate outreach or opportunistic in assessing its potential. Your approach counts for everything. And this is not (at least for the purposes of this discussion) about buying or leasing the outcome of the interaction. Once influencers are identified, we must merge what we've learned through the Conversation Prism process with programs, stories, and meaningful motives that appeal to them and ultimately earn their participation. If those bridges do not yet exist, we must construct them using only materials of relevance. And, I'm not talking about giving away trips, free products, or simply paying influencers to form alliances with your organization. While buying alliances may be an option, thinking beyond giveaways and promotions keeps your brand sharp and relevant, now and in the long term.

If we can establish and communicate a sense of purpose, we create a far more captivating and pertinent program that affects everything. *We are now engaging with justification and therefore serve a greater purpose.*

Identifying influencers is one thing. Engaging people and enticing not only their interest, but ultimately establishing an association and earning allegiance takes far more than interpersonal adeptness and a budget with which to purchase friendships.

We need to be acutely informed, open, and enlightened individuals who can engage others with both empathy and honesty. This intuition and awareness is earned through observation and immersion.

■ THE SHIFT FROM MONITORING TO ACTION

Are you listening?

Are you really listening, or are you just monitoring dialogues or mining data?

The role of monitoring serves as the eyes, ears, and heart of the organization and deserves support from a comprehensive system that connects to every essential node in the corporate and human network.

There's a difference and we stand to gain or lose ground based on our intentions and follow-up activities. The type of listening I'm referring to here isn't simply identifying updates or threads tied to keywords.

Listening requires a dedicated infrastructure and support system; essentially the ability to not just hear something and placate the concerns of people, but the capacity and alacrity to respond. We possess the power to grow through inflection and adaptation.

As social architects and engineers, we are responsible for paving the roads for information to freely travel between listening agents, spokespersons, decision makers, and ultimately to consumers and influencers (see Figure 19.1). Officially establishing a conversational workflow and infrastructure is how we:

➤ Recognize strengths and weaknesses.

➤ Improve products and services.

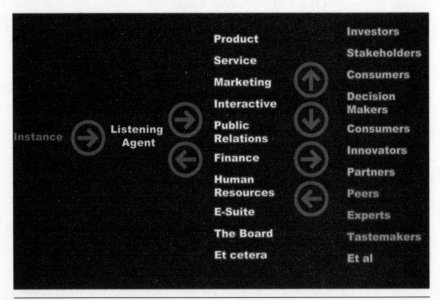

Figure 19.1   The Conversation Workflow

➤ Analyze competitive advantages and disadvantages.

➤ Maintain and improve existing and prospective employee relations and interactions.

➤ Ensure customer satisfaction and foster loyalty.

➤ Identify influencers and business prospects.

➤ Enhance processes.

➤ Warrant relevance.

➤ Expand market share.

➤ Strengthen valuation.

➤ Earn credibility and trust.

➤ Cultivate communities and encourage advocacy.

➤ Learn.

➤ Humanize.

➤ Create and ideate.

➤ Grow.

Someone has to take responsibility for the process of listening to and channeling conversations. It requires more than one champion to truly harness the potential of the interactive Web and power of community. Without a complete working infrastructure that channels conversations and feedback, and the resources required to effectively channel, scrutinize, strategize, reply, or counter, or simply act, we are being negligent toward our company and its customers.

In some cases, a community or listening manager will act as the central hub to all internal departments. In other cases, PR assumes the responsibility for listening, reporting, and analysis. In other organizations, the function of monitoring, observing, documenting, reporting, trending, and conversation management is outsourced to an agency that specializes in new media.

This is one of the most important roles in the transformation of any organization from an inward focus to an outward view. The intelligence and insight gathered during these exercises can tell us a great deal.

It's the only way to gauge the volume, velocity, and resources required to properly interpret, process, and address the situations that require our attention.

While jumping into social media is inevitable for many companies, the need to substantiate the effort in order to justify the shift in or creation of dedicated budget and personnel remains constant.

Before we can discuss ROI, we first need to understand the proportions of the investment required. The answers lie in the process of searching keywords and reading, watching, absorbing, and logging the responses you encounter through the Conversation Prism, and ultimately through the dedicated monitoring and channeling of important activity within your relevant networks.

■ X-RAY GLASSES AND BIONIC HEARING

We have the technology . . . we just need to know how to use it, and when, how, and to what extent.

The list of tools to identify influencers, unearth and listen to online conversations, and track their paths is extensive, and the available services will only continue to multiply.

Automation is helpful in that it saves time and conserves precious resources, and, in some cases, provides us with answers to questions we never knew to ask. Initially however, it's exposure as opposed to immersion. The systematic procedure for distinguishing, tracking, analyzing, trending, and reporting conversations and would-be influencers requires a direct experience in order to understand the differences in results between a hands-on approach and those run through algorithmic software.

To offer guidance on the next steps and to determine which tools to employ within your organization, I've developed a list of currently available solutions and services. Reviewing this list will enable you to start the process of uncovering the unknown and plotting your course of action. The decision about which solution to implement is yours to determine, as some will be more compatible with the infrastructure of your organization. I will include an up-to-date list on the website for this book.

POWER TOOLS: WHAT BRANDS TO USE TO GET THE JOB DONE

Sure, we know that every organization has its unique needs, and we each need to select the tools and services that fit our infrastructure, processes, and teams, not to mention our budget. But, no doubt you're curious as to what's being employed now. What tools are the market leaders using to discover their tastemakers, trendsetters, and market makers? How are other companies listening and responding to the front lines?[1]

Southwest Airlines uses a search tool from TweetDeck to track the conversations and sentiments regarding its own brand and its competitors—searching for terms such as "bag fee" and "frontier." As reported in the *Wall Street Journal*, a routine Twitter search uncovered a tweet referencing a Southwest Airlines flight that was preparing to make an emergency landing in Baltimore. The company had not yet released this information to its employees, including to Christi Day, the emerging-media specialist for the airline who discovered the tweet. Day investigated the matter at once, and continually posted updates to the company's Twitter page as the facts rolled in. According to Day, "the landing was uneventful, but Twitter followers appreciated the transparency and timely information."

Coca-Cola uses Scout (by Scout Labs) to monitor the comments on Twitter, as well as other platforms such as Facebook, MySpace, and even foreign language blogs. Scout rates each comment as positive or negative to help the beverage giant stay on top of public sentiment.

Whole Foods Market utilizes a tool from CoTweet to manage, track, and respond to the 300 to 500 tweets that are posted each day to the company's Twitter page. The tool tracks which tweets have been responded to, and which are still awaiting recognition and response. Whole Foods employees can also review any previous interaction and conversation threads with a customer to help them choose the most appropriate response. Likewise, Microsoft also uses CoTweet to manage its Twitter activity and ensure proper (and timely) responses to consumers.

■ SEARCHING THE SOCIAL WEB

➤ Search Engines

Collecta: Collecta is the first true real-time search engine that monitors not just Twitter but the update streams of news sites, popular blogs, and social media sites, including Twitter, MySpace, Digg, YouTube, and Flickr. Unlike a traditional search engine that displays indexed results, which are then ranked based on a series of links and ratings, results in Collecta are updated in your search stream as they happen—that is, as they appear online. Think Twitter Search, but for the entire Web.

Google Alerts: Offers e-mail updates of the latest relevant results for keywords on the Web, blogs, or some indexed social networks.

➤ Microblogs

CoTweet: A Web-based collaboration platform that provides case management for Twitter exchanges with customers, task assignment and follow-up, keyword/trend monitoring, and conversation threading.

FriendFeed: Now owned by Facebook, FriendFeed is a microblog that aggregates content from multiple networks into one easy-to-follow collective stream. Friends can follow, comment, share, and "like" updates, and also spark threaded conversations based on their activity. Since FriendFeed can import updates from multiple properties such as Twitter, Facebook, YouTube, Flickr, Delicious, LinkedIn, and roughly 50 additional services, it provides a highly curated source for curated search. The advanced search feature in FF allows users to search the entire network for keywords that are syndicated through all 58 networks within the community.

HootSuite: A professional Twitter client that manages the work-flow for multiple accounts. HootSuite's scheduling helps companies better control the pace of their outbound tweets to prevent aggravating their followers with tweet overload. HootSuite also offers brand monitoring/keyword tracking, Twitter search, and statistics.

Klout: Klout.com can reveal influencers based on topic. Sorted by level of authority on Twitter and soon, other social networks.

OneRiot: OneRiot (formerly Me.dium) crawls the links people share on Twitter, Digg, YouTube, and other social sharing services, then indexes the content on those pages instantly. The end result is a search experience that allows users to find fresh, socially relevant, human-curated content. It also displays a link to the person who first shared the item online.

PeopleBrowsr: A dashboard, and backend data analysis system, for managing communications across Twitter, Facebook, YouTube, FriendFeed and other social networks. The service also doubles as an integrated search network for each network it connects and offers the ability to track and manage automated or customer responses to the results for keywords—providing an all-inclusive communications management platform.

Google Query: Google Query will provide the ability to search microblogs similar to how users can search and sort data within Technorati, by date, influence, location, language, and so on. Here's the current description used in Google's localization service: Recent updates about QUERY. This is the MicroBlogsearch Universal result group header text. A Microblog is a blog with very short entries. Twitter is the popular service associated with this format.

Seesmic: A Web or desktop client that manages the lifestreams from Facebook and multiple Twitter accounts.

Twitter Search: Search.twitter.com, search.twitter.com/advanced, oneriot.com, Twazzup, Collecta.com, and so forth, provide the ability to search Twitter (and in Collecta's case, the entire Web) for real-time results related to a keyword. For a more detailed search based on timeframe, location, hashtag, people, and sentiment, try search.twitter.com/advanced.

Twazzup: Like Twitter Search, Twazzup displays the tweets in chronological order based on your keywords. The results also reveal other potentially relevant keywords, events, and hashtags associated with the subject matter you're researching, based on the patterns of those who collectively share similar updates. Results also include a list of top trendmakers, as well as related pictures, videos, and the most popular links related to your search criteria.

Tweefind: Provides search results that appear in order of user rank.

TweetDeck: Described as "air traffic control for Twitter," TweetDeck customizes and organizes the Twitter experience, manages multiple Twitter accounts, and offers search capabilities based on hashtag, brand, people, and so forth.

Twingly: Like Twitter Search, Twingly also provides results for other mainstream and niche microblogs such as Identica, Jaiku, and Pownce archives, among others. Also see Blogsearch.

Twitority: A generalized Twitter search engine solution that allows users to sort results by any, some, or a little authority.

➤ **Blogsearch**

Technorati: Considered the largest blog search engine in the world, Technorati tracks "blog reactions" (keywords) and blogs linking behavior.

Blogsearch.google.com: Similar to News.Google.com, Google Blog Search allows users to comb through blog posts for relevant discussions and identify authorities on any given subject. Google alerts are also available for blog search results.

Blogged.com: A community for identifying blogs and bloggers that cover particular topics from what's popular to "the long tail." Blogs are rated by the community as well as by blogged.com editors to provide a human perspective.

Twingly: Also provides "spam-free" search results of blogs discussing your keywords. Results can be sorted by Twingly rank (a vetted process of rating individual blogs), time, and language. Results include a link to the profile of the host blog.

BackType: Usually blog comments do not appear in traditional or blog search results. BackType is a conversational search engine that indexes and connects millions of conversations from blogs, social networks and other social media so people can find, follow, and share comments.

➤ **Forums/Usergroups**

BoardReader: Accurately finds and displays information within the Web's forums and message boards.

BoardTracker: A forum search engine, message tracking, and instant alerts system designed to provide relevant information contained in forum threads.

Go directly to the source:

➤ Google Groups
➤ Yahoo! Groups
➤ Ning
➤ Meetup

➤ **Conversation, Visualization, and Metrics Management Systems**

BuzzGain: A complete listening, influencer identification, relationship management and reporting solution, BuzzGain helps identify conversations containing keywords in blogs, media, and social networks as well as the influential voices behind those conversations. Using the integrated research tools and reporting tools, users can document and visualize trends, add commentary to results and publish customizable reports. It's free during its public beta period.

Spiral16: Unveils hidden patterns inside complex social media networks by providing a top-level view of data through visually rich, virtualized 3-D models. The platform also helps global brands monitor, manage, and analyze their social media presence to improve customer service, reputation, gather market intelligence, and understand conversations through sentiment.

Linkfluence: A research-based firm specializing in mapping, monitoring, and measuring trends and opinions on the Social Web. Linkfluence studies and offers solutions to visually map, monitor, and analyze social media activity and instances, and draws borders of conversational communities around brands/keywords to assess true impact on image and reputation.

PR Newswire Social Media Metrics: An intelligence tool powered by Sentiment Metrics that enables communications professionals and marketers to monitor, analyze, and measure the impact of what is being said about an organization, brand, spokesperson, or competitor. Social Media Metrics monitors over 20 million blogs, 5 million forum posts, and 30,000 online news sources, social networks, and microblogs, including Twitter. The system enables users to build customized searches to track keywords while simultaneously isolating specific geographic, demographic, and language parameters.

Scout Labs: A powerful, Web-based application that tracks social media activity and sorting through signals in the noise to help teams build better products and stronger customer relationships. The system provides a platform for monitoring, analyzing, and also managing follow-up and action.

DNA 13: Aimed at global enterprises, small agencies, and all sizes in between, DNA provides dashboard solutions that track and present reputation and visibility and also organize results and offer detailed analysis. Products include dnaMonitor and dnaEnterprise. Corporate positioning caters to communications and PR professionals.

HowSociable: Provides a free look into brand visibility metrics by allowing a user to enter a keyword, name, or phrase, and identify the content transpiring in 22 networks.

WhosTalkin: WhosTalkin.com is a social media search tool that allows users to search for conversations surrounding important topics. It serves as a hub for search results on blogs, news networks, social networks, video networks, image networks, forums, and tags.

FiltrBox: Real-time social media and Web monitoring, FiltrBox monitors thousands of mainstream news outlets, blogs, and social media in one place. By consolidating results in one dashboard, users can eliminate redundant searches and alerts. Users can also import their Google Alerts to manage noise, remove duplicate results, and consolidate disparate results feeds.

Radian6: Radian6 is focused on building a complete monitoring and analysis solution for PR and advertising professionals. The Radian6 listening platform monitors the Social Web to uncover conversations related to specific brands on millions of blog posts, viral videos, reviews in forums, sharing of photos, and twitter updates. It also provides the ability to analyze buzz about a company, products, issues, competitors, and outcomes of specific marketing campaigns and social media investments.

BuzzMetrics: Now part of Nielsen, BuzzMetrics delivers trusted brand metrics, meaningful consumer insights and real-time market intelligence to help clients apply the power of consumer-generated media (CGM) to their businesses. Nielsen BuzzMetrics uncovers and integrates data-driven insights culled from nearly 100 million blogs, social networks, groups, boards, and other CGM platforms. The services include brand monitoring, brand connections and customer relations, consumer insights, and brand campaign planning and measurement.

Trackur: A collection of online reputation monitoring and social media listening tools, Trackur scans hundreds of millions of Web pages—including news, blogs, video, images, and forums—and reports any discoveries that match relevant keywords.

Visible Technologies: Helps users listen to and learn what consumers are saying about their company/brand in the blogosphere and social media communities. It also fosters customer engagement by enabling users to effectively participate in these discussions by placing the right messages in front of the right audiences for a more direct connection.

Sentiment Metrics: Sentiment Metrics social media measurement dashboard enables users to monitor and measure social media and gain a necessary level of business intelligence to develop more targeted marketing, improve products, and increase profits.

TNS Cymfony: Provides expert interpretation of how corporate messages are picked up across traditional and social media sources, enabling the ability to measure results and discover trends that affect the bottom line. Whether the goal is to influence the brand perception during a new product release, marketing campaign, or even through a crisis, TNS Cymfony's market influence analysis tracks consumer preferences across traditional and social media sources and provides the ability for listeners to act and engage quickly to keep public perceptions on track.

BrandsEye: Traces and assesses online presences and provides a real-time Reputation Score for both the user's brand as well as their competitors. This allows companies to monitor the sentiments and opinions of their own customers, while making educated judgments about how to respond to attacks on their own online reputation.

Cision Social Media: Social media monitoring of over 100 million blogs, tens of thousands of online forums, over 450 leading rich media sites, along with a complete database of influential voices on the Web and in social media.

Techrigy: SM2 is a software solution designed specifically for PR and Marketing Agencies to monitor and measure social media. It works with the company's Social Media Warehouse system, which tracks blogs, wikis, message boards/forums, video/photo sites, mainstream media, blogs, microblogs, and social networks.

Trendrr: Tracks the popularity and awareness of trends across a variety of inputs, ranging from social networks, to blog buzz and video views downloads, all in real time.

SocialMention: A social media search platform that aggregates user-generated content from across the universe into a single stream of information.

Part

V

The Social Architect: Developing a Blueprint for New Marketing

The Human Network

Discovering the new influencers through network and link analysis[1] allows us to see the very people who define our markets. While network analysis enables us to uncover local patterns within networks, link analysis extends these observations to determine the associations between objects. Ultimately, what we should start to see and feel is something truly more profound than any one social network. We now begin to see the genesis of a *Human Network*, a term that I have interposed gradually throughout this book. Whereas the *Social Graph* (a term coined by Facebook's Mark Zuckerberg) is representative of the relationships we maintain within Facebook or any one social network, the Human Network is representative of the connections that link us to one another across multiple social networks. This is the true social network, one without boundaries or limitations for collaboration and communication. The Human Network is also how Cisco Systems defines the intersection where technology meets humanity.[2]

Technology is facilitating the social effect and it is most certainly connecting us in ways that truly make the world a much smaller place, one where we can participate in its definition and evolution—and also define our place within it.

■ BREATHING LIFE INTO THE HUMAN NETWORK

As individuals, our human network is composed of both professional and personal connections and they differ from each other based on shared interests as well as established relations online and in the real world. In many cases, we also maintain a life graph that represents the connections we actually maintain and foster in real life—hence our life graph will contrast with our social graph in applications such as location-based networking, accounting for some overlap.

The human network also illustrates the map of individuals with whom we can benefit from connecting. As a result of our research and observation in communities and networks, we can identify and discern tribes, tribal leaders, and specific individuals who can connect us with those individuals who can help us learn and motivate. We also garner perspective and empathy in the process. Additionally, we also recognize various patterns of connectivity, influence, and hierarchy. These connections and rankings are different within each network and also in the context that governs our study. For example, if a communications or public relations group commissioned the examination, the resulting network will contrast with the outcome of reviews conducted by customer service or human resources. Therefore, the human network will vary based on the nature of the dialogue.

Over the years, I have studied mapping and influence in much of my work where analyzing contextual relationships in online media from blogs to social networks to traditional media properties would dictate strategies and programming. In one such series, I observed how individuals establish conversational networks with or without forging links as a result. For example, on Twitter, if I were to publish a tweet on the subject of green technology, the responses I'd receive would differ from those who may feel compelled to retort, should I publish an update concerning healthcare. As reviewed earlier, those responses would also differ based on time and the opening of the attention aperture. In Twitter, I employed two services (which are free) to help analyze this activity. First, I would monitor the Twitter stream of a particular individual based on a theme. I would then run the tests again as that theme changed, usually a few weeks later. Using Twitter-Friends[3] and Mailana, I could visually map the conversational network related to themes for both inbound and outbound activity, thus establishing a snapshot of influence and reach. Figure 20.1 shows a graphic of outbound conversations, and Figure 20.2 depicts inbound messages.

The inbound network represents the individuals who respond to us publicly, and the outbound network is representative of those to whom we reply. Removing ourselves from this picture and inserting an already recognized influencer, we can use these tools to establish inbound and outbound conversational networks, based on the interaction over a period of time. We can then assess the caliber of those responding to determine weight and authority for possible inclusion in our resulting influencer map.

In the process of analyzing conversational networks, I realized that I could also connect individuals across multiple networks and remove the barriers between them. For the most part I did so manually,

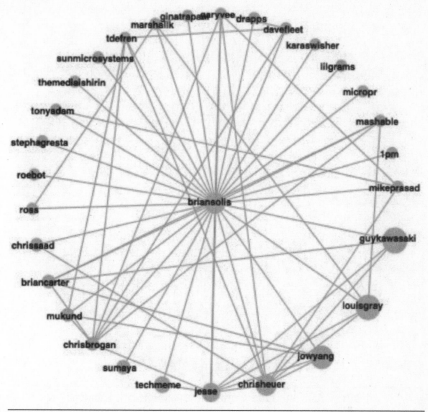

Figure 20.1   Outbound Conversational Network Example
Source: Twitter-Friends.

to ensure that my results were based on first-hand analysis and qualification of individuals based on preestablished authority, their published works, and the conversational and contextual networks they forged as a result.

■ THE HUMAN NETWORK: ALIVE AND CLICKING!

As a natural extension of work I was already performing at Cisco Systems, I was tasked with identifying digital and traditional influencers on behalf of the corporate communications team and based on the company's priority business units. It provided me an opportunity to further study influence, linking behavior, as well as where and how

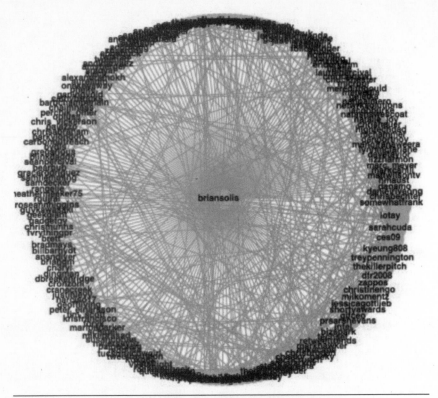

Figure 20.2   Inbound Conversational Network Example
Source: Twitter-Friends.

these connections were forged and ranked. While this is part of influencer research in general, it should not go unsaid that no databases or preexisting lists were used in this process. We let influence stand on its own merits to be discovered. If it wasn't discoverable, it wasn't influential.

For this project, I initially turned to Mailana and Klat.com as I was already versed in its structure and output.

Using the methodologies promoted by the Conversation Prism and the Conversation Index and also incorporating the systems for recognizing conversational networks, we pinpointed voices of authority, by subject, and analyzed how they connected to each other through their professional activity and interaction. In the process, we were able to reveal the human network representative of blogs, social networks, forums, and micronetworks as well as corresponding inner networks that showcased tighter, yet distributed pockets of influence and collaboration.

Essentially we applied the principles associated with network theory and envisioned through graph theory to humanize the landscape of influence.

Just for a bit of background, network theory,[4] as we applied it, represents the study of graphs that serve as a representation of relationships that are symmetrical, those symbolic of similar parts facing each other or arrayed around an axis.

To bring this human network to life, I turned to Pete Warden, creator of Mailana,[5] a social network analysis system. Warden was instrumental in the completion of this groundbreaking project, as he adapted his visual networking platform to integrate our research data into a visual and interactive map of influencers that spanned across networks and mediums, organized by business units and the manual assembly of established relationships (see Figure 20.3).

The human network embodies social network analysis, the mapping of relationships with social networks, network theory, link analysis, and graph theory, all fused into one hyperconnected comprehensive influencer network. Not only does this service provide a visual representation of relationships, it brings them to life. Contacts are clickable and the user can learn more about the individuals and their

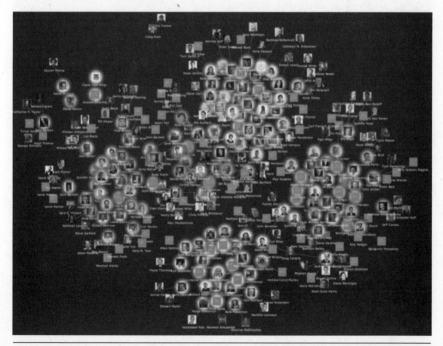

Figure 20.3   Visual Map of Influencers across Networks and Mediums

work. As each icon is clicked, it illuminates the connections that form distinct inner networks within the greater relevant net.

The mission of displaying the influencers and how they connect to each other was served. However, I continue to analyze network topology to learn more about centrality and the relative importance of nodes, edges, and hubs within each human network to better understand the influence of influence.

To further explore the behavior of hubs, nodes, hosts, intersections, connections, and distribution points, I contacted Stan Magniant, who at the time worked at Linkfluence, a research firm based in Washington, D.C., specializing in mapping, monitoring, and measuring trends and opinions on the Social Web.

Magniant and team assembled a heat map based on its interpretation of graph theory to create a network topology that revealed the inbound/outbound link behavior and also the corresponding level of influence based on the quantity of nodes pointing back to distribution points or hubs. After feeding data into the Linkfluence system, both a network topology and hierarchy were immediately apparent and, like the Mailana map, this too was alive and clicking (see Figure 20.4).

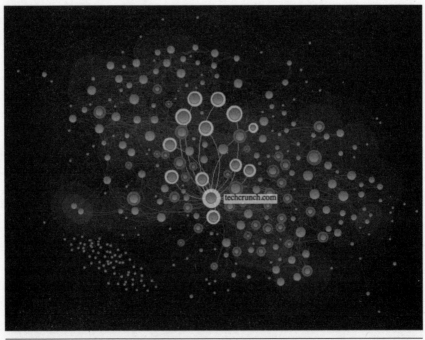

Figure 20.4   Linkfluence

Each node revealed inbound/outbound links and the interconnecting relationships and behavior they maintained. Influence and reach were suddenly evident and ready for exploration. We could view which individuals and properties consistently received the bulk of inbound links based on particular topics over time, while those linking back to primary sources also earned inbound links from peers at varying levels. Linkfluence revealed a hierarchical network structure that distinguished levels of influence and the corresponding networks of each.

Cisco's human network and its discernible structure and order introduced a new landscape of influencers and paths of influence to individual business units. These graphs were not only visualized, they were reinforced by the data collected during the process of discovery. The data would later prove crucial in justifying the work and findings, as decision makers require conclusive evidence and logical strategies to shift resources and attention in new directions.

■ VISUALIZING SOCIAL ORDER

Before we tackle the process of planning, I'd like to open a window onto the online behavior already observed and documented in social media to spark creativity and contemplation. Understanding these early analyses and hypotheses will allow us to factor potential human behavior into our programming and optimize their performance, immersion, and assimilation.

In social networks and online communities, the basis for cohesion, in its most simple interpretation, appears to be based on contextual exchanges and the viability of a mutually satisfactory reward system. We follow and connect with people we know, as well as those whom we admire, respect, and/or from whom we learn. We may also link to those we think will benefit from knowing us, and, in the process, take advantage of the swelling networks they create for personal or professional gain. Based on perpetual interests and those that temporarily distract us, our networks will shift, expand, contract, and morph, based on the individuals we align with at any given moment. Applying social order to social networks, no matter which school of thought you subscribe to, reveals the structure, social economy, and hierarchy, as well as the governing principles and culture. It is the hierarchy that conveys the balance of power and the contributing roles of each defining class.

Innovation is communicated through certain channels over time among the members of a social system.

■ PARTICIPATION INEQUALITY

In 1998, Steve Whittaker, Loren Terveen, Will Hill, and Lynn Cherny of AT&T Labs introduced us to the social theory of participation inequality within an online context in their research study, "The dynamics of mass interaction."[6]

Participation inequality refers to the phenomenon in social sciences that analyzes the differing levels of participation within diverse groups in a physical society.[7]

The findings of this paper would suggest that the effects of demographics (I'd argue psychographics) on conversational strategy demonstrated that common grounds theory would need to be modified to incorporate theories supporting weak ties and communication overload.

The study explored what, by any measure, is a social network in design, but more specifically defined as a newsgroup—an adaptation of bulletin board systems and the precursor to the Internet forums we are more familiar with today. Usenet was initially conceived by Tom Truscott and Jim Ellis in 1979.[8] The discoveries published by the authors foreshadowed much of what I've experienced in the new world of social networking.

Common grounds theory, as defined by this study, is a key principle for face-to-face conversations based on the establishment of mutual knowledge by which conversational contributions can be understood. This research found that "cross posting" (think syndication) and short messages (think Twitter) promoted interactivity. In fact, much like we hear today regarding social network fatigue or communication overload, this study also revealed that given the tremendous conversational traffic in Usenet, people were less likely to read or reply to long messages.

Earlier I suggested the term *psychographics* because in my research people are demonstrating the desire and the wherewithal to connect based on interest and/or knowledge of any given subject. An interaction can now be represented by a connection or follow, not just interaction.

When referring to the idea of "weak ties," the authors mentioned mathematical sociology and the examination of *interpersonal ties*, the information connections between people. According to research, interpersonal ties are usually categorized in one of three groups: strong, weak, or absent.[9] Weak ties represent the relationships we maintain with people outside our relevant networks. Unlike the contextual relations we maintain online today, weak ties provide diversity—an outsider's view. Quite simply, weak ties provide valuable perspective.

Perhaps most telling is the conclusion that mass interaction in online communities will require filtering in order to find relevant information.

■ PARTICIPATION INEQUALITY AND THE LAWS OF PERCENTAGES

The examination of the imbalances of participation inequality is not new and certainly maintains significance outside of the Social Web. There's much to learn about its dynamics through other examples that will offer a frame of reference for you to carry forward in your work.

Perhaps you are familiar with the 80/20 Rule, also known as the Pareto Principle—the law of the vital few and the principle of factor sparsity. It too studied the marvel of participation inequality, and is said to be the source of similar studies spanning almost every industry.

While the 80/20 Rule[10] is applied to circumstances, events, and businesses, the Web would introduce an even more divided landscape, one that would shift the balance of power between producers and consumers. If I mentioned that 80 percent of the content on the Web is created by 20 percent of the users, it might make perfect sense to you. After all, it seems quite possible.

However, in socialized networks and forums, the examination of participation inequality would eventually find that for every one person that posts, at least 99 other people are viewing content, but not posting in return. There are more readers than there are producers. Ben McConnell and Jackie Huba documented this behavior and named it the 1% Rule[11] in May 2006.

In their analysis, McConnell and Huba discovered similarities in the numbers reported by Wikipedia, Yahoo!, and ProductWiki. In June 2005, Wikipedia reported that 50 percent of all Wikipedia edits are done by .7 percent of users, and that 1.8 percent of users have written more than 72 percent of all articles.[12]

In February 2006, Bradley Horowitz shared his views on the scaling of online communities and, in doing so, created a pyramid that represents the levels and phases of value creation, in this case, Yahoo! Groups in particular (see Figure 20.5).[13]

Horowitz revealed:

➤ 1 percent of the user population, "creators," might start a group or thread.

➤ 10 percent of the user population, "synthesizer," might participate actively, and actually author content, whether starting or responding to a thread.

Figure 20.5

➤ 100 percent of the user population, "lurkers," benefits from the activities of the creators and synthesizers.

In October 2006, Jakob Nielsen introduced us to his interpretation of participation inequality for the Social Web, which further explored the studies published by AT&T Labs and Horowitz.[14] In summary, Nielsen observed that in most online communities, 90 percent of users are spectators, 9 percent contribute to a portion of interaction and content, and only 1 percent are responsible for a majority of the action within online communities (see Figure 20.6).

The 90-9-1 Principle found that 167,113 of Amazon's book reviews were contributed by a few "top-100" reviewers, with one prolific reviewer contributing over 12,000 reviews alone. In December 2007, MSDN Communities reported that 1,866 edits out of 10,851 total edits were made by the top five contributors. At the time, only .16 percent

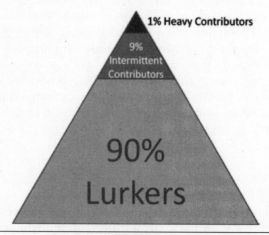

Figure 20.6

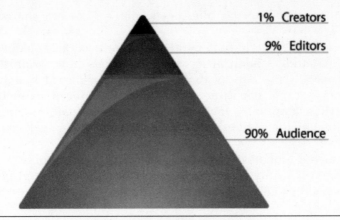

Figure 20.7

Source: Jake McKee and 90-9-1.com.

of all visitors to YouTube uploaded videos and .2 percent of visitors to Flickr uploaded pictures. Also, Nielsen found that blogs, in 2006, skewed the balance to 95-5-1, and Wikipedia's participation inequality was recorded with a 99.8-0.2-0.003 rule.

In 2008, "Community Guy" Jake McKee created a website dedicated to further exploring and explaining the 90-9-1 rule (see Figure 20.7).[15] McKee also offered a more polished image, with new descriptors to modernize the ideas:

➤ 1 percent Heavy Contributors was relabeled as 1 percent Creators.

➤ 9 percent Intermittent Contributors became 9 percent Editors.

➤ 90 percent Lurkers was renamed 90 percent Audience.

Based on my work and observations, I adapted the graphic to reflect the evolution of participation inequality and its ongoing struggle to capture the balance of power as it relates specifically to the state of adoption of each community, at a given point in time, on Rogers' Diffusion of Innovations Adoption cycle. Social media in general as compared to individual social networks will reside on different points at varying moments in time as each traverse across Rogers' DoI curve. We will find varying discrepancies in the equilibrium of engagement depending on time/place/state.

For example, as of September 2009, Facebook reported 300 million users worldwide. Collectively, they upload over 1 billion photos each month. Facebook also states that over 1 billion pieces of content

(Web links, news stories, blog posts, notes, etc.) are shared each month.

These numbers will only continue to grow, as Facebook becomes ubiquitous and as additional users as well as more sophisticated users embrace the site as their attention dashboard and host of their social graph. The same could also be true for other social networks. Thus, eventually, the 90-9-1 Rule might actually resemble the 80/20 Rule as the mediums move from left to right in Rogers' DoI graph.

As such, I amended the 90-9-1 graph based on my presumptions that we may already be moving towards a 90/10 Rule and possibly towards a shift to 80/20, as social media becomes omnipresent (see Figure 20.8).

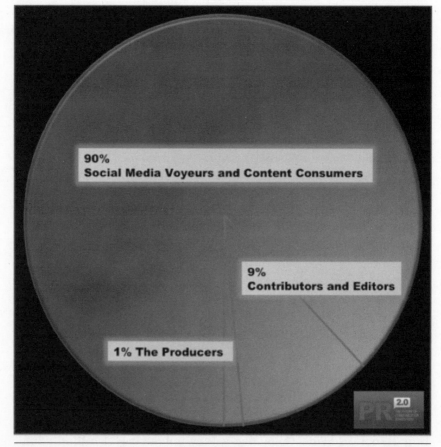

Figure 20.8

The new graphic is segmented to represent the behaviors of consumption as the rate of innovation, content production, and distractions increase at almost blinding speeds. As a result, 90 percent of users then potentially represent audience, consumers, and lurkers, and 10 percent of producers consist of the elite and also everyday contributors and editors.

■ SOCIAL TECHNOGRAPHICS

Whereas much of the previous discussion has focused on participation behavior within specific social networks, Forrester Research created Social Technographics®—a system for analyzing and classifying consumer participation in social technologies. For the past three years, Forrester documented this analysis in visual form, creating the Social Technographics Ladder to demonstrate and categorize individual activity across the Social Web.[16] Social Technographics Profiles places people who are online into overlapping groups based on their level of participation. (See Figure 20.9.)

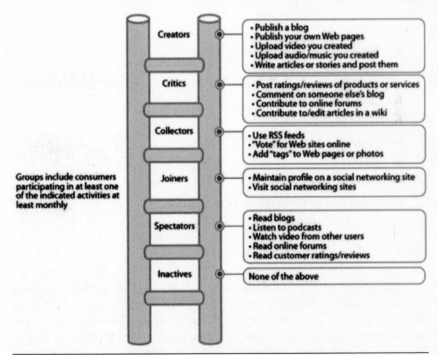

Figure 20.9   Social Technographics Ladder

Source: Forrester Research, Inc.

The groups are segmented as follows:

Creators:
➤ Publish a blog.
➤ Create and publish Web pages, video, audio, music.
➤ Write and publish articles or blog posts.

Critics:
➤ Post ratings/reviews of products or services.
➤ Comment on the blogs of others.
➤ Contribute to online forums.
➤ Write/edit articles and entries in wikis.

Collectors:
➤ Use RSS feeds.
➤ Vote for content online.
➤ Add tags to content.

Joiners:
➤ Maintain profiles on social networks.
➤ Visit social networks.

Spectators:
➤ Read blogs.
➤ Listen to podcasts.
➤ Watch videos.
➤ Read online forums.
➤ Read customer ratings/reviews.

Inactives:
➤ None of the above.

Along with the introduction of its most recent Technographics Ladder, Forrester published "The Broad Reach of Social Technologies,"[17] a report that found that more than four in five online adults in the United States now participate socially. (See Figure 20.10.) The role of spectator, at the very least, is now practically universal and therefore should serve as the final straw for those executives who

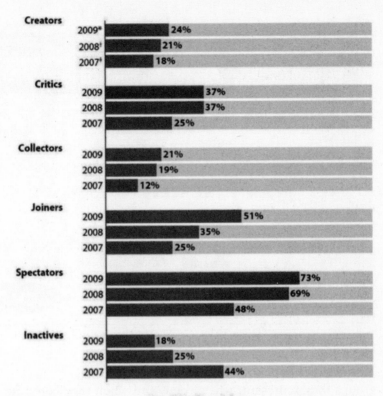

Base: US online adults

*Source: North American Technographics® Interactive Marketing Online Survey, Q2 2009 (US)
†Source: North American Technographics Media And Marketing Online Survey, Q2 2008
‡Source: North American Social Technographics Online Survey, Q2 2007

Figure 20.10   More Than Four in Five Online Adults Now Participate Socially
Source: Forrester Research, Inc.

withheld attention, time, and resources from organizing and orchestrating a strategic social effort (see Figure 20.11).

If social media were a scale or spectrum, we could simply divide it by elite content producers and consumers, contributing producers and consumers, consumers, and inactives, which might look similar to the 90-9-1 graph that I introduced earlier. What's important to understand when analyzing the Social Technographics Ladder is to establish where on the ladder your consumers and audiences are placed and to what extent. As such, your content, programming, and approach require a highly tailored and customized focus, voice, intent, and infrastructure that match and appeal to individuals and the

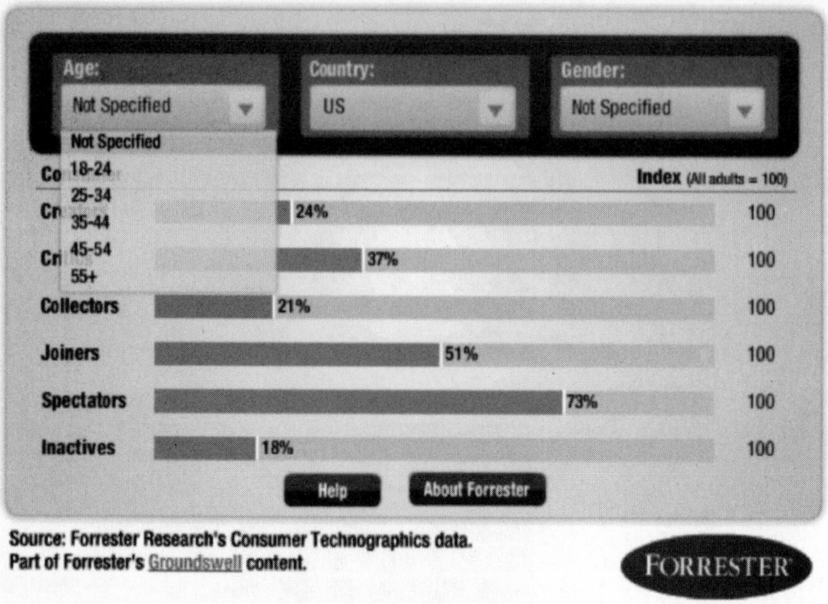

Figure 20.11   Consumer Profile Tool
Source: Forrester Research, Inc.

groups they represent, where, how, and when they consume and in turn respond.

To assist in this process, Forrester Research released an online Consumer Profile Tool that provides brands with Social Technographics, social profile information based on age group, country, and gender. Based on Forrester's survey data, you can view how participation varies among different groups of consumers, globally (see Figure 20.11).

■ TENETS OF COMMUNITY BUILDING

Ultimately, data is only as valuable as its incorporation into corresponding measures. This book is rich in research, information, theory, and experience and is intended to empower you with ideas, purpose, and direction. It is how the information in the book is applied that determines relevance in your world. The data that you gather is specifically relevant to your reality and what you discover, learn, and observe determines your next steps.

Applying Harold Lasswell's communication theory, which was originally introduced in 1949, we are to determine "who says what to whom in what channel with what effect."[18] As I introduced in my last book (*Putting the Public Back in Public Relations*, coauthored with Deirdre Breakenridge), in the Social Web we must analyze "Who says what, in which channel, to what effect; then ascertain who hears what, shares what, with what intent, where, to what effect."[19] This acknowledges that communication now continues after the initial introduction or encounter.

It is the connection between intelligence, intent, behavior, and people that explicitly and implicitly defines our community— ultimately determining our success. And, it is the collaborations between business units in the social realm that ensure cohesion, balance, brand presence, perception, and resonance.

Therefore, our job is to learn. The insights we garner will reveal specifically how and where to engage. At that point, everything boils down to community cultivation.

The world of business is accustomed to using acronyms and letters of the alphabet in helping its leaders become proficient in particular areas of study.

For example, in communications, we're taught how to employ "The Seven Cs," which include:[20]

➤ **Clear:** Ensure that your messages are clear, so that they are effective.

➤ **Concise:** Through brevity, there's clarity. Speak through the words that your intended audience is comfortable with, no more or less than absolutely necessary. Eliminate buzzwords.

➤ **Concrete:** You have a choice in your writing to use concrete (specific) or abstract (vague) words. While each has a place in business writing, concrete terms are typically more accurate and believable.

➤ **Correct:** Accurate and correct content ranges in characteristics from the value and comprehensiveness of expertise shared on any given subject to spelling, grammar, punctuation, and format.

➤ **Coherent:** Messages must make sense. They must be digestible. They must connect with those who come into contact with them. A message's flow and processing should be seamless.

➤ **Complete:** Information must be complete and definitive, ensuring that more questions are answered than raised.

➤ **Courteous:** Establishing goodwill is as much a function of delivery as it is format. Ensure that messages and stories are thoughtful and worthy of the intelligence and emotions of those whom we're trying to reach.

Moving along the alphabet, we're also presented with the Four Ps of Marketing, also known the Marketing Mix, which was originally introduced by Harvard professor Jerome McCarthy and Phil Kotler in the early 1960s.[21]

The Four Ps are:

> **Product:** A tangible object or service.

> **Price:** The price that the customer pays as determined by market factors such as market share, competition, material costs, product identity, and perceived value.

> **Place:** Also referred to as the distribution channel, *place* is the location where a product can be purchased.

> **Promotion:** Communications employed to promote the product in the marketplace, ranging from advertising, public relations, word of mouth, point of sale, direct mail, events, marketing, and now, social media.

Many have suggested that a fifth "P" should be included, to cover the role of people in the marketing mix. This is truer today than ever before.

In 1997, Bob Lauterborn, professor of advertising at the University of North Carolina and coauthor of *The New Marketing Paradigm: Integrated Marketing Communications,*[22] adapted the Four Ps and focused on the customer instead of on the product. His Four Cs of Service take into account that consumers are growing in influence and that companies need to determine how to send the right message at the right time in the right way to the right person. Instead of building and pushing products—for example, "build it and they will come"—the Four Cs champion the consumer's individual wants and needs.[23]

Attributes of the Four Cs of Service include:

> Product evolves into **Commodity.**

> Price becomes **Cost.**

> Place becomes **Channel** or **Convenience.**

> Promotion shifts to **Communication** (although one could argue now that the Social Web ushered in an era of conversations and collaboration over communication and promotion).

In 2004, Professor Koichi Shimizu of the Josai University Graduate School of Business Administration adapted Lauterborn's Four Cs into a framework for recognizing and leveraging the customer's role in business.[24] Shimizu introduced the world to the 7Cs Compass Model,

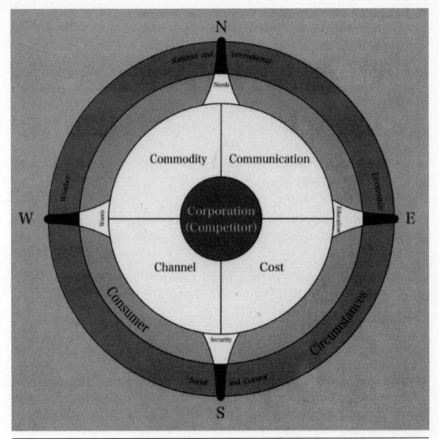

Figure 20.12   7Cs Compass Model

which portrays customers as encircling companies and companies at the center of marketing activities, and also includes the role of consumers in addition to customers.

The 7Cs Compass Model (see Figure 20.12) includes:

1. Corporation and Competitor.
2. Commodity.
3. Cost.
4. Communication.
5. Channel.
6. Consumer.
7. Circumstances.

The compass points in the model represent:

➤ **N = needs:** Analysis of customer needs—unsubstantiated opinions—some of which cannot be converted into concrete commodities.

➤ **W = wants:** The substantiated needs to expect commodities.

➤ **S = security:** The safety of commodities and production processes and the post-sale warranty.

➤ **E = education:** A consumer's right to know information about the commodities.

The compass points are balanced by navigational bearings that help businesses understand associated circumstances:

➤ **National and international:** Related to politics and law. I would add that consumer wants and needs and corresponding commodity relevance apply to the cultures uniquely in national and international circumstances

➤ **Weather:** Weather and natural environments are still uncontrollable and worth proactive consideration. I suggest that weather can also represent socioeconomic environments and their supporting ecosystems and habitats (for example, individual social networks versus real-world societies).

➤ **Social and cultural circumstances:** Representative of the social system and problems of a nation. The following seven human cultural factors need to be included in marketing analyses:

1. Basic values and attitudes.

2. Motivation.

3. Learning capacity and achievement orientation.

4. Technical know-how.

5. Social discipline.

6. Sense of responsibility for the common good and the community.

7. Capacity for flexible adaptation to a changing environment.

➤ **Economic circumstances:** Related to national circumstances, but also including factors such as energy, resources, international income and expense, financial circumstances and economic growth, and so forth.

As interactive media earns prominence in today's society, the laws of marketing, customer service, product development, and ultimately, community cultivation recognized the roles of customers, consumers, influencers, peers, competitors, among many other factors. Social media is the great equalizer and as such, we look again to the alphabet to help build a socially aware framework to serve as a creative inspiration for finding people and establishing the relationships that will serve as the foundation for community building.

As in all forms of marketing and communications, principles and methodologies will continue to evolve. In the past several years alone, many social media pioneers have shared their views for documenting the ethos, governances, and ethics that serve as the undercurrent for community cultivation.

Chris Heuer, the founder of Social Media Club and new media innovator, discusses the Four Cs for a social operating system:[25]

➤ **Context:** How we frame our stories.

➤ **Communications:** The practice of sharing our story as well as listening, responding, and growing.

➤ **Collaboration:** Working together to make things better and more efficient and effective.

➤ **Connections:** The relationships we forge and maintain.

Heuer binds together the Cs through a framework of values:

➤ Be human.
➤ Be aware.
➤ Be honest.
➤ Be respectful.
➤ Be a participant.
➤ Be open.
➤ Be courageous.

In November 2008, social maven David Armano introduced his version of the Four Cs of Community (see Figure 20.13):[26]

➤ **Content:** Quality content is ideal for attracting the audience necessary to build community.

➤ **Context:** Understanding how to meet people where they are; creating the right experience at the right time.

Figure 20.13

Source: © David//Armano darmano.typepad.com.

➤ **Connectivity:** Designing experiences to support microinteractions.

➤ **Continuity:** Providing an ongoing, valuable, and consistent user experience.

In July 2009, Gaurav Mishra, CEO of social media research and strategy company 20:20 WebTech, contributed a guest post to Beth Kanter's blog in which he proposed a 4 C's Social Media Framework (see Figure 20.14):

➤ **Content:** Social media transforms consumers into creators.

➤ **Collaboration:** The facilitation and aggregation of individual actions into meaningful collective results through conversation, co-creation, and collective action.

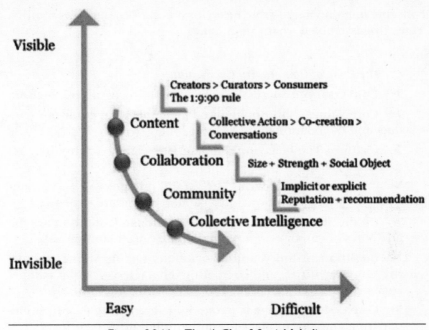

Figure 20.14   The 4 C's of Social Media
Source: Gaurau Mishra (www.gauravonomics.com).

➤ **Community:** Social media enables sustained collaboration around shared ideas over time and across space.

➤ **Collective intelligence:** The Social Web empowers us to aggregate individual actions and also run sophisticated algorithms to extract meaning.

In his post, Mishra captured a core quality of community development that should not go overlooked, which also reinforces our initial discussions on social objects: "People don't build relationships with each other in a vacuum. A vibrant community is built around a social object that is meaningful for its members. The social object can be a person, a place, a thing or an idea."

One can conjure any order of Cs or Ps to further the dialogue. I've assembled these examples and theories for you because each represent intrinsic values that will improve our work in identifying individuals and groups and also the methods necessary to establish and foster flourishing and interactive communities. However, there are some gaps—some terminology was either inferred or absent, yet the concepts remain vital to growing a vibrant and dynamic community. Thus, I've assembled what I refer to as C^3.

C^3: The Code of Community Cultivation

➤ **Conversation:** Successful communities thrive on interaction.

➤ **Core values:** Philosophies and principles that guide our conduct and the relationships we forge.

➤ **Culture:** The behavior characteristics of the community we define and shape.

➤ **Cause:** Our conviction, our intent, our mission.... Without cause, we lose motivation and a supporting reward structure.

➤ **Credit:** Recognition, paying it forward, and attention are the attributes of empowerment and thus a stronger community.

➤ **Coalition:** Affinity and associations require liking, sympathy, commonalities, and compelling characteristics that compel someone to align with other people or with something else.

➤ **Conversion:** Change is paramount. The ability to shift someone from one state or place to another is powerful, transformative, and part of any ongoing community program.

➤ **Commitment:** Without resolve, passion, or drive we cannot expect to inspire others to join or remain part of our communities. We are the catalysts. We are contagious. We must establish and convey our conviction to ensure loyalty and camaraderie.

➤ **Compromise:** In order to grow and evolve, we must adapt, which requires us to listen and feel the feedback from our community. This is how we learn and innovate.

➤ **Champion:** Without champions, the ability to scale growth becomes difficult, if not impossible. We must instill enthusiasm and empower champions to help us extend our reach.

➤ **Compassion:** Empathy and sympathy are instrumental attributes for feeling the state, experience, and emotions of our peers and influencers in order to understand the people we are trying to reach.

➤ **Confidence:** In order to convey expertise, insight, and passion authoritatively, confidence is the key to believability.

➤ Also includes the Cs from the previously mentioned examples: Content, Community, Continuity, Collaboration, Connectivity, Collective Intelligence, Context, Communication, Customer, and Consumer,

And of course, as in any business, the most important Cs to consider in any new media program include the C-Suite:

➤ CEO: Chief Executive Officer

➤ COO: Chief Operating Officer

➤ CMO: Chief Marketing Officer

➤ CTO: Chief Technology Officer

➤ CIO: Chief Information Officer

➤ CFO: Chief Financial Officer

➤ CSO: Chief Security, Strategy, or Social Officer

➤ And all other CxOs[27]

The underlying principle of any relationship-based program is that communities tend to reward selflessness, even if we are inconspicuously accomplishing our goals in the process of growing our networks and corresponding communities. Give your audience something to believe in.

Chapter 21

The Social Marketing Compass

Creating a Social Media Plan

Failing to plan is planning to fail.

— UNKNOWN

■ THE CALM BEFORE THE STORM

Depending on the drivers for engagement and the state of adoption in the Social Web, our first steps might require either the creation of a fresh social media plan or one based on the state of the existing program and the assessment of what is currently in motion, what's lacking, and what it should include. In both cases, our work in the Conversation Prism and Index must prove complete and irrefutable. It serves as the social map for planning and defining our approach.

Now we have one more step to undertake in order to draft a market-ready social media blueprint, one that is inclusive of all activity currently in effect now or in the developmental stages within your organization. For smaller companies, this process is straightforward. Nonetheless, we must conduct an audit that surveys the Social Web for any existing social profiles, objects, and accounts that are already in use or were created earlier and now remain dormant. This allows us to assemble the fragmented pieces that may exist and also assess the state of affairs, caliber of content, and relevance of accounts to evaluate and regroup. As a result, some accounts may remain, some may be reorganized, others may become inactive or erased altogether. These actions will be determined by the results of the Conversation Prism research.

For intelligence purposes, we should also review the activity of our competitors. This deserves ongoing attention.

This step is designed to unearth any potential landmines or surprises to ensure that anything you do from this point forward is highly orchestrated. Contingent upon the specific results of this internal probe, our next steps may differ a bit. The risk that we're attempting to minimize right now is the dilution of the brand through rogue accounts created by individuals with good intentions, but not bound to a plan or centralized purpose. Without governance or organization, the brand's image can quickly spin out of control with each new unplanned profile or social object created and placed into practice. For larger enterprises, this threat may already be a reality, and the extent of the damage caused will vary.

Your job is to reel in everything that is already in play concerning your brand, or spark new programs for the uninitiated.

■ THE SOCIAL MARKETING COMPASS

Before we tackle the official process of creating or amending an existing plan, here is one last exercise that will help us maintain focus and perspective. The fabric of our plan should be woven from threads of ethics, purpose, and principles and bound by salient business goals and objectives. Inspired by the term *moral compass*, I created the Social Marketing Compass (again with the artistic talents of JESS3), to serve as our value system when defining our program activities. (See Figure 21.1.)

A compass is a device for determining orientation and serves as a true indicator of physical direction. The Social Marketing Compass points a brand in a physical and experiential direction to genuinely and effectively connect with customers, peers, and influencers, where they interact and seek guidance online.

No infographic is complete without further explanation, and while its design may be extraordinary, it means nothing if we don't understand how to use it.

➤ The Brand

At the center of the compass is the brand; essentially, everything you do will revolve around it.

Figure 21.1

Source: Brian Solis and Jesse Thomas (http://Jess3.com).

➤ The Players

Fundamental to any program, the players define how, when, why, and to what extent our activity is intermediated across the Social Web. They include:

➤ **Advocates/stakeholders:** Those individuals who maintain a stake in the brand and the success of the company, through emotional, strategic, or financial investment—and are usually among the first line of external champions.

➤ **Traditional media:** Reporters, journalists, analysts, and other forms of mainstream and vertical media who already reach our intended audiences.

➤ **New influencers/trust agents:** Individuals who focus a noteworthy portion of their updates, content, and voice on particular topics, industries, or markets.

➤ **Champions:** Whereas advocates and stakeholders have skin in the game to some extent, champions are merely inspired to share their experiences and views because they are passionate, compelled, or incentivized.

➤ **Bloggers/market makers:** Bloggers and market makers represent what some refer to as the "A-list." This elite group can steer, shape, and galvanize activity that moves markets based on their views.

➤ **Tastemakers/Magic Middle:** Tastemakers and the magic middle are distinct from new influencers and trust agents, and, depending on the industry, serve as a subset of them. In their own way they make markets and spark trends based on their activity. Tastemakers are the trendsetters and, in the Social Web, they usually boast notable followers and connections who emulate their behavior, whether it's explicit or implicit, on behalf of the tastemaker. The term *Magic Middle* was coined by David Sifry,[1] who at the time was CEO of Technorati, the world's largest blog network; he defined this group as bloggers who maintained an inbound link volume of between 20 to 1,000 links.

Now, I refer to the Magic Middle as any group of content creators who remain focused on a topic and have earned a substantial audience because of their experiences, views, and perspective.

➤ Platform

Every initiative, inclusive of those groups of individuals who define our markets and ensuing behavior, requires a platform upon which to connect, communicate, and congregate. These platforms represent existing and also emerging categories that are worthy of our attention today and tomorrow:

➤ **Mobile:** Any network that unites groups of targeted individuals through interaction on mobile devices.

➤ **Social dashboard/microsites:** As discussed previously, social dashboards and microsites aggregate distributed social presences into one experience for channeling activity, providing information, fostering community, and guiding perception and impressions.

➤ **Widgets and applications:** Widgets and applications are portable services that spark interaction in a variety of networks, from mobile devices to Web-based social networks. They create an immersive experience designed to perform a dedicated function including tasks, games, interaction, learning, and other forms of entertainment and engagement within a dedicated, embeddable environment, while branding or conveying messages in the process.

➤ **Forums and groups:** Web 1.0 still rules, and through research we learn that communication and influence is still widespread in forums and groups where people not only communicate with each other every day, they also organize events, manage projects, and teach and learn from one another on almost every topic imaginable and unimaginable.

➤ **Blogs:** Web-based blogs, in all of their shapes and sizes, deserve a tremendous amount of attention, as they are still among the most active and influential news sources, besides traditional media. Not only do they hit mainstream audiences, they also focus on dedicated, vertical communities and nicheworks that equally contribute to your total market.

➤ **Social networks:** Of course social networks are a primary forum for today's social media interactions and therefore require a dedicated focus. As we've repeated so often in these pages, our attention is necessitated in popular networks as well as the nicheworks dedicated to our areas of interest.

➤ **Content creation:** The development and syndication of social objects carries the ability to reach people in almost every medium today, and will only continue to expand as technology advances. We are now in the content publishing and distribution business.

➤ **Events (offline and online):** The cultivation of communities is important online and also in the physical locales where we meet our customers, advocates, peers and influencers. A fusion between online and offline communication is critical and therefore mandatory.

➤ **Microcommunities:** While many refer to these services as microblogs, the truth is that they are not in any way, shape, or form reminiscent of blogs, nor is the behavior that they stimulate. We focus on them as dedicated platforms due to their unique interactions, communities, efficacy, and reach.

➤ **Channels**

The platforms that host relevant activity are supported, interconnected, and piped through channels that help increase, focus, or syndicate our mission through words, videos, pictures, audio, and other social objects and engagement tactics.

Through these channels we can amplify our messages while simultaneously increasing our digital footprint and brand reach and resonance. Even though some of this content may seem repetitive, I am including it again for the sake of context, as it relates to planning.

➤ **Aggregation:** Channeling information from multiple sources into one stream, microsite, dashboard, or feed.

➤ **Crowd-sourced:** Funneling information from targeted groups for a specified occurrence.

➤ **Curation:** Selecting highly poignant information and content from various, qualified sources and feeding it into strategic online accounts and social mediums.

➤ **Search engine optimization (SEO):** SEO increases the visibility of content, sites, and destinations within traditional search.

➤ **Promotion:** In the Social Web, going viral is a rarity. In order for anything to garner presence and visibility, online or offline, inclusive of front channel and back channel, promotion is imperative.

➤ **Syndication:** Beam social objects from one account to many networks simultaneously, in order to appeal to distinct communities within each.

➤ **Social media optimization:** Enhancing the properties of social objects to increase their chances of being found within their respective social networks, as well as in social and real-time search engines.

➤ **Participation/engagement:** Although promotion helps increase awareness for messages, stories, personalities, profiles, and objects in general, the process of "unmarketing" through partici-pation and engagement speaks volumes.

➤ **Portability:** The easier we make it for individuals to engage and transport social objects, the more we increase the likelihood of them doing so. Everything, of course, starts with the creation of compelling and remarkable content/media supported by the integration of embed codes, linkbacks, tweetability, promotion within the social graph, and also widgetizing the experience.

➤ **Content streams/activity streams:** Funneling our disparate feeds into dedicated channels allows discerning contacts to fol-low our updates in a variety of formats. I highly recommend creating multiple activity streams focused on particular areas of interest in addition to a corporate fire-hose. This proactive filter-ing helps followers receive only the information in which they're interested.

➤ **User-generated content (UGC):** Developing a cooperative ecosystem is not only engaging, it's empowering. User-generated content is a highly efficient and useful form that fosters dialogue, garners valuable feedback, and sparks word of mouth.

➤ **Emotions**

The socialization of the Web is powered by people, and it is a move-ment that is bound by the same natural laws and rules that govern human behavior. Successful branding is made possible when individ-uals can establish a human and emotional connection. In social net-works, the brand is represented by *you* and, for that reason, we must factor compassion, care, and feeling into our planning. Connect from the heart.

➤ **Reciprocation:** The gesture of a response is far more powerful than we perceive. It is the act of paying it forward that actually contributes to the caliber, quality, and value of dialogue and inter-changes. As influence is both democratized and equalized, giving back is a symbol of respect and gratitude.

➤ **Empathy:** Understanding the sentiment of another related to material interaction and experiences humanizes the context of an experience and conversation. You must *become* the very people you're trying to reach and in order to do so, our understanding must extend beyond training and embrace real-life exposure.

➤ **Recognition:** Identifying the contributions of others and pro-moting or responding to worthy individuals and instances are parts of how we cultivate communities and build relationships. From "thank you" to "I'm sorry," the symbolic deeds of acknowledgement, admittance, and identification serve as powerful forms of validation.

➤ **Core values:** The attributes that define the principles and standards of a brand are reinforced or diminished by its conduct. If we wish to attract influential peers, we must stand for something with which people can identify and associate. We must represent purpose. Our brand and our actions either encourage affinity or they don't.

➤ **Resolution:** The practice of solving problems, disputes, and other correlated issues is a focus and a mission that contribute to those actions that indeed speak louder than words. And, if we're to be measured by them, then let our commitment to resolve impediments speak for itself.

➤ **Empowerment:** Providing the authority to achieve something not possible before the encounter instills confidence and advocacy and sets the foundation to scale community development. Empowerment alters the balance of engagement and transforms interactions into relationships.

➤ **Humanization:** Conveying and embodying a human voice and character in all we do in interactive media, from the creation and distribution of social objects to engagement with individuals, is most effective when we personalize our approach. The Social Web is alive and powered by our ability to identify with others through direct interaction or by coming into contact with their personas, as attached to the content they interact with, share, or produce.

➤ **Honesty:** Be honest and virtuous in all interactions and not misleading whatsoever in any scenario in order to achieve your objective. Be truthful. If you don't have an answer or information, say so. If what you represent doesn't measure up in a particular setting, admit it. Focus on strengths and opportunities. Do not spin.

➤ **Reward:** Sometimes recognition isn't enough to satisfy someone for their contribution. The act of rewarding someone is a sign of appreciation. Rewards can span from monetary items to discounts to free products to access and special privileges. The consistent performance of rewarding community behavior fosters increased activity through positive conditioning.

➤ **Value proposition:** When humanizing our stories and interactions, it is the value proposition that speaks directly to specific markets. Many times marketing either attempts to generalize features or capabilities for the masses or simply reiterates the value propositions as dictated by internal management.

➤ **Be believable:** Words such as *transparency* and *authenticity* are overused in any discussion related to socialized outreach and therefore lose a good deal of their essence and meaning. It is more convincing and consequential in any encounter if you are *believable*. This can be passionate, exuberant, and contagious, unlike transparency or authenticity. Give me something to believe in.

➤ **Sincerity:** Your biggest objective moving forward is to earn and continue to gain trust. In order to do so, your actions must exclude pretense and instead enrich interactions through the exchange of genuine feelings and intentions.

■ CREATING A PLAN: DEFINING THE FUTURE, NOW

To quote personal time management author and expert Alan Lakein, "Planning is bringing the future into the present so that you can do something about it now."

A standard does not exist for drafting and implementing a targeted social media plan—and for good reason. Its content is unique to your brand, and therefore its documentation and output are also distinct. This section will offer the framework, but will require your perspective and insight to complete the design.

So far, we have assembled the content for this plan with most of the needed items residing in the data collection process that is used to listen and quantify the conversation index.

➤ Volume
➤ Relevant networks
➤ Sentiments
➤ Perceptions
➤ Reach
➤ Divisions currently affected
➤ Share of voice
➤ Themes/trends
➤ The state of social affairs
  ➤ Current accounts and activity
  ➤ Competitive intelligence

Now we need to place that relevant information into a plan of action. This sample template for defining marketing plans has been amended to serve our purposes. This example is intended to put into action our recommended programs, based on the strategies that match existing market behavior. Regardless of the size of the organization, this plan is designed to serve at the brand level. Dedicated social media programs will also require specific plans at the program and departmental levels, as one plan cannot encompass the total program required across the organization and still maintain integrity, accuracy, and, most important, comprehension and the wherewithal to execute and manage.

■ SOCIAL MEDIA PLAN OUTLINE[2]

OUTLINE

I. Executive Summary

This is where we make our case. By providing a tight, organized, and high-level summary of intentions, tactics, and metrics supported by observations and analysis, we officially begin the process of gathering support.

The executive summary sets the stage through the documentation and communication of our research, insights, and discoveries, and the recommendations inspired by the very people we wish to reach.

II. Purpose

Based on the exercises performed through the Conversation Prism, the Conversation Index, the Brand/Personality Identity Cycle, the Social Audit, and the review of the Social Marketing Compass, we must distill our sense of purpose so that it resonates with our team. It deserves a spotlight here as it places the rest of the plan in context.

III. The Challenge and Opportunity

This section is used to communicate the specific challenges associated with engagement, based on existing data in order to set expectations and establish a frame of reference. No challenge is complete without also identifying and communicating the opportunities discovered in our studies.

IV. Situation Analysis

Company Analysis
➤ Goals

➤ Mission

➤ Core values

➤ Culture

➤ Strengths

➤ Weaknesses

➤ Relevant networks (The Conversation Prism)

➤ Current activity and sentiment (Conversation Index)

➤ Share of voice (Conversation Index)

➤ The state of our digital footprint (Social Audit)

Competitor Analysis
➤ Market position

➤ Strengths

➤ Weaknesses

➤ Current activities and sentiment

➤ Digital footprint

➤ Share of voice

Divisions/Business Units Impacted by Existing Conversations
➤ Service, Marketing, Product Development, PR, etc.

Brand Personality
➤ Include brand attributes as related specifically to this program

V. Market Segmentation

Customer Analysis
➤ Types/segments

Segment 1
➤ Description

➤ Challenges

➤ Value drivers

➤ Social networks and communities of interest

➤ Influential blogs

➤ Decision process
➤ Perception
➤ Sentiment

VI. Review the 4 Ps of the Social Marketing Mix

Based on the 4 Ps associated with the typical marketing mix (product, price, place, and promotion),[3] we can adapt these principles to our social marketing mix to document and communicate our assessment and corresponding strategy for each relevant network and recommended program.

➤ **Place (distribution):** Highlight the relevant networks and communities for participation and/or distribution of social objects.

➤ **Participation:** Refers to the social object, network, and/or engagement strategy you recommend, by network.

➤ **Purpose:** Much more than the goal for each program, purpose aligns the corresponding cause, value, and intent we bring to the conversation in each case.

➤ **Promotion:** Discuss how you will specifically promote each program within and around each network and object. Also communicate the logistics and budget required for each program.

VII. Strategies by Network, Community, and Blog Categories

Each relevant network will require a specialized strategy and approach based on our fieldwork.

Network A
➤ Recommended activities
➤ Culture/social climate
➤ Social objects necessary
➤ Production schedule
➤ Timeframe
➤ Resources required
➤ Roles and responsibilities
➤ Budget
➤ Goals and projections

Network B
➤ Same as Network A

Blog Group A
➤ Recommended storylines and engagement strategies
➤ Timeframe
➤ Resources and supporting information and content required
➤ Budget
➤ Goals and projections

Blog Group B
➤ Same as Blog Group A

VIII. Conclusion

This is where you can share realistic and creative ideas that get decision makers thinking about the possibilities and potential that emerging social media now holds, as supported by your diligent analysis and as presented through your creative and informed perspective. Use this section to also provide recommendations on next steps for improving the social facade in general, as well as suggestions for business units not yet specifically included in this plan.

Remember this, however; with new ideas, new politics and dynamics unravel. You are essentially a change agent helping to solidify the company's ability to compete now and in the future. In the future, those around you will realize the latent advantages for not only the business, but for their individual careers. Stay strong and unswerving. This is your work.

As my good friend Hugh MacLeod says in his book, *Ignore Everybody*, "Good ideas alter the power balance in relationships. That is why good ideas are initially resisted."[4]

Once your idea garners acceptance and velocity, you will find yourself surrounded by supporters and backchannel detractors. But make no mistake: it's because your ideas are substantial.

As we learn through success and failure, in order to compete for the future, it is our nascent acceptance of champions and their creativity that enables us to surpass those companies that don't.

Divide and Conquer

Building Marketing and Service Teams Around Social Media Programs

Over the years, I've explored the drivers that propel businesses into the social world, analyzing their initial steps and observations, and planning and implementation processes, as well as how they assess and apply resources.

The most common motives to experiment or dive into social media are spurred through a proactive position of innovation, competition, and championing, or from a reaction-based set of circumstances that created necessity or a sense of urgency.

It's a moment characterized by "Ah-ha" or "Uh-oh...."

■ SOCIAL MEDIA TAKES A COMMUNITY EFFORT

If we've learned anything in this book thus far, it's that any one person or group does not own socially rooted conversations; they simply map to them. In fact, your customers are among the most influential stakeholders present today, and without guidance or participation, they may aimlessly steer the impressions and perceptions of your brand. The simple truth is that everyone owns socialized media, including "*you*." Perhaps it's better said this way: The conversation is omnipresent and not defined, steered, or controlled by any one entity. We are merely participants in a greater production. We determine our role as an engaged organization as well as individuals in cooperation with the powers that be.

Truthfully, many departments will be forced to socialize, and therefore require social programs at the departmental level to be executed at the departmental level and perhaps managed by a centralized group that most likely oversees other areas of branding, marketing, or communications simultaneously.

In the meantime, without organization, unity, and direction, the risk and likelihood for social anarchy prevails. If we pay close attention, we don't need to look far to observe and pinpoint the disjointed efforts of even the best brands engaging online and the discontinuity and fragmentation in their use of social networks and participatory programs that seem only to muddle and dilute branding efforts and the state of existing equity and resonance.

■ FLUIDITY THROUGH DECENTRALIZATION AND CENTRALIZATION: ASSEMBLING AND CONDUCTING AN ORCHESTRA

Many of the cases that I'm reviewing these days demonstrate either a decentralized or centralized approach to social media. To give us clarity into the process of organizing teams and established hierarchy, think about an interactive media program as an orchestra. There are few, several, or many musicians who comprise an ensemble, representing a variety of different instruments arranged to perform particular pieces as rehearsed and intended.

Decentralized media is either intentional or simply the victim of an overambitious company tackling social media across the organization, without a hub or gravity to integrate holistically and cohesively. Using the orchestra analogy, this is less representative of a unified, structured group and more similar to a group of jazz improvisers. In some cases, the free flow and unscripted jam of these musicians fuses to create something truly incredible. In others, listeners are lost in the disarray and lack of structure of the music and the competing soloists. In jazz, however, musicians are usually virtuosos in their own right, in contrast to the users on the Internet who are participating in the socialization of corporate culture and communications, among whom very few are truly maestros.

Harmonious social media programs are the result of organization, rehearsal, and arrangement, and inspired by talent, leadership, and imagination. These groups are directed by an individual or team that coordinates the roles and contributions of those involved. Someone must assemble the players, synchronize their positions, and guide the flow of the production. It's the only way to strategically score and present an integrated performance. And each player is selected because they've either auditioned or proved their merit. Simply said, they have earned the right to represent the brand.

Even though the doctrines guiding the evolution of the Social Web profess democratization, within a business or brand it's impossible to scale and perform harmoniously without leadership, instruction, and administration. What's constant, however, is that without the establishment of structure from the onset, it's either impossible or improbable to reel in existing efforts to redesign the social architecture. Instead, the process of correcting existing processes is reactively addressed with new or adapted policies.

■ THE SOCIETY AND CULTURE OF BUSINESS

The true value of a more socially aware and focused mindset can positively impact every department within an organization to create a more powerful, harmonious, and effective unity that together builds and nurtures a respected, active, and trusted brand. It's how we learn, channel, and escort valuable feedback within the company that offers the opportunity to improve relevance and leadership, which are so critical in a time when attention spans are elastic and ever thinning.

Our presence is requested in more than one channel and in more than one capacity.

In any case, where new and emerging media is permeating the existing corporate culture, the behavior and culture of the workforce is disrupted. Aside from the usual politics, lobbying, ambition, and ambivalence, the adaptation and socialization of existing processes and systems is inevitable. However, the role of the workforce in its introduction, adoption, and success is crucial. Consequently, we must account for the human factor in anything we do while moving forward. It is they who will lead us into the future.

■ MEETING OF THE MINDS: CONSENSUS AD IDEM

The creation of a New Media Board of Advisors can help steer the natural permeation and evolution of new media within the organization. This body is designed to help foster collaboration and cooperation, advise decision makers, and organize and manage the division of labor. This taskforce should include participants from each affected group to provide perspective, balance, and intellectual and human capital.

The socialization of every department will lend support and direction to myriad important conversations taking place, currently without you, across the Web. Having representation from each is critical to organization, buy-in, and practice.

The Board of Advisors should be structured as any standard board used to advise businesses in general to help make critical decisions that have positive impacts on the bottom line, as well as on community development.

The anatomy of the board should include the following representatives (where applicable):

➤ Legal
➤ Finance
➤ Product
➤ Service
➤ Marketing
➤ Communications
➤ Executive management (VP level or higher)
➤ Sales
➤ HR
➤ Web
➤ IT
➤ Research
➤ Interactive
➤ Advertising/branding
➤ Community Manager

The list should also include any individual or individuals who are passionate about social media, either personally or professionally, to a certain extent. While their expertise may or may not add value to strategic discussions and calculations, their experience is invaluable and their energy is transmissible. We can all learn from each other.

■ OUTSIDE THE INSIDE: ESTABLISHING AN INSIDER PROGRAM

Internal advisors are instrumental in the definition of programming and also in the establishment of protocol and the solidification of a chain of command required for the design, management, and execution of a campaign. Once a program is in the process of creation or refinement, an outside point of view is also helpful. In addition to the creation of an internal board of new media advisors, I also recommend either the addition of outsiders to the team through the inclusion of strategic partners, or the formation of an Insider Program to counsel the team on ideas, activities, and performance. This program can either incentivize or reward its members through pay or products/services, or simply for credit and recognition.

For example, Intel Corporation inaugurated a group known as the Intel Insiders, of which I am a current advisor, to offer guidance on the company's new media events, initiatives, and objectives. Other board members include Tom Foremski, Frank Gruber, iJustine, Cathy Brooks, Sarah Austin, and J. D. Lasica. We were specifically tasked with reviewing new product and program initiatives to offer input and suggestions prior to or following their introduction. I also was involved with the review and planning for the company's use of Twitter under the @Intel moniker. This advisory board has been in place for almost two years and its members serve voluntarily, without compensation. However, Intel is a household brand and a global brand, and therefore association offers value for all involved. When reviewing smaller or emerging brands and businesses, "insiders" or outside advisors have been compensated with shares or a stake in the company, percentage of revenues, with gifts or products, and or simply appreciation and recognition.

An Insider Program should feature the perspective of those who can impact perception, reach, and velocity, or those who are directly or indirectly affected by the actions of the company or its competition:

➤ Market partner
➤ Customer
➤ Investor
➤ Influencers, enthusiasts, and advocates
➤ Industry expert
➤ Delegates from any relevant external agencies

■ EXAMPLE: NEW MEDIA BOARD OF ADVISORS

➤ Governance

The role of a New Media Board of Advisors offers value beyond its creativity, innovation, and resource and content management. The

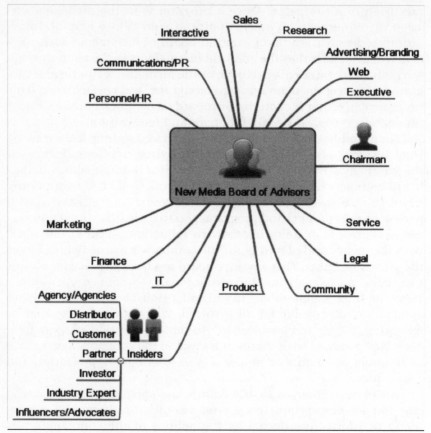

Figure 22.1   New Media Board of Advisors

board regulates the strategy and activity from the creation of accounts and profiles, assigning responsibilities, establishing conversational workflow and adaptation and response processes and channels (see Figure 22.1).

The board's strength lies in its ability to not only contribute to or define guidelines and policies, but to also enforce them when necessary.

In order for the board of advisors to run seamlessly, altruistically, and equitably, members would act wisely to elect an individual as its chairperson to oversee interaction, communicate status to executives, and also communicate direction back to the team, as well as to ensure productive collaboration. While much of this activity is brand new, and the rules are just now catching up to the required internal transformation, sovereignty and jurisdiction is vital in these initial, yet critical, phases. I suppose that's the true essence of new media. It's always new. . . .

In the long term, though, as the company learns and adapts to emerging media, the board may no longer be necessary or of any consequence. Eventually, the teams persevere and master the art and science of these new mediums and methodologies—while adhering to the greater good and mission, of course. Eventually, everything folds back into the grind or routine, however you may view it. For now, however, we have much to learn, and we're doing so, together.

➤ **The Mission**

The charter of the new Media Board of Advisors is to establish inbound and outbound processes and management protocol, answer questions, encourage inventiveness, educate, and assemble the teams responsible for engagement. Without a mission, we are bound to very little. And in this case, anarchy is not represented in the form of an overdue insurrection or revolution due to oppression. It is representative of the chaos of misdirected, competing, and potentially brand-damaging social networking, profile creation, activity, and engagement.

We need a democratic parliament to act on behalf of the people in our markets and the people within our organization. Namely, the mission of the Social BoA (sBoA) is to distinguish between hype and resolution or, as referred to in the geek world, shiny-object syndrome versus real-world applications. With the right team, the whole is better than the sum of its parts; hence the first act of this governing body is to establish its mission.

The constitution of the sBoA is hereunder relegated to:

➤ Establishing guidelines and policies.

➤ Auditing and documenting the state of the brand in the social realm.

➤ Passing through an initial round of the Conversation Prism to establish a beta version of the Conversation Index.

➤ Documenting the New Media Style Guide.

➤ Customizing and applying the principles and ethics of the Social Compass.

➤ Overseeing and guiding content production and management.

➤ Organizing the effort to discover and define the personality of the brand as well as the associated personal brands of those who represent it.

➤ Ensuring that online and representative brands and associated personalities are in alignment.

➤ Evaluating competitive and market behavior.

➤ Constructing and introducing social architecture and workflow.

➤ Identifying and recognizing capable and worthy representatives internally prior to scouting outside the fold, in order to assemble the most capable and exemplary teams.

➤ Ensuring that resources are collaborating and performing as intended.

➤ Maintaining a standard of education to ensure that all who are involved progress and develop over time.

➤ **Assembling a New Media Taskforce**

The Internet, for better or for worse, has a long memory. As a result, the board will help guide us, using our Social Compass in addition to the established guidelines and policies that serve as the foundation for everything we do moving forward.

The initial challenges are both similar and unique to each organization. Size, shape, and state of affairs determine where many begin and who joins the fray. Small businesses, for example, will have owners and/or employees who wear multiple hats in order to build a framework and engage. Larger organizations will have to recruit and progress at a pace that is compatible with their cultures and infrastructures.

The structure of this team will fluctuate from company to company and vary in size and shape, from small businesses to entrepreneurs to blue-chip corporations. What remains constant is the need for structure, organization, and thoughtful execution.

The taskforce works in concert with the board, but is unique in its mission. In my experience, the board is clear in its structure and goals, but it's not necessarily adept in the execution area of new media. Ideas and objectives aside, a specialized taskforce is also necessary to help transform corresponding strategies into functional reality across the organization.

Within every business, at least one person or persons emerge as either definitive champions or resident specialists. If this doesn't occur, hire a qualified individual immediately. This person or individuals will serve as the leaders of this new team (and, yes, I'm officially recommending that you add a new role and team to the organizational chart) and will serve as an internal new media agency, while the

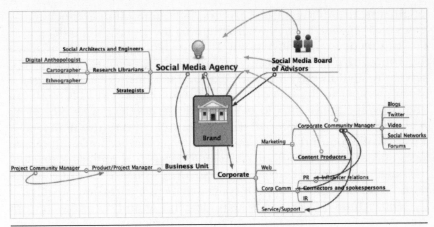

Figure 22.2   Workflow Evolved

organization itself adapts to outside influences in order to contribute to its direction in the market.

➤ Organizational Transformation: Redesigning the New Marketing Landscape

During these crucial stages in the organizational transformation process, an internal expert can provide direction and in some cases support to help each division begin the process of socialization or refresh its current approach, according to a logical and useful method.

Figure 22.2 illustrates this new media infrastructure. It is a representation of the realignment of organizational and resource structures that I have successfully architected and implemented within many companies. In this case, I spotlight a model used within a particular Fortune 500 business.

■ EXAMPLE: INTERNAL TASKFORCE

At the center of the chart is the brand. The board of new media advisors advises the brand and, in turn, feeds the business units and corporate teams dedicated to marketing, Web, communications, and service. Those divisions can then tap the internal wisdom of the internal new media taskforce for help as needed. The taskforce thus retains a team of experts and mavens either on staff or through consultant relationships. Note the areas of expertise and resources that could benefit the new media agency, such as digital librarians, architects and engineers, anthropologists, cartographers, and ethnographers (new roles and responsibilities are highlighted later in the chapter).

In this diagram, the community manager reports to the marketing function, providing the general team with information, data, and advice related to the corporate brand. Each business unit assigns a team member to the task of community management as it relates to their specific areas of focus to engage at the product or service level. This member would interact with the brand community manager to ensure collaboration and support. The project-level community manager may also serve another, specified role, such as project or product management, content creation, and so forth, and provide project community management support as needed or in a part-time capacity.

For example, if PR needs help identifying and mapping new influencers, the taskforce can help through direction, education, or execution. When the marketing team needs to reach trust agents or tastemakers through a direct marketing or sponsored tweeting initiative on Twitter, the resident experts will have access to best practices, partners, and most likely an idea of who these tastemakers are and where they communicate.

■ EXAMPLE: ORGANIZATIONAL TRANSFORMATION

In this example (see Figure 22.3), we visualize the new organizational landscape as it integrates the role of new media experts into the hierarchy of business processes. While off to the side in the image, the social media management function and its supporting resources serve as a central facility to provide cross-functional direction, support, and knowledge to all teams and divisions with a role tied to any outward or inward interaction through new media channels.

While the group reports to a high-level corporate function and/or the new media board of advisors, it is designed to serve almost every applicable division and discipline.

The Social Media Agency maintains day-to-day responsibility for many core functions and is empowered to serve and also police its peers within the organization:

➤ Conversational Alerts, channeled to the impacted person or team.

➤ Counsel on specific programs and initiatives specific to each unit or division.

➤ Ongoing advice and best practices.

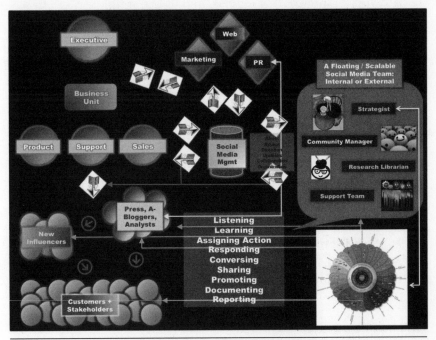

Figure 22.3   New Marketing Organizational Transformation

➤   Contributed content, personnel, and programming to the internal educational program.

➤   Listening at the corporate level and assigning actions based on proactive or reactive scenarios.

➤   The documentation of best practices.

➤   Training based on specific initiatives.

➤   Execution on behalf of business units and teams when applicable and necessary.

➤   The creation of specialized teams around programs or the facilitation of external resources to help where appropriate.

➤   Assessment of resources and associated costs per campaign.

➤   The ability to identify influential communities and influencers.

➤   The state and sentiment of the brand and competitors within the Social Web.

➤   The culture of primary communities and the opportunities for immersion.

➤   Trends.

➤ Internal audits on social usage, content production, distribution, and engagement.

➤ Listening/monitoring/documenting—intelligence gathering and trend analysis.

➤ Engagement in the networks and groups where relevant conversations are pervasive and warrant participation.

➤ Content creation.

➤ Conversation management and trafficking.

➤ Influencer and tastemaker identification and networking.

➤ Product and service refinement.

➤ Community management, empowerment, and cultivation.

➤ Event hosting and franchising.

➤ Story development.

➤ Humanizing company and product messaging and redefining the online journey and experience associated with the online presences associated with specific brands/products.

■ NEW ROLES AND RESPONSIBILITIES IN THE ERA OF EMERGING MEDIA

In February of 2006, Intel announced that it was in the process of hiring more than 100 anthropologists and other social scientists to work alongside its engineers.[1] Intel believes that in order to humanize its company, it must humanize its products. So much so, that the company placed three anthropologists as managers in business units: Eric Dishman in Digital Health, Genevieve Bell in Digital Home, and Tony Salvador in Emerging Markets. Pat Gelsinger, a senior vice president at Intel, in an interview with MIT's *Technology Review* magazine emphasized the impact of these new scientists having influence in more than just tactical product development: they're also playing a key role in long-term strategic planning.[2]

Nokia has also integrated the role of social sciences into its research and design. The company hired Jan Chipchase[3] to observe and understand how mobile design fits into and affects lives, societies, and cultures.[4] In an interview with *New Scientist*, Chipchase shared insight into his mobile research in the emerging and rural markets around the globe: "We do research in such communities because these are the places in which we can best learn about the kinds of mobile use that will become mainstream in other parts of the world. We find these communities to be incredibly innovative in the way they use their mobile phones."[5] The following are other roles that social science can play, in which they will affect and benefit everything from marketing communications and public relations to product development and service programs to advertising and sales to company culture and management behavior:[6]

➤ **Content producers:** Creates content necessary for client/company interaction with customers, peers, and influencers, including videos, images, Web pages, blog posts, policies and guidelines, tweets, wikis, comments, online experiences, profiles, and so forth. In many cases, connectors and industry experts/strategists wear this hat and assign the creation of important content to either content producers or other members on the team with direct experience, or simply produce it themselves.

➤ **Digital sociologists:** Observes the cultures, trends, and behaviors associated with communities, networks, and forums, and compares the interactivity around keywords and brands to contribute to engagement strategies, customer service policies, and improvements and product modifications.

➤ **Digital ethnographers:** Ethnography is the branch of anthropology that deals with the scientific description of specific human cultures. For those projects where a deep study of online culture and communities is critical, an ethnographer is ideal for documenting a descriptive study of a particular human society.

➤ **Research librarians:** Complements or augments in-house or contract sociologists by analyzing relevant keywords used by customers, listening to and documenting conversations by content and sentiment, charting volume and frequency within social networks, identifying and analyzing true influencers and tastemakers across media, blogs, and social communities, and presenting data and charts for analysis by strategists.

➤ **Community managers:** Listens to conversations in social networks, forums, and the blogosphere documented by research librarians or through their own process; assigns relevant dialogue to appropriate team leads; manages the workflow and response status; and in most cases is the first line of response.

➤ **Digital or social architects:** Digital or social architects are responsible for building the online bridges between the company brand and consumers via widgets, sites, online dashboards, blogs, social newsrooms, social media releases, wikis, social networks, fan pages, forums, groups, and any other application, platform, or group responsible for hosting content, conversations, and interactivity.

➤ **Social engineers:** Engineering can create the roads and highways that connect a brand to its audiences and communities. Engineers can also observe behavior and trends within communities in order to inspire new product designs, programs, and corporate initiatives to align more closely with the needs and desires of its consumers.

➤ **Connectors:** Informed individuals and teams that can connect stories to influencers and inspire activity, direction, and conversations. Connectors act based on intelligence, empathy, sincerity, and the ability to truly "bridge" a story to someone else in a way that's specific and compelling to them as an individual and also as it relates to their audience and social graph.

➤ **Industry experts/strategists:** Someone has to act as the conductor to this all-star orchestra. Qualified individuals have mastered the art and science of attaching new and traditional media to the bottom line of their business and also possess a deep understanding of and experiences with customer empathy, market trends, and the governing technology that connects the people within desired market places.

➤ **Cartographers:** Those responsible for visually mapping relationships, linking patterns and influences in social maps of relevance (per the Conversation Prism) and interaction, among other ties.

These new, adjoined job functions create a new level of services that complement existing, traditional, and necessary corporate activities. The opportunities are limited only by the imagination of those responsible for engendering change from within.

Part

VI

A Little Less Conversation, a Little More Action: Rising above the Noise

Chapter 23

A Tale of Two Cities

Social CRM and Relationship Management

■ WEB 2.0 AND THE EVOLUTION OF CRM 2.0

As in Charles Dickens's novel, *A Tale of Two Cities*, this chapter is set amidst a revolution that depicts the quandary facing individuals who stand for something more significant than the status quo. While not as dramatic or profound as the experiences depicted in Dickens's book, a tale of two cities exists between the current state of affairs in customer relationship management and the idea of what relationships should symbolize for today's businesses, amidst this social mutiny.

The foundation for CRM, customer relationship management, was set in the 1980s and was traditionally viewed as the technology and doctrines governing marketing automation, sales automation, and customer service.

As Web 2.0 gave rise to a genre of social computing and collaboration, the enterprise infrastructure, business paradigm, value chain, and workflow were forever transformed. Processes and methodologies were suddenly placed under the microscope finding the search for new opportunities for efficiencies and innovation, and thus Web 2.0 spawned an era of Enterprise 2.0. In the process, CRM experienced a renaissance and was ripe for a new name to reflect the impact of Enterprise 2.0 and Web 2.0 on customer management. While many suggestions were introduced, this new generation of CRM was captured most effectively as CRM 2.0. Led by Paul Greenberg (author of the best selling book *CRM at the Speed of Light*), Axel Schultze, Christopher Carfi, Mei Lin Fun, Brent Leary, and Andrew Boyd, among others, CRM 2.0 would rise alongside Enterprise 2.0, reaching its apex in innovation and visibility in 2007 and 2008.[1]

Axel Schultz created a wiki dedicated to exploring and defining the new landscape for CRM 2.0, http://crm20.pbworks.com, which served as a collaborative working group that united technology innovators and industry thought leaders.

Several definitions were presented in the wiki to capture the spirit, state of technology, and promise of the CRM 2.0 movement.[2]

Paul Greenberg contributed:

> *CRM 2.0 is a philosophy and a business strategy, supported by a technology platform, business rules and processes, designed to engage the customer in a collaborative conversation to improve human interactions and provide mutually beneficial value in a trusted and transparent business environment. It is the company's response to the customer's ownership of the conversation.*

In November 2008, William Band of Forrester Research published a report entitled, "CRM 2.0: Fantasy or Reality?"

Band described the state of new CRM and the need to evolve its infrastructure to adapt to the proliferation of social computing. The report was described this way:[3]

> *The rise of Social Computing means that customer relationship management (CRM) professionals must find innovative new ways to cope with the emerging phenomenon of "social customers." Forrester talked with nine early-adopter companies and reviewed the social technology capabilities of six leading CRM solutions vendors to understand the business tactics and new technologies that CRM professionals are using to achieve the five objectives of social customer strategy: listening, talking, energizing, supporting, and embracing. Best practices for supporting next-generation customer management—CRM 2.0—are rapidly emerging. In fact, leading-edge organizations are actively using social technologies to forge new and tighter relationships with their buyer communities, and social technologies are driving business results. Now is the time to take action to start gaining the practical experience you need to break out of old mindsets and grasp new opportunities.*

The conclusion was best summed up by using Band's own words: "Those who wait to join in will find it increasingly hard to catch up."

Indeed. But while CRM 2.0 was gaining support, social media was rewriting the playbook for customer influence and interaction.

Social media emerged in parallel as a pervasive and sprawling ecosystem for breeding influence and set the stage for something more significant and consequential than CRM 2.0.

While CRM defined an era and captured the processes, systems, and ideologies that promoted streamlined relationship management, CRM in and of itself didn't imply social interaction, engagement, participation, or internal adaptation. And although CRM 2.0 was rooted in thoughtful and visionary intentions and efforts, its lifespan was finite.

The 2.0 moniker truly represented the next generation of CRM technologies and corresponding outward and inward philosophies to improve the automation of sales, marketing, and service. It most certainly served its time, but it didn't meet the requirements and demands of a more socially aware society that was empowered by the technology and rewarded for its participation through recognition, authority, and the ability to incite change and response.

If we examine the common themes among the definitions of CRM 2.0 cited previously, as well as those published in papers, stories, and blog posts over the years, we uncover the attributes that ultimately paved the way for what would later earn official recognition as Social CRM (sCRM):

➤ Philosophy

➤ Business strategy

➤ Technology platform

➤ Collaboration

➤ Conversation

➤ Human interaction

➤ Human culture

➤ Customer

➤ Experience

➤ Social

➤ Relationships

The migration from CRM 2.0 to sCRM represents a shift from managing customers to listening to and engaging with them.

Social CRM reflects the maxim of social democracy and forged a decree that crowd-sourced governing principles and innovation, forcing companies to take heed and adapt to the will and influence of its peers and customers through public forums and networks.

The customer was now recognized as the social customer.

Starting in 2007 and 2008, Social CRM gathered momentum. Brent Leary,[4] Paul Greenberg, Filiberto Selvas,[5] Ross Mayfield,[6] Jeremiah Owyang,[7] and I,[8] along with among many others, rallied support for a more "social" form of customer relationship management.

In July 2009, Paul Greenberg officially shifted focus from CRM 2.0 to Social CRM in his post, "Time to Put a Stake in the Ground on Social CRM":[9]

> *The debate and discussion about what defines Social CRM a.k.a. CRM 2.0 vs. its traditional parent has been going on for about 2 years pretty regularly and started, according to thought leader Graham Hill almost a decade before that.*
>
> *Personally, I'm done defining it and am moving on. I think enough time has been spent trying to decide what we're calling it and what it is. I think that we've reached the point that though there is no one point of view, there is a general idea of what we have. So this post, which will be on ZDNET and PGreenblog is my stake in the ground for the definition of Social CRM.*

The shift in the outward focus and inward adaptation of organizations that recognize the power and extent of online conversations will soon discover that the "C" in sCRM slowly disappears.

■ TWITTER AND SOCIAL NETWORKS USHER IN A NEW ERA OF RELATIONSHIPS

My foray into the Social Web and D2C (direct to customer) engagement as a complement to traditional media harkens back to the early days of bulletin boards, which would later evolve into communities such as Yahoo! Groups and ultimately social networks, as well as the emerging era of websites created by HTML-efficient enthusiasts who shared news, thoughts, rants, and observations related to their passions and interests. These influential sites would serve as the precursor to blogs.

But here we are, years later, and mainstream brands are finally starting to pay attention. We're waking up to a new world of opportunity that changes nothing less than how, what, where, to what extent, and with whom we communicate.

The Internet was the harbinger for individuals to establish authority and control.

Forums and websites would lead to next generation, sophisticated, and polished forums, social networks, and blogs to extend reach and the impact of influence, creating a paradigm-changing movement that would forever transform business dynamics.

Even though millions of consumers active in the Social Web beckoned for participation from brands, it would take Twitter, and a couple of years of incredible growth, to serve as an undeniable catalyst for the reinvention of CRM and how we identify, track, respond to, and manage online conversations that are pertinent to brand perception, leverage, satisfaction, and resonance. Twitter essentially made everyone in the world of CRM and CRM 2.0 pay attention. It sparked the change for how brands truly engage across the Conversation Prism, a.k.a. the Social Web, and served as the guiding concepts for the formalization of sCRM.

Twitter and Twitter Search have ushered in a real-time, "now" genre of interaction that is findable, creating dedicated ecosystems that transform and support how we as consumers share and discover relevant information, at will.

Online discussions, rants, and observations are either alarming and motivating brand managers or luring them into entrapment scenarios. But the reality is that real-time dialogue fuels connections and perceptions in the statusphere, blogosphere, online communities, and the Social Web in general. It's this swelling tsunami of chatter that will only intensify and heighten as it forces a new genre of Social Customer Relationship Management. As such, Social CRM is no longer a debate nor an option for businesses.

It necessitates brand involvement from almost every outward facing department, not only marketing, sales, channel, and service, to proactively share answers, solve problems, establish authority, and build relationships and loyalty, and to do so one tweet, blog post, update, and "like" at a time.

In the world of business, social media forces companies to augment the offshoring of reactive customer service with the nearshoring of proactive engagement. The conversations that power social media spark a sense of urgency for brands to identify influential voices and talk to customers where and when relevant conversations are transpiring.

In an interview with Jon Swartz of *USA Today*, Bill Tolany, global coordinator of integrated media at Whole Foods Market shared his views on the new service landscape, "Social media is a natural extension of customer service."[10]

Whole Foods has more than 50 Twitter accounts and growing—tweeting on topics as specialized as cheese, wine, and specific items, with each participant trained through the integrated media department.

In the same article, Swartz interviewed Elissa Fink, vice president of marketing at Tableau Software, to discuss how Twitter was improving the experience for users of the company's business software: "The more ways you provide customers to contact you, you're more likely to satisfy them. It shows you're listening to them."

And as Salesforce.com CEO Marc Benioff observed in *USA Today*, "Brands aren't about 'messages' anymore. Brands today are conversations—and today the most important conversations are happening through social media such as Twitter, Facebook, and MySpace."

Dion Hinchcliffe documented the rise of sCRM and the advantages of using social software to reinvent customer relationships on his blog at ZDNet.[11] He observed that in sCRM "the elimination of decades of inadequate communication channels will suddenly unleash a tide of many opportunities, as well as challenges, for most organizations." Hinchcliffe also observed four key aspects of Social CRM:

1. **A social environment:** Customers must be able to create an identity and perceive other customers, as well as individual workers, and be able to interact with both types of parties in a Social CRM environment.

2. **Customer participation mechanisms:** While discussion forums are very open-ended and can be used for many types of participation, Social CRM becomes more strategic when there are participation mechanisms that are driven by the specific needs of the organization or its customers. These might include social customer support, competitive contests, innovation/prediction markets, or joint product design, perhaps with finely tuned controls (such as Kluster[12]).

3. **Shared collective intelligence:** Web 2.0 applications are most successful when they create a shared repository of information created by the joint participation of their users. Good social CRM tools will make sure that the directed activities of a social CRM environment are accumulated, discoverable, and reusable. The artifacts of these activities are likely customer problem resolutions, product improvements, sales opportunities, and so forth. In other words, *"relationships that get better the more people use them"* would be a good way to paraphrase one of the key mantras of 2.0 applications in a CRM context.

4. **Mechanisms to deal with conversational scale:** There is still a fear that deploying social tools to interact with online customers en masse will create unexpected costs or increased overhead as thousands—and in some organization's cases—millions of customers try to engage with them.

To help us visualize the sCRM architecture, Hinchliffe created a helpful infographic entitled "The Social Business Front Line: Customer Relationship Management."

In this graph, he places the sCRM management network between businesses and customers where partnerships are forged and cultivated. Also connected to the sCRM network are workers who oversee and participate in relevant interactions and also a silo that captures collective intelligence through community-generated activity.

With sCRM, as in social media, the focus is on people placing the onus on the company's front line to ensure productive collaboration and brand resonate. Hinchcliffe marks this through five Key Attributes of the Social Business Front Line:

1. Social environment
2. Crowd-sourced results
3. Community-driven
4. Joint accumulated value
5. Scalable relationships

■ WHEN THE "S" IN sCRM STANDS FOR SELF-SERVING

I'd be remiss if I didn't at least share with you some of the more controversial ways that sCRM is channeling its inner CRM through the automation of consumer and prospect engagement. Not unlike many of the direct marketing initiatives, spanning from e-mail to snail mail, sCRM is already emulating the one-way broadcast systems that new media missionaries have so diligently rallied to socialize. See Figure 23.1. If we think that for one minute marketers, executives, and salespersons will forget all that they've learned through their years of profiteering through one-dimensional sales and marketing initiatives, we're highly mistaken.

In one such example, a television network used Twitter and an sCRM system (described in the tool section) to promote a new series. In this case, the back channel proved lucrative to the promotional campaign. Using a Twitter-based framework similar to systems employed by e-mail marketers, this freely available sCRM Twitter

Figure 23.1   The Social Business Front Line: Customer
Relationship Management

Source: From http://blogs.zdnet.com/Hinchcliffe.

application enabled network marketers to search Twitter for all tweets related to the actors of the program. The software automatically followed each person using the branded Twitter account (the show), sorted the tens of thousands of reciprocating follows by influence and relevant keywords, and then automatically sent pre-scripted messages via DM (direct message) to each person—without human intervention. The promotion of the show was deemed a success, with over 100,000 individuals qualified and over 20,000 DMs sent in a single push.

This particular initiative was solely focused on one-way promotion. None of the responses from the back channel effort were ever read, acknowledged, or addressed. It's the difference between broadcasting and contributing value.

But imagine if they were one in the same. The system actually accommodates both outbound and inbound sCRM—remember, most tools should embody technology and the supporting ethos of relationships management. As responses arrive, the system, along with a program manager, could have easily assigned conversations to the appropriate individuals representing designated groups.

To embrace inbound conversations is truly what the "s" represents in sCRM. It's a shift in mindset and purpose—all it takes is a plan and a supporting process or team.

For example, on any given day on Twitter, movies, music artists, TV shows, and products literally become the talk of the town—well, of Twitterville,[13] at least—with many actually earning enough momentum to become trending topics (roughly 4,000 tweets per hour). These priceless conversations represent one part of an sCRM process. We know their level of interest on the subject. Basically, we have the tools right now to capture that dialogue, gather intelligence, and channel the data into databases for immediate response and engagement programs and/or future campaigns. But right now, most businesses are missing this opportunity to capture this vital input. These invaluable opportunities are fleeting into the digital horizon.

■ VENDOR RELATIONSHIP MANAGEMENT (VRM)

In December of 2006, Christopher Carfi wrote about Vendor Relationships Management on his blog, The Social Customer Manifesto, and offered a simple, but important message, "This [VRM] needs to be on your radar."[14]

Carfi documented the history and development of VRM, tracing back to its roots in 1999 when the concept of vendor relationship management was referred to as TEKRAM (market spelled backwards).

Doc Searls made the case[15] for consumer-powered influence in respect to vendor management, and Mike Vizard coined VRM in response during a Gillmor Gang podcast in September 2006.[16]

Paul Greenberg responded to Carfi's hosted discussion on VRM with an observation that would serve as one of the movement's credos: "The vendor and customer have to collaborate to optimize the relationship. It is no longer one-sided. That means that the customer's management of the relationship is the recognition of the partnership that successful implementation demands and there has to be skin in the game on both sides."[17]

VRM at its core is reciprocal to CRM, capsizing the concept of talking at or marketing to customers and shifting the balance of power in relationships from vendors to consumers. Like CRM and sCRM, VRM is representative of a mission and parallel philosophy, as well as supporting tools and technology ecosystem—think Priceline and Lending Tree from a product perspective and Get Satisfaction and Uservoice from a service angle.

As described by VRMLabs, VRM is a customer-vendor locked see-saw: "Customers and vendors are a locked see-saw with one hugely outweighing the former. Like with a real world see-saw[sic], the fun is spoiled for both. Giving individuals tools to redress the balance, the pressure from customers should level the players."[18]

VRM is the symmetry of customer and vendor participation and collaboration, and the implementation of the relationship into "relationship management."

As such, Project VRM was established by industry leaders and champions to ensure that the oscillation between customer and vendor is uniform. Project VRM is a development effort at the Berkman Center for Internet and Society at Harvard University, and is led by Doc Searls, a fellow with the Center. It is a community-powered wiki with real-world sources, extensions, and implications that foster discussion, participation, and partnerships between technologists, market experts, customers, and vendors to establish guidelines and platforms to improve the relationships between vendors and customers. As noted in the "About the Author" page of Project VRM, "It is Doc's [Searls'] belief (and this project will test his hypothesis) that VRM is required to bring a useful and productive balance of power between vendors and customers, supply and demand—for the good of both—in the marketplace."[19]

When reviewing the progression of CRM and its supporting categories and descriptions, the word "automation" was omnipresent. As we've learned from our time together, automation is a word that's usually absent from the descriptions of social media and sCRM—this is especially true in reference to engagement, listening, and participation.

In the end, the goal of VRM seeks to enhance the relationship and interaction between demand and supply by providing more efficient and mutually beneficial solutions for "demand" to partner with "supply."[20]

As in any relationship, in order for VRM to have a positive impact, vendors must find compelling incentives, while customers seek solutions through newfound empowerment.

VRM represents hope and challenges in order to define paths to resolution and coalition.

Tools aside, it's your role and actions in the engagement equation of Social CRM that serve as the cadence to future dialog and ultimately shape brand personality and allegiance with every beat of your social rhythm.

■ THE VALUE OF SOCIAL CUSTOMERS

In Paul Greenberg's *CRM at the Speed of Light: Social CRM Strategies, Tools, and Techniques for Engaging Your Customers*, he discusses the correlation between advocacy (evangelism) and loyalty.[21]

One way to measure advocacy is via a Net Promoter Score (NPS), a trademarked metric system developed by Fred Reichheld, Bain & Company, and Satmetrix. Introduced by Reichheld in a 2003 *Harvard Business Review* article "One Number You Need to Grow,"[22] the NPS analyzes how businesses can create more "promoters" and fewer "detractors." Reichheld expounded on this idea in his 2006 best-seller, *The Ultimate Question: Driving Good Profits and True Growth.*[23]

The key to NPS is evaluating the value inherent in the answer to a very simple question, "How likely is it that you would recommend our company [or product] to a friend or colleague?"

The answer is rated between 0 to 10 and based on the score, the respondents are grouped into one of three categories, detractors (0–6), passives (7–8), and promoters (9–10). The next step is to then get feedback on why they scored as such in the attempt to empower advocacy.

In 2003, Dr. Kumar and Werner Reinartz published the "Mismanagement of Customer Loyalty" a pioneering study on the connection between customer profitability and loyalty.[24] Their findings concluded that *not all loyal customers are profitable, and not all profitable customers are loyal.*

Did you catch that part?

If anything, the social customer is, at the very least, becoming much more prominent and influential than ever before.

In 2008's *Managing Customers for Profit: Strategies to Increase Profits and Build Loyalty,*[25] Dr. Kumar introduced a series of new equations and ideologies. Among them, Customer Brand Value (CBV) and Customer Referral Value (CRV) extend Customer Lifetime Value to anticipate customer behavior and quantify social value and potential profitability. For the purpose of this discussion, and the book in general, let's examine CRV for a moment. Dr. Kumar defines CRV as the ability of managers "to measure and manage each customer based on his ability to generate indirect profit to the firm."

Like Reichheld, Dr. Kumar studied the alacrity of consumer referrals. However, the difference between the work of Reichheld and

Kumar is the extent to which the original question "would you refer this to someone you know" is asked and answered. Dr. Kumar believes that the true value lies in the answer to the question, "did you actually make the referral?" and what happened next: "Did they actually become a customer?"

While businesses analyze the breakdown in activities to improve sCRM, we can identify active voices online, whether or not they're customers or prospects, as the social customer isn't the only candidate and catalyst for advocacy, direction, and action. The true promise and future of relationship management lies among "The Social."

■ VRM + sCRM = SRM

Ross Mayfield, founder of SocialText, developed a versatile dashboard for enterprises seeking to collaborate internally with coworkers and externally with customers and stakeholders. He often references the engagement iceberg,[26] where only a small portion of customer conversations and engagement are truly visible, while most occur beneath the water line and thus, out of view. Mayfield also notes that the nature of the dialogue and how conversations progress throughout the Web usually requires more than one person or department to engage.

As we've covered practically everywhere in this book, each online conversation worthy of response can be directly matched to specific divisions within an organization and usually rank in this order:

1. Support
2. PR
3. Marketing/brand
4. Sales
5. Product development
6. HR

Once we listen, we find conversations inevitably map to specific departments. Thus, the identification and associated nature and sentiment tied to social capture and response mechanisms require purpose and resolve from the specific disciplines they touch and affect. As a result, when we view conversations as they map interdepartmentally, the "C" in sCRM begins to disappear. (See Figure 23.2.)

Thus, the highlights and observations tied to real-time activity demonstrates the reality that every department eventually needs to socialize and thus, much like the divergence between CRM and CRM

Social ~~C~~RM = Social Relationship Management (SRM)

Figure 23.2

2.0 and that of CRM 2.0 and sCRM, sCRM now starts to represent something much bigger than only social customer relationship management.

Therefore customers are now merely part of a larger equation that also balances vendors, experts, partners, and other influencers.

sCRM and CRM look at the value of a customer using a variety of tools and methodologies such as Customer Lifetime Value (CLV) and Customer Lifecycle Management, the value of commerce that can be attributed to the customer relationship over time.

We're moving away from an era of simple listening, monitoring, and responding, to an age of direct engagement (reactive and proactive) in concert with the management of this activity. It's rooted in our ability to essentially become the *person*, not only the *customer*, whom we want to embrace and inspire. As such, existing customers and prospects are only part of a much more sophisticated equation. Or said another way, customers are now playing one of the leading roles in a more elaborate production, sharing the stage with other cast members that represent all facets of business workflow and governing marketplaces.

■ NO BRAND IS AN ISLAND

Social relationships management (SRM) is a credo aligned with a humanized business strategy and supporting technology infrastructure and platform. SRM recognizes that all people, no matter what system they use, are equal. It represents a wider scope of active listening and participation across the full spectrum of influence mapped to specific department representatives within the organization using various lenses for which to identify individuals where and how they interact.

SRM adopts a doctrine that champions:

➤ Collaboration over conversation.
➤ Listening over intermittent searching and research.
➤ Action and resolution instead of monitoring.
➤ Personalization over automation.

Relationships management or SRM is much more than engagement strategies and tactics. It requires completely revamped tenets and infrastructure to support relationships and the necessary empowerment and management through technology and resources.

■ THE EVOLUTION OF RELATIONSHIPS IS JUST BEGINNING

The "now" Web is powerful. The "next" Web is consequential. With each step, we are building new bridges, networks, and channels. The evolution of the Web is absolutely changing the way people communicate, research, and ultimately make decisions.

While sCRM is designed to ensure that proactive and reactive support is pervasive, managed, and streamlined, CRM, as a foundation, is much more than technology. It is representative of a total customer-centric approach and the organization's philosophy for how it views, empowers, and continues to earn the business of its customers.

The migration from CRM 2.0 to sCRM to SRM was fueled by the humanization and democratization of brands and the acceptance that social networks, communities, and tools are important and essential to brand and relationship management. Online conversations and their focus would dictate who should lead these efforts, what rules they need to abide by, as well as the philosophies and commensurate planning and organization of resources and content.

In the Social Web, a brand's perception and reputation is in the hands of the new influencers—those customers, peers, and prospects who leverage social media to voice their views, opinions, and questions. SRM is thus defined by how and when a brand discovers and engages in these discussions, which determine the brand's impact, reach, and resonance.

The true shift represented by the social and real-time Web is not simply the ability to surface relevant conversations as they happen, it represents the opportunity to learn from public sentiment and the indicators that they signal to create a more aware, responsive, and adaptive organization that proactively leads communities through action.

It's not what you say about the brand, it's about what *they* say about it that counts.

Chapter 24

The Contrast between Earned and Paid

When Paying for Friends Makes Cents

Twitter and social networks in general are luring users into a Web of both interconnected and extended connections—forging potentially valuable relationships with the individuals whom we know and those whom we admire, respect, and one day hope to know.

The race to extend one's social graph across the statusphere is laying the groundwork for a more formidable platform to share one's thoughts, opinions, observations, messages, and agenda. This is as true for individuals as it is for marketers, sales organizations, and brands.

■ BUYING FOLLOWERS VERSUS EARNING FRIENDS

As Twitter's civilization personifies the natural tendency to extend the connections that strengthen the network, individuals also share the desire to participate in the expansion. As such, we, as a dedicated online society, grow in prominence.

As personalities, the path between where we are and where we would like to be is defined by our actions and the practices we embody. We have a choice to increase our congregation organically or through prescribed measures. Brands too, face the same crossroads.

Earning friends versus buying followers is a short cut that can quite possibly build stronger, vibrant, and targeted communities.

Yes, the thought of buying followers is questionable at best and, in most cases outside of social networking, it's easy to view it as corrupt.

We've witnessed the onslaught of packaged systems for increasing followers, connections, and even achieving "our dreams" on Twitter and other social networks. In the end however, you get what you pay for. These pyramid and "get rich quick" schemes do not create a sustainable and scalable network that functions as a holistic and dedicated entity tied to a cause or focus.

Trend/keyword marketing or hashtag exploitation are two very different tactics that attempt to yield similar results. Trend and keyword marketing are usually reactive in their composition. Reactive campaigns are rooted in the discovery of online conversations related to particular keywords, for example:

"I'm looking for help with HDTVs."

"I am so upset with X company, their service is absolutely horrible."

"I'm in the market for a new hybrid car."

"Can anyone recommend a great place for pizza around Brighton?"

Someone within the marketing or service departments for related or competitive organizations invests a portion of the day identifying these target conversations and then replies to them in the public timeline with a response aimed at providing resolution, answers, or direction. This practice aims at generating goodwill, advocacy, and, hopefully, new followers and customers.

Companies who do this extremely well include Dell, Comcast, Southwest Air, JetBlue, Virgin America, H&R Block, Wells Fargo, Bank of America, Sprint, Home Depot, Cisco, Panasonic LiHD, and many, many others.

However, there is a dark side to this practice and it is usually driven by shortsightedness, underestimation, greed, lack of respect, or naiveté.

While some are harmless, others are downright abominable.

On the more harmless end of the spectrum, The Home Depot Center (Not Home Depot, but the venue in Southern California sponsored by Home Depot) tracked keywords such as "skateboarding" as a way of promoting an upcoming ESPN X games. Each time a keyword was discovered, the person or team running the @HomeDepotCenter Twitter account would respond with "@username, Skateboarding!!! We love that the @espnxgames are back @TheHomeDepotCenter! Check out HomeDepotCenter for presale code. Follow us!"

While this form of communication is essentially benign, it doesn't necessarily bode well for those users choosing to follow them. If you looked at http://www.twitter.com/homedepotcenter around June 26, 2009, you would have read pages of similar tweets to various individuals. As a follower, each one of these tweets would have appeared in your timeline and would have most likely driven you to *un*follow them.

■ #HASHTAGS

Hashtag marketing can assume either a proactive or reactive model. And unfortunately, in some cases, the examples I'll share (and there are those I don't dare mention) are simply unspeakable.

Hashtags or tags are keywords or terms assigned to a piece of information. This type of metadata helps describe an item and allows it to be found again by browsing or searching. Tags are chosen informally and personally by the item's creator or by its viewer, depending on the system.[1] Hashtags are also used for forming groups, such as #engagebookclub, or for expressing a state of mind, thought, or observation, such as "I am so tired after work, what to do? #timetorelax."

Similar to the reactive nature of conversational/response marketing, reactive hashtag marketing seeks to solve or uncover dialogue related to user-defined topics. While keywords are somewhat similar, #hashtags are user-introduced subjects specifically tied to a theme. For example, if you are having an issue with your cable service, you could tweet, "Ugh, my cable service is out again in Providence. #nameofprovidersucks." If others who are experiencing similar issues see your tweet or update, they could also express frustration and include the same hashtag at the end of their post.

As we've seen over the last two years, @comcastcares has actively monitored conversations related to keywords, tied to or around Comcast, with priority given to those keywords and hashtags such as #comcastsucks or "hate Comcast," in order to solve problems and ultimately convert negative experiences into neutral or positive results. It's this shift in perception that quite possibly converts antagonists into advocates.

■ HASHTAGS: A PROACTIVE APPROACH

Hashtag marketing can also assume a proactive approach when brands deploy campaigns designed to trigger word of mouth around a keyword in the attempt to garner rapid and extensive momentum that earns a spot in Twitter's coveted list of Trending Topics. Initially many startup companies experimented with auto-tweets that would automatically post to Twitter as people registered for new services or downloaded new software applications.

For example, when Co-Tweet, a Twitter client for social CRM applications, and Tweetboard, an embeddable forum for hosting threaded discussions that stem from Twitter, were soliciting new users, they required interested parties to Tweet @cotweet or @tweetboard in the public timeline in order to request access. Eventually the tweets became bona fide trending topics, which carried the companies to a more prominent level of visibility, and also aroused curiosity among those wondering what their friends and peers were tweeting about.

Over time, companies envisioned new, creative methods for igniting trends on Twitter. Moonfruit, a free website creator, stirred things up on Twitter and the blogosphere when it announced a Twitter promotion to celebrate its tenth anniversary. The company announced that it would give away 10 Macbook Pro laptops in 10 days to selected individuals who either retweeted the suggested message proposed by Moonfruit, "Celebrate 10 years of Moonfruit and win a MacBook Pro http://bit.ly/96bxC #moonfruit," or creatively used the #moonfruit hashtag in a tweet. All entrants were encouraged to tweet often to increase their chances of winning. The caveat? They had to follow @moontweet in order to find out if they won.

This program is referred to as a "Tweet to Win" campaign and it's straddling the line between spam and fair game.

Not only did Moonfruit become a trending topic, the account skyrocketed to over 40,000 followers almost immediately and ultimately increased visibility for its Web design services. Did it also increase sales? Yes, it did. The account now hovers just under 30,000.

According to an article in ClickZ,[2] a news and expert advice resource for digital marketers, Moonfruit founder Wendy White was overwhelmed by its success. The promotion resulted in a 600 percent lift in site traffic and doubled user sign-up for service trials in just a few days. "The response has been beyond belief, far more effective than other marketing channels," White reported.

In this case, the company not only amplified its community and potential reach today and in the future, it also extended its value proposition across the social graphs of trusted individuals who opted to tweet as part of the contest. Friends become a powerful catalyst for extending the reach by applying a filter to content. But, they can tarnish friendships and potentially erode confidence if their tweeting is misused. This is something for both brands and individuals to consider—as their participation in these campaigns can have negative impacts on their connections, inadvertently straining relationships by causing an imbalance in the routine that defines an acceptable signal-to-noise ratio.

Twitter is already experimenting with the manual removal of certain trending topics, based on whether or not they're legitimate.

No matter if it's a "Tweet to Win" or a "Tweet to *insert action here*," campaign, gaining friends and followers via a public timeline strategy is a finite strategy without a long-term strategy in place.

■ OFFERS AND SPECIALS

When it comes to earning friends and followers by offering specials via Twitter, no one leads the way quite like @Delloutlet. In June 2009 the company reported over $3 million in sales directly tied to Tweets promoting specials available solely on Twitter.

@delloutlet currently boasts over 1.4 million followers seeking exclusive deals available only on the microcommunity.

However, it's not just the big boys who can brandish authority on Twitter to the tune of tens or even hundreds of thousands of new followers and millions in new sales. Small businesses are demonstrating the power of Twitter and the rewards for giving back to the community as a way of earning friends and followers.

One of the most oft-cited examples of a small business cultivating relationships on Twitter and building a vocal and loyal community is @NAKEDpizza. Backed by Mark Cuban, Naked Pizza is an all-natural and "good for you" pizza joint in New Orleans that bears the motto: "Doing it one day at a time. We care. We really do."

Naked Pizza has earned each and every one of its roughly 5,000 followers on Twitter by Tweeting interesting information (related and unrelated to pizza), recognizing customers, answering questions, and listening to local conversations relevant to their business. Based on listening exercises, Naked Pizza followed the right people and, in turn, many followed them back.

In an interview with *Advertising Age* magazine, Jeff Leach, Naked Pizza cofounder, explained, "Every phone call was tracked, every order was measured by where it came from, and it told us very quickly that Twitter is useful. Sure, there's the brand marketing and getting-to-know-you stuff.... But we wanted to know: Can it make the cash register ring?"[3]

Indeed, it did. On April 23, 2009, the company reported that Twitter accounted for 15 percent of total sales that day.

When Naked Pizza is discussed as a small business that's blazing the trail on Twitter, Berry Chill (@YogiJones) isn't far behind.

Berry Chill has three locations in the Chicago area and uses Twitter to send out "Sweet Tweets" to draw new and existing customers in the door. Typically, the special requires the recipient to show that they're followers on Twitter, and as a reward they can receive discounts or even a free yogurt. One such promotion recorded over 1,100 yogurt giveaways.

Michael Farah, founder and CEO of Berry Chill, attested that Twitter was increasing the customer base and attested to Twitter's use as an inexpensive acquisition tool: "Our last big promotion gave away $5,500 worth of product—but sales were the same as the day before. The people who were existing customers standing in line attracted people who hadn't tried it."

■ PAY PER TWEET

Izea debuted to both accolades and controversy its Sponsoredtwts (@spontwts), a Twitter advertising/pay-for-tweet service that complements its other sponsored conversation, Pay Per Post blog offering. Izea is credited with creating the sponsored conversation market in 2006 with nearly one million conversations funded to date. The company defines sponsored conversations as a social media marketing technique in which brands provide financial or material compensation to bloggers in exchange for posting related content about a product, service, or website on their blog, and now on Twitter, also.

Sponsoredtwts has effectively experimented with several public campaigns that have achieved the goals set forth by the brands that sponsored conversations on Twitter and has helped many companies achieve their objectives and happily serve as referrals to other businesses.

If it's anything similar to its blog program, Izea plans to recruit Twitter users in droves and reward them with monetary compensations or product incentives.

Brands that have successfully used the pay-per-post service include 1-800 Flowers, Beaches Resort, Black&Decker, Bumble Bee Tuna, Disney, Ford, Hamilton Beach, Hewlett Packard, Kmart, Microsoft, MTV, Overstock, Paramount Pictures, and Universal Music.

Izea is not alone in this market. Twittad is a Social Media Affinity Network that connects advertisers and peer-to-peer Twitter users through creative ad campaigns rooted in paid tweets. Paid tweets start at $3 each.

In one campaign, Craftsman Tools turned to Twittad to drive signups and buzz for its NASCAR VIP Pass Giveaway. Craftsman ran the giveaway through multiple advertising channels, and even James Eliason, President/CEO of Twittad, is the first to remind people that the pay-per-tweet model should always be used in conjunction with other forms of online and offline advertising.

Twittad came up with 15 different tweet messages that users could select; this number helped ensure variation in the messages, so that followers wouldn't see the exact same message from multiple users. Each Twittad user sent three tweets during the week-long campaign. Twittad and Craftsman saw multiple retweets and sharing among friends who were fans of NASCAR. Click-throughs were fast and furious for the first five minutes after a tweet was sent and then tapered off from there (as a result, Twittad wisely spaced out accepting users into the campaign, to smooth out the traffic pattern over the seven days).

As for hard results, the numbers are impressive. The Twittad campaign reached 1,575,000 followers on Twitter. And Craftsman saw approximately 4,000 sign-ups as a direct result of the Twitter campaign, as well as growth in followers to their @Craftsmanclub account.

Another pay-per-tweet solution is Ad.ly, a self-service platform for real celebrities including Kim Kardashian, Brooke Burke, Nicole Richie, and Dr. Drew, as well as the Internet famous on Twitter and the advertisers and marketers looking to leverage their social graph, emotional reach, and associated fandom. Tweets range from the low hundreds to several thousand per tweet. Ad.ly CEO Sean Rad is quick to stress the importance of matching the right publisher with the right advertiser. By selectively targeting appropriate celebrities (and their audiences), Ad.ly tweets can successfully tread the line between advertisement and relevant content (although they're always disclosed as paid advertisements).

There are risks involved here that any brand manager should consider before being lured by the promise of word of mouth, celebrity association, and prosperity. It's the differences between visibility and presence, hype and realization, and earned versus paid. Granted, as in any celebrity endorsement campaign, including Weblebrities, a product and brand benefit from the value of association. But since we're referring to words, we must choose them carefully—as well as the voice used to share them, regardless of the stature.

The Federal Trade Commission is monitoring this activity closely to ensure that disclosure is readily visible and comprehendible, whether it's a post or a tweet. The penalties for not properly disclosing that these conversations are sponsored is not only damaging, it's very public.

As a result of the evolving level of influence inherent in the Social Web, the notice incorporates several amendments to the FTC's guidelines concerning the use of endorsements and testimonials in advertising and blogging, which address endorsements by consumers, experts, organizations, and celebrities, as well as the disclosure of important connections between advertisers and endorsers.

In October 2009, the Federal Trade Commission released its final revisions to the guidance it gives advertisers on how to keep their endorsement and testimonial ads in line with the FTC Act. The Guides were last updated in 1980.[4]

■ BUYING FRIENDS AND FOLLOWERS

There are foreseeable benefits and monetization opportunities for those brands and individuals who can build a vibrant and dedicated community organically, as well as through mindful programs that offer compensation and premium perks. However, the question is: How can this process be expedited while still investing in a flourishing network without compromising the brand or consequential relationships within social networks and in the real world? Better yet, how can it be done without alerting the FTC to any potentially questionable practices?

uSocial (http://usocial.net/twitter_marketing/) offers the ability to purchase followers. This company is breaking new ground in the Twitter marketing space, but soon will be one of many follower-focused marketing services to emerge as Twitter gains in popularity and prominence.

While it may seem insincere to "buy" friends, it is, according to uSocial, a completely opt-in process and therefore may make sense for any company looking to ignite its community service for Twitter or any other social network. Technically, you're purchasing a series of individuals who subscribe to receive updates and will still require the same community development work to transcend the community from one of recipients to potentially one of advocates.

Leon Hill, chief executive of uSocial, described the process of finding and recruiting followers as more of a matchmaking service. It starts with searching Twitter and identifying what users are interested in and where they're geographically located. Users are in full control over which accounts they follow and ignore.

At press time, uSocial boasts a roster of over 150[5] customers and offers the following menu of services:

➤ 1,000 followers for $87.

➤ 2,500 followers for $147.

➤ 5,000 followers for $230.

➤ 10,000 followers for $372.

➤ 25,000 followers for $869.

➤ 100,000 followers for $3,479.

uSocial also offers a variety of social marketing services that could help boost visibility based on goals within specific social networks. For example, the company can help brands reach the front page of Digg, Yahoo! Buzz, or any other social bookmarking site. uSocial claims that it can deliver in excess of 100,000 unique visitors in less than 24 hours. Personal experience places that number closer to the range of 10,000–20,000. However, combined services could indeed generate over 100,000 unique visits over the course of a month through a cumulative social marketing campaign.

In the world of traditional marketing, buying or renting lists is not uncommon; in fact, the practice is commonplace. However, the difference between push marketing and social engagement is intention and value. Lists are just lists. Whether we're buying followers, earning them through promotions and special offers, or pushing content to the front page of social bookmarking sites, we are bound by the prevailing ethical and moral boundaries defined in the rules of engagement.

Social media should not be driven by a campaign mindset. This is a long-term strategy that should not fade. Even if some day social media simply becomes synonymous with service and community development and advocacy, the governing principles still apply.

We must continuously ask and answer the question: "Why are we trying to increase our followers?" and then do the things it takes to earn and capture their attention for the long term.

We earn the relationships we deserve.

The New Media Scorecard

Measuring Investment Returns

One of the most fascinating aspects of socialized media is its ability to track and measure almost anything that matters to your business—as it unfolds. With the right tools, we can peel back the layers between the digital and real worlds to reveal the actions, behavior, perception, advocates, influencers, trends, hot zones, and sentiments of the communities that define market places.

Whether you realize it or not, you are already making progress. To ease us into this complex and diverse discussion, I've peppered the materials needed to build a framework for relevant business metrics throughout this book.

In the Social CRM chapter (Chapter 23), we learn how to measure customer value and influence. Earlier in the book we examine the processes associated with identifying and establishing authority. We also review methods for discovering communities of influence and capturing relevant activity in order to institute a measurable Conversation Index. In addition, we learned how to define experiences, establish desired direction, and track and measure activity. Each step forms a foundation of metrics that serve as benchmarks moving forward—focused specifically on the programs and goals as implemented at program and brand levels and organized and managed by chartered business units within the company. After all, while the need to measure initiatives is pervasive, we have no basis for comparison without benchmarks.

There are several schools of thought when it comes to measuring the effectiveness of new media. In this chapter, we'll explore the tools and methodologies that translate activity into tangible value for your business and its management infrastructure.

Our first step, however, is to understand who within the organization is already measuring Web activity and immediately become part of the process. Typically the Web team or data analyst(s) maintain control of valuable online performance information, usually sourced from Web analytic tools such as Omniture or Google Analytics. While they're measuring and seeking data as it relates to the experience of online visitors, much of what they do is aligned with your work. Working together, your roles will adapt to more effectively translate data into business value. This analysis will impact and shape current and future campaigns.

■ THE DISPARITY BETWEEN SOCIAL MEDIA ADOPTION AND MEASUREMENT

While the allure of new media is hypnotizing, bewitching us to leap before looking or fire before aiming, its value and magic are truly revealed in the behavior and ensuing analysis that stems from our involvement.

In its first annual Social Media Survey published in 2009, PRWeek and MS&L discovered that 49 percent of companies do not have a specific approach regarding the use of social media on behalf of the company.[1] Without focus or purpose, what can we possibly measure? Equally interesting and troubling, *66 percent of companies reported that they have not made changes to products or marketing efforts based on customer feedback garnered in the Social Web.*

In the same survey, companies reported the top applications for social media, which demonstrate the opportunities and extent of where measurement can apply and benefit the organization, once it's embraced:

➤ 47 percent: Manage and monitor customer feedback.

➤ 40 percent: Reach key influencers.

➤ 39 percent: Understanding the consumer and competitive landscape.

➤ 32 percent: Creating brand communities and fan pages.

➤ 31 percent: Media relations.

➤ 31 percent: Lead generation.

➤ 28 percent: Product launches.

➤ 19 percent: Product reviews.

➤ 6 percent: Monitoring conversations.

Indeed, we now have the ability to incite change directly and indirectly and track the resulting reactions and responses as they travel from community to community and person to person, transcending the boundaries between the digital and real worlds.

Twitter, for example, is considered a dream come true for marketers and advertisers. A study conducted by Interpret LLC discovered that people who use Twitter are much more receptive to advertising than the average Internet user.[2]

Engaging without analysis is akin to driving aimlessly, without direction or purpose.

Measurement is the key to relevance and future successes.

■ ■ ■

Here are just a few ways that change agents are measuring the ROI of social media:[3]

> ➤ Best Buy measures the ROI of its internal "Blue Shirts Nation" community in terms of lower turnover rates.

> ➤ The National Association of Manufacturers measures the ROI of its blog in terms of greater access to the halls of Capital Hill.

> ➤ Dell measures the success of its IdeaStorm community both in terms of lower support costs and in the number of new ideas generated.

> ➤ SeaWorld reached out to roller-coaster enthusiasts with its social media program and measured its ROI in terms of lower outreach costs as well as tickets sold.

■ ROA: RETURN ON ACRONYMS

One of the most commonly asked questions in new media marketing is often voiced by someone who is usually unqualified to appreciate the response.

You know the question. We hear it all the time.

"What's the ROI of this?"

While many think it, the initial answer is usually suppressed: "I dunno, what's the ROI of anything we do? What's the ROI of customer service? What's the ROI of PR? What's the ROI of branding? What's the return on human resources? While we're at it . . . what's the meaning of life?"

I'm only partially kidding.

What if we asked the question this way: "How can we measure ROI if the 'I' stands for ignorance?"

As I always say, ignorance is bliss until it's not.

The truth is that we need to have answers. The good news is that the answers are available. If we don't know them, we must seek them. We just need to know what to look for and where.

In traditional business return on investment is calculated by dividing net profits after taxes by total assets.[4] For example, if you invested $50,000 and the investment was worth $75,000 after two years, your annual return on investment would be 25 percent. To get that result, you divide the $25,000 gain by your $50,000 investment, and then divide the 50 percent gain by 2.

In new media, ROI now also includes:

➤ **Return on participation, return on engagement, or return on involvement:** The review of activities, patterns, reactions, and results associated with direct interaction or through social objects.

➤ **Return on experience:** The analysis of the effects of experience through design aesthetics, engagement, and words.

➤ **Return on influence:** The study of the impact of influence as it reverberates across communities and resulting behavior.

While experts play with the "I" in ROI or x in ROx to reflect other measurement scenarios, in order to truly garner insight and value from the gauging of our activities, we must first define the "R," or return. Defining the "R" allows us to analyze behavior and activity as it applies to the business. Return on investment is a bona fide analysis related to business finances. Its value is indisputable—even in the seemingly elusive world of social media.

This is done initially by asking a handful of simple questions:

➤ What are we measuring and why?

➤ What does success look like?

➤ How will we know when we get there?

➤ Are there incremental milestones worth noting?

➤ Who else within the organization benefits from our work and how would they measure meaningful results?

Observing the literal translation of the "I" as investment, we must also factor in the corporate assets that power any and all business initiatives:

➤ Intellectual capital
➤ Resources
➤ Finances
➤ Campaign costs

As inexpensive as social media is considered to be in comparison to traditional programs, there are always fixed costs associated with any activity.

In June 2008, I published an early formula for calculating the "I" in ROI based on the research results from the Conversation Prism and Index studies.[5]

■ THE ESSENTIAL GUIDE TO SOCIAL MEDIA: RESOURCES—PERSONNEL AND BUDGETS

➤ Activities to Meter

➤ The average frequency of relevant conversations.
➤ Identify the more active hubs and communities.
➤ The context of the conversations in order to determine time and variety of resources required.

➤ Resource Assessment Formula

Number of average relevant conversations per day per community.

Multiplied by the quantity of relevant communities.

Multiplied by 20 (average minutes required to research and respond and also monitor for additional responses), variable +/– dependent on the case, usually +.

Divided by 60 (minutes).

Equals the amount of time required and in turn, the resources and associated costs required depending on internal labor (salaries/hourly rates), external consulting fees, plus cost of equipment and other necessary resources.

■ THE SOCIAL BAROMETER

Over the years, I have established the criterion to measure my work as it specifically relates to the companies and the business units each custom initiative was designed to benefit. Along the way, I have also maintained a spectator perspective, as I've documented the evolution of the interactive media landscape. Much of this is so new and exciting that businesses are diving in out of perceived or defined urgency without investing resources in acquiring, assessing, and embracing existing and modern techniques for evaluating participatory programs.

However, there are best practices tied to soft and explicit metrics that we can implement to justify and judge our work. Depending on the level of sophistication and also primary focus and purpose of your business, the combination of these calculations will vary in relevance and importance.

As we assess the methodologies, formulas, and criteria required for creating a blueprint for measurement, we must identify the attributes that are important to the organization as well as those that will receive buy-in at the departmental and executive level.

Don Bartholomew, a social media and public relations research and measurement consultant, observed that communications professionals, for example, often confuse "outputs" with "outtakes" or "outcomes"—basically confusing exposure with action.

He proposed a metrics taxonomy to help us truly understand our mission for measurement:[6]

Exposure: To what degree have we created exposure to content and message?

Engagement: Who, how, and where are people interacting/engaging with our content?

Influence: The degree to which exposure and engagement have influenced perceptions and attitudes.

Action: As a result of the effort, what actions, if any, has the target taken?

Bartholomew also defined three zones of measurement: "websites" on the left side (measured by Web analytics), "social networks" in the center (measured by content and behavior analysis) and "offline" on the right side (captured by audience research):

From the left, companies or brands control, own, or manage websites—corporate sites, Facebook pages, Twitter accounts, LinkedIn pages, and blogs by way of example—and create content that consumers may engage with. This zone is measured primarily by Web analytics. In the middle are the actual social networks and conversations between individuals. In this zone we are interested in data sets that cannot be gathered solely using Web analytics packages. How often is the brand being mentioned in conversation? What is the sentiment of the comments? How often is the brand being recommended and by whom? Content and behavior analysis, including tracking technologies, are the primary measurement tools in this zone. The third zone represents all the real-world, offline transactions that may be of interest. Did someone visit the store or attend an event? Did they buy a product? Did they recommend the brand or product to a friend over coffee?

■ START WITH THE RESULTS, THEN WORK BACKWARD: DEFINING GOALS AND OBJECTIVES

We can't measure what we do not recognize as value. We cannot measure success if we don't know what success looks like. It is for these very reasons that we must first establish our day-to-day programs and incremental campaigns around the end-result—as shaped by the research work performed in the listening and observation stages of the Conversation Prism.

The queen of measurement, K.D. Paine (Katie Delahaye Paine), observed that the importance value of social media is what happens because of it. Therefore she suggests that we actually consider dropping "Media" from social media when it comes to measuring its effects.[7]

K.D. recognizes that the metrics required for measuring the effectiveness of social media are new and different from anything currently used in marketing: "We need to be working closely with the data geeks and the market research folks and measure the things that happen faster and better because of social networking."

K.D. outlined a change in business habits and efficiency as a foundation for metrics:

➤ Process improvement
➤ Time to market
➤ Number of new product ideas
➤ Number of suggestions

➤ Length of time it takes to find a solution to a problem

➤ Efficiency with which a product is launched

➤ Level of social capital

➤ Churn rates among your customers and/or employees

➤ Cost of recruitment

Therefore, establishing objectives and tying activity back to the results we desire both require planning and calculation.

To help, K.D. Paine created an immensely helpful Measurement Program Checklist (edited to reflect the lessons shared in this book).[8]

MEASUREMENT PROGRAM CHECKLIST BY K.D. PAINE

Step 1: What Are Your Objectives?

1. What are your organization's key goals for this year?

2. What are your department's key goals for this year?

3. What do you hope to accomplish with your measurement report?

➤ Get budget approved.

➤ Increase budget.

➤ Increase head count.

➤ Get more internal support.

➤ Get more external support.

➤ Justify my existence.

➤ Get a raise.

➤ Get promoted.

Step 2: What Audiences Are You Targeting?

List all that apply, not just the following common ones. (If in doubt, put all the executives and marketing people in your organization in a room and ask them.)

➤ Media

➤ Prospects

➤ Customers

➤ Partners
➤ Employees
➤ Governments
➤ NGOs
➤ Communities
➤ Investors
➤ Thought leaders
➤ International community
➤ Other

How does a good relationship with your various target audiences benefit your organization?

1. Increases sales.
2. Increases attendance.
3. Increases donations.
4. Increases likelihood of desirable legislation passing.
5. Increases preference.
6. Increases awareness.
7. Improves employee retention.
8. Improves employee loyalty.
9. Improves customer retention.
10. Improves customer loyalty.
11. Improves likelihood of purchase.
12. Attracts new customers.
13. Attracts new prospects (Lead generation).
14. Attracts new donors/potential donors.
15. Increases amount of purchase.
16. Increases frequency of purchase.
17. Boosts stock price.
18. Increases profitability.
19. Reduces turnover.
20. Decreases time to market.
21. Decreases number of complaints.
22. Decreases absenteeism.

Step 3: Set Priorities

Prioritize your audiences with this exercise: You have a total of 100 points to allocate. Award those points to the audiences that you have identified in order of their importance to your organization, based on your answers to questions in Step 2.

Step 4: Determine a Benchmark

Who or what keeps your boss/client up at night? In other words, what are the competitive threats or perceived competitive threats to your organization? Select from the following list to determine what you will be comparing your results to:

➤ Competitor(s)/peer companies

➤ Industry benchmarks

➤ Yourself over time

➤ Last year's results

➤ Last quarter's sales and/or Web/commerce metrics

Step 5: Select the Right Measurement Tool

If your objectives (see Step 1) include "increase awareness," improve products/service "attitude change" or "education," you will need to conduct an online audit in social media to determine the state and establish a benchmark.

If you are seeking to measure sales and leads, you should be tracking website traffic and conferring with the sales team to document numbers, referring sources, and existing hurdles. If you are measuring influencer relations, or presence, you will need to consider the following criteria in your measurement efforts:

➤ Tone of coverage.

➤ Share of voice versus the competition.

➤ Share of discussion versus the competition.

➤ Share of spokesperson visibility.

➤ Degree to which you have communicated key messages.

➤ Degree to which you are favorably or unfavorably positioned on key issues.

➤ Audience reached.

➤ Prominence of coverage—the visibility of your brand within the story.

➤ Dominance of coverage—the extent to which your brand dominates the coverage or is subservient to another brand.

➤ Proactive versus reactive media.

➤ Key analysts quoted.

➤ Type of analyst quoted.

➤ Important trust agents and tastemakers.

➤ Key reporters.

➤ Key publications, blogs, and communities.

➤ Key topics or subjects.

➤ Key message and value propositions, list below:

1. _____

2. _____

➤ Prominence:

   ➤ Employer of choice

   ➤ Investment of choice (financial strength)

   ➤ Vendor of choice (good/best value for the money)

   ➤ Environmentally responsible

   ➤ Market and thought leadership

   ➤ Other:_____

➤ Influencers and key spokespeople:

   ➤ Company spokespeople (provide names)

   _____

   ➤ Competitors' spokespeople (provide names if available) _____

   ➤ Industry analysts

   ➤ Financial analysts

   ➤ Government officials

   ➤ Educators

   ➤ Other

Pat LaPointe at Marketing Measurement Today developed a framework for approaching social measurement in response to one of the most common questions he faced: "How should I measure the value of all the social marketing things we're doing, like Twitter, Linked-in, Facebook, and so forth?"

LaPointe's answer was as commonsensical as it was poignant, "*Why* are you doing them in the first place? If you can't answer that, you're wasting your time and the company's money."[9]

SOCIAL MEASUREMENT FRAMEWORK BY PAT LAPOINTE

1. Fill in the blanks: "Adding or swapping-in social media initiatives will impact _____ by _____ extent over _____ timeframe. And when that happens, the added value for the business will be $_____, which will give me an ROI of _____. This forms your hypotheses about what you might achieve, and why the rest of the business should care.

2. Identify all the assumptions implicit in your hypotheses and "flex" each assumption up/down by 50 percent to 100 percent to see under which circumstances your assumptions become unprofitable.

3. Identify the most sensitive assumption variables—those that tend to dramatically change the hypothesized payback by the greatest degree based on small changes in the assumption. These are your key uncertainties.

4. Enhance your understanding of the sensitive assumptions through small-scale experiments constructed across broad ranges of the sensitive variables. Plan your experiments in ways you can safely *fail*, but mostly in ways to help you understand clearly what it would take to *succeed*—even if that turns out to be unprofitable upon further analysis. That way, you will at least know what won't work, and change your hypotheses in #1 above accordingly.

5. Repeat steps 1 thru 4 until you have a model that seems to work.

6. In the process, the drivers of program success will become very obvious. Those become your key metrics to monitor.

The frameworks proposed by K.D. Paine and Pat LaPointe represent methodical approaches to help us assess performance as compared to expectations with tangible business performance metrics.

■ AUTHORITY: THE ABILITY TO GALVANIZE ACTION AND QUANTIFY IT

Revisiting influence as I define it (the ability to inspire action and measure it), essentially the world of metrics opens up new opportunities well beyond company mentions and traditional website analytics. Suddenly "hits" or mentions mean very little if we are not observing what happens after the impression is made. Measuring traffic, hits, views, and referring sources requires purpose, a front-end in which we can engage, define and capture measurable activity, monitor, assess, and adapt. It is important to focus on performance and establish our key performance indicators (KPI) in advance, which will allow us to track progress and execution of our programs.

In social media, performance data is typically organized as follows (whether intentionally or unintentionally):

➤ Volume

➤ Engagement

➤ Action

Remember, no matter how many formulas you review or trends you observe, in order for metrics to be accurate and meaningful, they have to apply to your world. Therefore any combination of Volume, Engagement, and Action can define success and failure, which ultimately determines your level of authority and influence.

➤ Volume

Volume is symbolic of brand presence, the frequency with which it appears, its amplification, and its reach across the Web. It represents the extent to which your brand appears and resonates online, as defined by the communities, conversations, and people behind the surrounding activity.

In order to better understand how to recognize and quantify volume, we must define the characteristics and associated attributes with defining individual value:

➤ **Dialogue:** The quantity of discussions transpiring in the front and back channels, taking the shape of questions, answers, suggestions, and general interaction around the brand, as documented by networks and the Social Web as a whole.

➤ **Themes/memes:** Trends, topics, and discussion threads related to the brand, without direct influence from the brand.

➤ **SEO and SMO:** Linkbacks and links to the brand site, page, or a branded social object with value symbolized in the form of Page Rank, Relevance, and Authority.

➤ **Sentiment:** The perception of the state of the brand at any moment in time—the process of attempting to shift sentiment in the "conversion" section is the difference between volume and action.

➤ **Customer satisfaction:** The state of customer fulfillment and gratification (see details in Chapter 23).

➤ **Audience:** The size of individual communities, networks, and social graphs, measured independently as well as in aggregate.

➤ **Engagement**

One of the most compelling aspects of interactive media is represented in the moniker that I just used: interactive media. It's indicative of two-way exchanges and it's measurable as such. I describe engagement as the time spent with the brand, either individually, in a community environment, or through direct interaction. Engagement metrics are captured through the impact garnered from conversations with brand representatives, time spent viewing or taking action around social objects, as well as browsing, viewing, and interfacing with branded online content.

Engagement can include:

➤ **Conversations:** Direct exchanges tied to the brand, represented through comments, blog posts, Tweets, and Retweets, wall posts, and shares—as eConsultancy says, "An engaged customer is a highly valuable one."[10]

➤ **Time:** The duration spent viewing or interacting with the brand, a social object, or content, from widgets to pages to profiles to conversations.

➤ **Social graph/relationships:** The size and shape of a social network tied to a person or a brand, measured by quality and quantity.

➤ **Fans/followers:** The number of individuals subscribed to receive the updates in social networks and communities.

➤ **Interaction:** The level in which people contribute information, social objects, and other content to brand hosted communities and networks.

➤ **Registrations:** Individuals who proactively register or subscribe to information, content, offers, and so forth.

➤ **Bookmarking:** The process of publicly sharing favorite content through social bookmarks, "favorites," and "likes" (which are all discoverable and calculable).

➤ **Traffic:** The cumulative activity directly at or around a site, page, profile, or social object.

➤ **Views:** Less about Web pages or more specifically tied to the viewing of specific social objects, such as videos, images, and widgets.

➤ **Shares:** The act of sharing content and objects across the Social Web.

➤ **Immersion:** The depth of interaction or engagement with online content, applications, conversations, or social objects.

➤ **Conversion**

Action is profound in both its value to the bottom line and in its ability to reveal and convey meaningful and discernible statistics. The ability to capture and measure action, if tied to calculated social programs, and meaningful business metrics is among the most salient forms of assessing return on investment as a true performance equation. Whereas volume and engagement capture the state of brand perception engagement and presence, action reveals the activities that directly contribute to business health and profitability. This is why social media programs should feature carefully designed calls to action combined with the ability to capture and analyze the data on the backend—in real time.

Quantifiable data points and key performance indicators and measurable tactics can include:

➤ **Conversions:** The process of transforming individuals from one state to something of greater value, such as prospects and visitors into customers, or customers into advocates.

➤ **Click-throughs:** Crossing the chasm between social presences and objects to branded sites and microsites rife with calls to action—transcending from the virtual into real-world customers and users.

➤ **Offers:** Social media is expected to be a tremendous catalyst for individualized deals, discounts, exclusive offers, specials for products, services, and also local transactions. Airlines are measuring the response for special fares they offer in social networks; local businesses are documenting responses tied to specialized programs designed to lure prospects and transform them into customers; these efforts link to sales as a metric.

➤ **Ratings:** Customer review sites are repositories for brand experiences and sentiment, without astroturfing these sites, customers can be encouraged and directed to share positive thoughts.

➤ **Increased sales:** If @delloutlet can attribute approximately $3 million directly to its twitter stream, Blendtec can recognize a 500 percent increase in sales, and other brands can realize increased revenue through its engagement specifically in the Social Web, integrating social programs and barometers designed to trigger and capture sales is within your grasp.

➤ **Data capture/registrations:** Growing lists of targeted prospects and customers is ideal for increasing relationships as well as direct communications channels—the number of individuals who share information either goes up or down based on your activity.

➤ **Conversations/share of voice:** As discussed previously, conversations and share of voice are identifiable and measurable, providing a lens and revealing the state of presence and sentiment as a solitary number or in comparison to competition at any point in time, over time.

➤ **Sentiment conversion:** While sentiment is a reflection of volume and state, the act of shifting sentiment is a strategy and tactic that is both identifiable and measurable

➤ **Customer/acquisition/retention/referrals/loyalty:** Customer interaction and recognition improves satisfaction, loyalty, and future revenue—assessing the cost of customer acquisition and retention using other forms of marketing and service programs and media compared to the costs associated with your social programs. As a metric, Zappos.com (a wholly owned subsidiary of Amazon.com) reports that 75 percent of its annual $1 billion in sales are from repeat customers.[11]

➤ **Lead generation:** The number of new prospects acquired through specific new media initiatives compared to other programs and dedicated performance.

➤ **Feedback/change:** Capturing thoughts and feedback through online voting and survey initiatives can be measured in change and interaction—the value of a brilliant idea is priceless.

➤ **Visitors/traffic:** Whether we're pointing people to a particular place or steering activity and responses based on our interaction, traffic is measurable and indicative of interest and movement.

➤ **Downloads:** The number of people who get something in exchange for something, for example, a downloaded widget, custom wallpaper, a white paper, coupon upon completion of registration, following, becoming a fan, and so forth.

➤ **New markets:** The establishment of new markets and channels based on engagement in nicheworks.

➤ **Participation/membership:** Capturing affinity is instantaneous in its results and value, designing programs around membership drives (such as a fan page, group, etc.) reveals the growth rate of a community (dialogue and interaction also become factors).

➤ **Cost savings/avoidance:** What did the company save by applying feedback and insight gleaned from the Social Web, solicited through either feedback or direct interaction.

■ THE Cs OF MEASURING ACTION THROUGH COST

Yes, more Cs! For those in the online marketing and advertising world, this section will be remedial. However, since social and participatory methodologies and programs are transforming many disciplines within the business, we are creating hybrids of professionals who now need to become a jack-of-all-trades as well as a master of some.

The Cs in this case refer to cost, which can represent the "I" in ROI, as it serves as a benchmark for measuring the true price associated with activity—taking the form of monetary and resource assets. Their meaning and value in the era of interactive media is often debated, but using the law of "it depends," any one or combination of these Cs can help you measure what specifically matters to your business.

Cost per impression (CPM): The cost of acquiring eyeballs through impressions. Payment is often triggered by mutually agreeing upon activities such as a click-through, registration, sale, and so on. The CPM deal is calculated by multiplying the CPM rate by the number of CPM units. For example, one million impressions at $10 CPM equals a total price of $10,000. The amount paid per impression is calculated by dividing the CPM by 1,000—for example, $10 CPM/1,000 impressions = $.01 per impression.[12]

Cost per click (CPC): The cost or cost-equivalent paid per click-through or a campaign where payment is based on impressions, not clicks. For example, impressions are sold for $10 CPM with a click-through rate (CTR) of 2 percent. 1,000 impressions × 2 percent CTR = 20 click-throughs. $10 CPM/20 click-throughs = $.50 per click.[13]

Click-through rate (CTR): The analysis of activity that sends a viewer from one place to a place of designation. It is the average number of click-throughs per hundred ad impressions, usually expressed as a percentage. The CTR measures the percentage of people who clicked through a media asset to arrive at a destination site. It is used as a measure of immediate response, but not to show the overall response.

Social media is encouraging metrics that identify real business value, resulting in less interest in click-through rates and more interest in conversion rates. Active and high click-through rates don't necessarily guarantee good conversion rates, with the two rates often sharing an inverse relationship.[14]

Eric Von Coelln, who evaluates the numbers behind social media marketing and gaming, assessed the click-through rates after tweets to benchmark engagement. Von Coelln analyzed tweets that contained links from powerhouse brands, including @Zappos, @JetBlue, @SouthwestAir, and @ZyngaPoker. His study found that 1 to 3 percent of active followers actually click-through to view the content.[15] Hence, CTR in this case didn't necessarily amount to much more than a benchmark number, but if we explored the activity that transpired after the click-through, we could assess conversion rates or, as you see next, the ability to recognize the effects of social actions.

Cost per action (CPA): A model in which payment is based solely on qualifying actions such as sales or registrations. The actions defined in a CPA agreement are tied to conversion, with sales and registrations representing the most common transactions. The CPA model resides at the opposite end of the C spectrum from CPM, with the CPC somewhere in the middle.[16] Affiliate marketing, for example, is one of the most often referred to performance-based models, where merchants and advertisers determine what actions they choose to reward and how much they are willing to pay for that activity.

Cost per engagement (CPE): CPE is a performance-based metric that assumes advertising impressions are free. Advertisers and marketers only pay based on user engagement, wherein a prospect interacts with the content. Examples include polling, games, rollovers, tours, downloads, and so forth.

Another form of CPE is analyzing the fixed costs associated with existing resources such as employees, contractors, and services. We can measure time associated with activity designed to produce results or drive action. Knowing the cost of time spent to yield an outcome gives us the ability to capture and assess engagement over time as it relates to specific goals.

■ THE ENGAGEMENT PHASE

New media is an equalizing medium. As such, the social objects and engagement strategies that are introduced through online communities provide much more value than exposure and branding.

In one such case, David Berkowitz, senior director of emerging media and innovation at 360i, proposed CPSA,[17] a new pricing model for social media that factors the cost per social action. CPSA is connected to distinct social qualities that lead to either new relationships (such as through "viral" referrals or acquiring new followers and fans) or deepening existing relationships (such as through "likes," comments, responses, and ratings). Berkowitz proposed that the primary benefit of CPSA is that it offers marketers a program where they know that they are paying specifically for social and relationship-oriented programs.

Engagement value and presence differ from network to network and from community to community. For example, the rate at which people are exposed to and thus interact with an object or person in Twitter is different from the rate in MySpace, which is different from YouTube or Facebook. Embedding calculated and productive action within any existing framework allows you to capture a "cost per social action," not as a standard industry metric, but as a form of tailored measurement within predefined and understood paradigms. That activity can be measured within each network regardless of the "C" program mentioned previously, as well as in the "free" programs we pursue through direct engagement—responding, interacting, sharing content, introducing objects, and so on.

Procter & Gamble became one of the first companies to launch a results-based online ad model that rewards publishers for consumer engagement.[18] P&G, which owns brands such as Gillette, Pampers, and Pantene, will offer financial incentives for publishers where its campaigns receive greater engagement, beyond ad or content views, sign-ups, game play, and so on. The move essentially forces publishers to assume a proactive role in embracing accountability and also inspiring creativity to effectively partner with brands to cultivate meaningful interactions with audiences.

In response to P&G's announcement, Jack Wallington, program manager at the Internet Advertising Bureau (IAB), seemed to support

P&G, but added a note of caution: "It's not the way the whole market is heading, but looking at more than traffic is a good thing. But even with CPE and other statistics, people are missing a trick in terms of branding power. Even if users don't click-through, they could still be engaged. I hope P&G takes that into consideration."[19]

Jerry Lloyd-Williams, digital strategy director at U.K.-based media agency Mediacom, believes that CPE requires accountability, making the media buy a more collaborative experience. Mediacom, for instance, worked with Volkswagen and *Times Online* to create a CPE campaign, "A Life More Streamlined," for the Volkswagen Passat. The *Times Online* was compensated each time a person watched a video, listened to a podcast, or downloaded material.[20]

The data, of course, changes from network to network, but it is this information that must be uncovered through industry research or through direct consumer analysis to create an internal benchmark for your activity.

Charlene Li, founder of the Altimeter Group and former social analyst at Forrester Research, conducted a social engagement review in conjunction with Wetpaint of the 100 most valuable brands, as identified by *BusinessWeek*/Interact.[21] The ENGAGEMENTdb 2009 Report observed the engagement programs as well as their performances.[22]

The team critiqued the brands on the extent (breadth) of engagement across the Social Web as well as level of engagement (depth), such as whether they reply to comments made on blog posts or respond to consumers on Twitter, and so forth. Each brand was given a numerical score.

The top 10 ENGAGEMENTdb brands with their scores in 2009 were:

1. Starbucks (127)
2. Dell (123)
3. eBay (115)
4. Google (105)
5. Microsoft (103)
6. Thomson Reuters (101)
7. Nike (100)
8. Amazon (88)
9. SAP (86)
10. Tie: Yahoo!/Intel (85)

As we're enthralled in the exploration of engagement metrics such as CPE, social actions, or engagement, the ENGAGEMENTdb report did find a correlation between engagement and financial performance.

But even more interesting is that we also looked at the financial performance of the brands, grouping the companies with the greatest depth and breadth into a group called "Social Media Mavens." These mavens *on average* grew 18 percent in revenues over the last 12 months, compared to the least engaged companies who *on average* saw a decline of 6 percent in revenue during the same period. The same holds true for two other financial metrics, gross margin and net profit.

The metrics we establish are derivative of the mission, purpose, and presence we embody throughout the organization and are truly measured by how our intentions are conveyed through the champions and advocates we empower. This sentiment and philosophy is echoed in Li's introduction of the ENGAGEMENTdb report:[23]

The study also looks at the engagement best practices of four companies: Starbucks, Dell, SAP, and Toyota. Some of the key findings include:

➤ *Emphasize quality, not just quantity.*

Engagement is more than just setting up a blog and letting viewers post comments; it's more than just having a Facebook profile and having others write on your wall. Don't just check the box; engage with your customer audience.

➤ *To scale engagement, make social media part of everyone's job.*

The best practice interviews have a common theme—social media is no longer the responsibility of a few people in the organization. Instead, it's important for everyone across the organization to engage with customers in the channels that make sense—a few minutes each day spent by every employee adds up to a wealth of customer touch points.

➤ *Doing it all may not be for you—but you must do something.*

Start you must, or risk falling far behind other brands, not only in your industry, but across your customers' general online experience.

➤ *Find your sweet spot.*
Engagement can't be skin-deep, nor is it a campaign that can be turned on and off. True engagement means full engagement in the channels where you choose to invest. Thus, choose carefully and advocate strongly to acquire the resources and support you will need to succeed.

We're learning that social media engagement is tied to all outbound forms of marketing, service, communications, branding, and relationship management. It's less about talking "at" people and more about collaboration and movement, which offer more value and quality to people on both sides of the equation and thus ensures measurable impact.

■ THE RAZORFISH SOCIAL INFLUENCE SCORE

In mid-2009, branding, social, and experiential marketing and advertising firm Razorfish released a Social Influence Marketing Report.[24] In the report, Razorfish proposed a Social Influence Score. Global Social Media leader Shiv Singh described the new metric as an attempt to bring clarity to the chaos: "Brands . . . can't just push messages out. Whatever they do or don't do, they need to measure."

The score is the representation of online conversations related to a brand and then further categorized by brand and comparative industry sentiment. It is designed to capture the state of brand health.

The formula is as follows:

1. Calculate the total number of conversations regarding a brand.
2. Categorize by sentiment (positive, neutral, and negative).
3. Subtract the number of negative mentions from the sum of positive and neutral comments.
4. Divide the resulting number by the total number of conversations—this produces the net sentiment.
5. Divide brand-specific net sentiment by 100 times the net sentiment attributed to each industry to produce the SIM score. Example of the SIM Score for GM

Net Sentiment for the Brand:
  Positive Conversations: 22,355
  Neutral Conversations: 80,764

Negative Conversations: 19,127
Total Conversations for the Brand: 122,246
Positive + Neutral – Negative Conversations:
  103,119 – 19,127 = 83,992
Net Sentiment/Total Conversations:
  83,992/122,246 = 0.68
Net Sentiment for the Industry:
  Positive Conversations: 399,431
  Neutral Conversations: 1,465,720
  Negative Conversations: 241,372
  Total Conversations for the Industry: 2,106,523
Positive + Neutral – Negative Conversations:
  1,865,151 – 241,372 = 1,623,779
Net Sentiment/Total Conversations:
  1,623,779/2,106,523 = 0.77
SIM Score:
  83,992/1,623,779 = 0.051 × 100 = 5

■ SHARE OF VOICE

Another way to establish brand health and establish share of voice now and over time is to use the techniques shared in the chapter discussing the Conversation Prism and Conversation Index.

It recognizes the state of awareness and reputation to not only measure, but also to inspire rapid evolution.

By listening to the conversations on the Social Web, we can capture the following data using a period of time (a particular month for example):

1. Number of conversations related to brand/product within all relevant networks (blogs, Twitter, Facebook, etc.).
   a. Categorize conversations by networks of relevance.
   b. Sorted by business unit (Marketing, Service, Product, Communications, etc.).
2. Sentiment (Positive, Neutral, Negative).
3. Repeat this process for key competitors.

This data should be captured in the form of a matrix or report so that we can refer to it every month.

To determine Share of Voice and the State of Sentiment, we simply capture the total number of conversations and organize it as such:

Share of Voice: Total Conversations in the Social Web compared to brand/competitor share:
➤ Your brand represents X percent
➤ Competitor A = X percent
➤ Competitor B = X percent
➤ Competitor C = X percent
➤ Competitor D = X percent
➤ Total = 100 percent

Sentiment Score:
➤ Total positive, neutral, or negative conversations divided by total number of conversations, including positive, neutral, and negative for a particular span of time (example: 12,000 positive conversations divided by 25,000 total number of conversations = 48 percent).
➤ Compare results to competitors for each state of sentiment.

■ COMPARATIVE DATA ANALYSIS

In almost every form of measurement, the need for comparative data is prevalent. At the campaign and brand level, a snapshot of time and activity is necessary to serve as a benchmark related to the state of brand-specific activity as well as that of the competition. Whether it's the Conversation Index, the Social Influence Score, or existing data that reveals sentiment, traffic, and activity volume, sales, action, competitive intelligence, and so forth, we must first establish a benchmark for every program by which to compare future socialization of resources and objects.

For example, how much are you paying now to acquire customers and prospects or market share using other marketing channels and using the preceding metrics?

Everything we discuss and review serves as the base to compare our work and results to internal initiatives and in direct comparison to the efforts of our competitors. Thus, we learn and adapt to create more engaging and holistic programs that are measurable and versatile. By defining what it is we need to grow, we can determine what it is we need to measure, which dictates the social programs we employ and how we ultimately engage.

In the end, the best thing to measure is the predefined activity you plan on capturing. Give them something to talk about. Give them a reason to connect. Moniter, document, and measure everything that happens as a result.

Conclusion

And here we are...

You and I have traveled a great distance to reach this point in time and place—collaboratively reaching a state of higher awareness and wisdom in our odyssey. You are to be commended and hopefully rewarded for your commitment and investment in deciphering this perpetually transforming new media landscape. Remember, you play an active role in its evolution and definition. As we've learned, new media is a great journey in which the destination is immaterial, but the stops along the way account for everything. The intelligence you've absorbed up to now and all that you will master through practice in the time to come shapes your professional and personal future and fortune.

I'd like to take this opportunity to leave you with a few parting thoughts before we continue our expedition together in the other mediums that follow this book. Remember, the companion site for this book, http://www.areyouengaged.com, will include many lessons and stories that did not make the final cut for the book, as well as current stories that continue to capture and define the progress of interactive media. The site will serve as a resource to continue your education through examples, best practices, observations, and updates, as well as providing you with any additional resources you will need to effectively support your efforts as you blaze new trails.

■ YOU ARE MORE INFLUENTIAL THAN YOU MAY REALIZE

As a result of reading this book and embracing the principles, lessons, and methodologies contained within, you have effectively pondered and assimilated the ethics of the new media movement that resonate

347

with you today and will reverberate throughout your work tomorrow. Indeed, the future of new media is up to you. As such, we must strive for higher standards through innovation, accountability, purpose, and the ongoing sharing of our knowledge to improve the foundation for new media literacy.

While I've shared case studies and examples in this book and also in the companion site, remember that those stories are merely illustrations for what's possible in the context of the business and established goals and metrics designed to measure their effectiveness. The true purpose of this book is tied to the ripe opportunities that await your creativity and brilliance. New media thrives on its interdependence with cutting-edge technology systems and new ideas. The channels and tools for communicating are always changing, but it's the people we are trying to reach and the laws of communication and behavior that remain constant. Their actions and words tell us everything we need to know. It is your responsibility and duty to build the bridges between your communities and your brand and mission, inspired by prevailing case studies and as guided by your intuition.

The problem with creativity is that it's usually constrained by spoken and unspoken rules that govern the process of ingenuity.

If I host a brainstorming session and place a box in the middle of the room and say, "Here's a box, now think outside of it," I unwittingly place parameters around your imagination. Sometimes brilliance is channeled through our fieldwork, without the limitations of the proverbial "box" that's placed before us.

Therefore there is no box.

As we draw our experiences in this book to a close, the truth is that our partnership is only beginning. I look forward to connecting with you online and in person one day soon.

I'm grateful for this opportunity to share my experiences with you. In the process of writing this book, I too have learned a great deal. So thank you.

All that's separating you from where you are and where you want to be is time and experience. Your dedication, aspiration, and motivation already serve as the foundations for success. It's why you're here.

Now, let's get to work.

Glossary

Aggregator: A tool, application, or process, that pulls together multiple feeds from content sites and brings them together in one place.

Astroturfing: A synthetic "grassroots" effort; a falsely positioned, paid, or deceptive campaign to generate buzz, visibility, and word of mouth (WOM).

Authenticity: The practice of being authentic, true, and genuine in online interactions.

Authority: Someone who is an expert or recognized pundit or influencer on a particular subject.

Authority (2): The stature earned for a person, blog, content, destination, or network as measured by linkbacks (links to the particular destination) or connections (friends/followers) or comments, views, or tweetbacks (retweets or tweets of reference), or votes/thumbs up/+1s/Diggs, or a combination of some or all of the above.

Being Yourself/Being Human: Part of the problem associated with social media is disingenuous behavior. Social media thrives on authenticity and sincerity. The practice of being human, being yourself, or disclosing that the persona is representative of something else that's calculated and intended. Anonymous interaction is discouraged and usually disregarded.

Blogroll: A list of related, inspiring, relevant, or friendly blogs as listed on any given blog.

Brand-Jacked: The act of assuming the presence of a person or brand in social networks. Squatting (taking or assuming a username before the true brand owner can grab it) in any given network is also a form of brandjacking.

Brandstream: This is a trademarked term used to describe a brand's use of an activity stream or lifestream.

Citizen Journalism: Everyday people reporting on news, events, and experiences through blogs, microblogs, micromedia, video, audio, comments, and so forth.

Cloud: The cloud is essentially a metaphor for the Internet. It ties to cloud computing and serves as the backbone and hosting infrastructure for social media applications, services, and networks. The cloud can host online applications, services, published content, storage, data, user information, and so forth.

Cloud Computing: Any application or service that is hosted in the cloud and accessed through a client, such as a computer, smartphone, gadget, appliance, and so on. Applications and services that are served through cloud computing mimic the capabilities associated with software applications, but don't necessarily require the traditional hardware and support infrastructures to create, install, and manage them.

Comment Spam: The practice of artificially and thoughtlessly promoting content or products in the comments section of any blog, social network profile, group, fanpage, wiki, or content page. Strategically discussing the solution/service/person as it relates to steering content helpfully without coming across as spam, snake-oil, or as a sales pitch is not comment spam.

Connection: The link between people, themes, topics, keywords, and/or content.

Consumer-Generated Media (CGM)/User-Generated Content (UGC): The content created by users or consumers and added to social media properties and communities. For example, blog posts, comments, reviews, votes, videos, pictures, podcasts, online documents, tweets, and status updates are all forms of user-generated content.

Conversation: The published online dialogue that transpires between one or more people in and around ideas, content, updates, themes, and events. Conversations can be synchronous, tied to real-time updates and responses, threaded in one string of related content, updates, and responses, or asynchronous, where the dialogue is not tied to time and place and distributed across social networks. (Twitter hosts asynchronous conversations; responses to blog posts or online content from other blogs, microcommunities, or other social networks through links also represent asynchronous dialogue.)

Creative Commons: Creative licensing by CreativeCommons.org offers a social media–friendly licensing architecture that allows people to use and share content based on the terms defined by the content creator or host. It frees up the usage patterns usually limited by traditional copyrights (all rights reserved) in exchange for credit, links, or some other form of gesture or recognition.

Crowd-Sourcing: The process of tapping the wisdom of crowds to create content, solve problems, answer questions, contribute to the evolution of a product or service, define governance associated with rules or politics, and so forth. Wikipedia is the most frequently used example for defining crowd-sourcing. Digg is considered a crowd-sourced news community.

Dashboard: A central hub for a variety of actions and capabilities, similar to the desktop of a computer screen. It refers to the items you place within a fixed area to streamline your activities associated with reading, publishing, responding, listening and monitoring, and updating.

Disclosure: The ethical measure of stating your intent, association, and/or goals associated with content or activity.

Embed: The process of integrating or adding a piece of content into another piece of content or place. YouTube provides embed code for its videos to enable users to place an integrated video and player in blogs, Web pages, and online profiles to share and serve information without forcing the visitor to click-through to YouTube in order to watch the video.

Engagement: The steps in participating in an online conversation through direct interaction or a response through direct or indirect words in and around the content source or publisher.

Favorite: "Favoriting" content or updates in social networks for review or sharing at a later date. It's also used as a form of bookmarking.

Feed: Content that can be viewed through other related or outside services. A blog updates its feed using RSS (really simple syndication) with every newly published post that can then be read by someone else who subscribes to the RSS feed using a feed reader such as Google Reader or Netvibes.

Flog: Fake blogs, comments, or reviews that promote content, products, brands, or services by pretending to be something or someone else without disclosure.

Folksonomy: The indexing of content by a greater collective of people through tags, labels, descriptions, titles, or keywords. Flickr and YouTube are powered by folksonomy in order to help others find the content they need. It's the process of matching content to content-seekers and serves as the undercurrent for effective social media optimization (SMO).

Gadget: A tiny application that performs a specific function on a Web page or social network profile. iGoogle is an example of a service that provides a custom experience based on the gadgets users install on their iGoogle desktop. Gadgets are virtually unlimited in variations and capabilities. They can include mini services to check weather, interact through instant messaging clients, update Twitter, check stocks or sports scores, translate sentences or words into other languages, read RSS feeds, and so on.

Hashtag: A keyword, keyword string, or theme preceded by a pound or number sign "#" and used to index and categorize content in networks where folksonomy is not directly supported. For example, hashtags gained prominence in Twitter as a way of associating tweets to topics. This book could carry the hashtag #socialmediamanifesto or #socialmedia or #SMM.

Hat Tip: The gesture of publicly recognizing someone or something as a source of content or information.

IRL: "In real life" refers to behavior offline or in the real world, which can sometimes be quite different from online behavior or activity.

Keywords: The word(s) used to describe content, media, destination pages and sites, and communities to boost visibility and ranking when someone searches for related information. Webmasters use keywords to describe and promote websites in search engine results, often referred to as search engine optimization (SEO). Keywords are also used to promote content when someone searches within a social network or a blog search engine. This is referred to as social media optimization (SMO).

Lifestream: A dedicated channel to aggregate the content produced on various social networks such as Flickr, YouTube, blogs, comments, and so on, into one easy-to-follow and easy-to-interact-with stream. FriendFeed, SocialThing, and Chi.mp are considered services for creating, hosting, and following lifestreams. Also referred to as an activitystream (related to similar activity, not necessarily sourced by the same person or brand) and brandstream (the channeled activity produced by a brand). The Facebook NewsFeed is also considered an activitystream or lifestream as it collects updates from the outside networks and communities you designate.

Like: Similar to "favoriting," "liking" is a token of gratitude and appreciation for content and updates shared in social networks such as Facebook and FriendFeed.

Linkback: A way for Web and content publishers to receive notification when other publishers link to their page or media.

Linkbait: Refers to the intentional publishing or promotion of content or destinations to provoke a response, usually in the form of a linkback. Since links contribute to the authority of a host, it helps boost their ranking and thus motivates publishers to use controversial methods to bait linked responses. If not done carefully, it can have negative repercussions.

Listening: Monitoring conversations and activity online related to keywords.

Liveblog or Livetweet: Sharing updates in real-time (as they happen) in blog posts, Twitter, or other social media platforms to keep readers or followers up to date with events as they unfold.

Livecast: Streaming video or audio live to document an experience or gather viewers and publishers together at a fixed moment in time to interact around the subject.

Mashup: The fusion, mixing, and matching of two or more applications or services to create or enable something new. Google Maps is a popular service that is often mashed up with other services. For example, Twittervision shows tweets and twitters on a map, based on any given location, to show where people are tweeting from in real-time.

Meetup: A service for facilitating and discovering events related to any given topic, theme, or interest. When you host an event that is housed at meetup.com, it's generally referred to as a meetup.

Meme: A theme that spreads on the Internet quickly. A memetracker can channel related activity and updates in one place to follow progress and information.

Participation: Engaging in online activity and also creating and contributing content that potentially resonates with people on any given subject within related communities and networks.

Pay It Forward: The act of paying homage or respect and calling attention to someone else in recognition of their contributions.

Permalink: The permanent link or URL for a destination or specific piece of content or media.

Relationships: While they may mimic ties in the real world, social media relationships usually refer to the exercise of connecting with like-minded individuals. These relationships can be fostered as a means of instilling and cultivating loyalty, advocacy, and activity. As in any relationship, there is an expected give-and-take value associated with interaction. Much more than a "two-way" street, people on both sides of the relationship must view the connection as mutually beneficial and productive over time.

Return On Investment (ROI): Return on investment is the system by which we measure the effectiveness of our initiatives related to time, resources, and capital compared to what was received in return. Over the years, especially in social media, ROI has been adapted to measure specific nuances of initiatives. ROI can also stand for return on influence, return on involvement, return on innovation, and relevance of interaction, among others.

Retweet: Retweeting, or simply RT, is the process of sharing someone else's tweet in order to extend the visibility of the original tweet and also recognize the originator in the process. For example: RT @briansolis Engage! is now available in bookstores online and near you; see www.areyouengaged.com.

Social Capital: The amount of personal wealth you garner through participation, engagement, contributions, and paying it forward as measured by reputation and authority. This is referred to as "personal brand worth" or, as Tara Hunt calls it, "The Whuffie Factor."

Social Economy: The people and technology that contribute to and define the vibrancy, prosperity, direction, and health of the Social Web.

Social Graph: Originally used in reference to the network of friends, associates, peers, and contacts that one maintains in Facebook, the social graph is essentially a personal network for facilitating communications and sharing information and content. Social graphs can span across multiple networks or reside in one primary community.

Social Operating System (OS): Social operating system is a term that I initially used to refer to the applications, widgets, gadgets, and services (online social networks and microcommunities) that we use to effectively communicate and navigate within our social graph.

Statusphere: Another term I used to describe the new ecosystem for sharing, discovering, and publishing updates and micro-sized content on social networks and microcommunities that reverberate throughout social networks and syndicated profiles, resulting in a formidable network effect of movement and response.

Stream: A river of information that is aggregated from a series of distributed content and presences across the Social Web.

Syndication: The opposite of aggregation, social syndication is the process of sharing one piece of content produced in one network across multiple networks without having to manually update each and every maintained account or profile manually. Ping.fm, TubeFilter, and Utterli are a few of many examples that facilitate syndication.

Tag: A keyword used to describe content in social networks and blogs.

Tag Cloud: A visual collection of the most often used tags generated by user, URL, page/profile, or themes, as dictated either by description tags or by the most often used words in any given post, site, or collection of media.

Tastemaker: Also referred to as taste neighbors, these individuals are considered influencers and trendsetters within their immediate sphere of activity or social graph.

Thread: A visual flow of tracking and presenting related conversations and responses within blogs and blog comments, microcommunities such as FriendFeed, social networks such as Facebook, or using special tools such as JS-Kit echo of Disqus, or a combination of all of the above.

Trackback/Tweetback: Similar to a linkback, a trackback or tweetback lets a blogger know when another blogger has linked to their blog or tweeted about their post.

Transparency: Its original definition referred to honest and authentic participation in social media. Over time, I've argued that the term *transparency* can be misleading in the sense that being yourself may not be enough to warrant a desired response, or that it wouldn't necessarily support or best present the brand, company, or service represented if the individual personality did not match the corresponding persona and prestige.

Trending Topics: Popularized by Twitter, trending topics are the most current themes that people are discussing related to keywords or hashtags at any given moment.

Tribe: Popularized by Seth Godin, "tribes" refers to dedicated communities around a particular theme, cause, or movement. I believe that in life we are either hosts or we are guests. In this example, we either belong to a tribe or we lead it. In social media, we have the ability to effectively thrive in both in order to build a cross-network tribe rich with advocates and enthusiasts.

Trust: The reward for genuine participation and helpful collaboration in social networks and blogs.

Tweet: Trademarked by Twitter, tweet refers to an update shared on Twitter.

Tweetup: Similar to meetup, Tweetups refer to events organized on Twitter that result in an IRL (in real life) event.

Twit/Twitterer/Tweeps/Tweeple: Someone who tweets on Twitter.

Value: The substance and essence contributed to an online exchange or act of sharing information.

Views: The number of times a piece of content, media, or online destination was viewed by people. Many services attempt to track the number of unique views based on the IP address (an ID or Internet protocol address that's specific to a computer or device accessing the Web through any online access provider) to qualify and quantify the amount of views. Instead of counting how many times one particular system watches a video, it will only count it as one view to provide a more accurate reflection of popularity and activity.

Viral: The act of media or content getting shared within and across social networks. This is often confused with the impression that through viral marketing, content itself can elicit the desire to share. However, it's people that ultimately make something viral and therefore they require attention when introducing interesting content that offers the potential of legitimately going viral.

Virtual Goods and Gifts: Products that are made available for free or for purchase to use or share with others within social networks. In Facebook, you could offer a virtual birthday cake as a gift to recognize someone's special day and call attention to the act within your (and their) social graph. Other virtual goods include drinks, badges, games, and so on.

Virtual World: A social network that offers an immersive 3D world that is constructed outside of reality to create its own experience. Second Life and World of Warcraft are leading examples.

Vote: The act of promoting content, people, or media within specific social networks. Votes (Diggs on Digg, Stumbles on StumbleUpon) can go up or down.

Widget: A self-contained website, ad, game, network, service, or application that is embeddable on websites, profiles, blogs, and other online properties.

Word of Mouth (WOM): Not necessarily derived from social media, but most certainly practiced and studied as a part of it, word of mouth refers to the phenomenon that occurs when people actively and fervently share content, media, or information across the Web. As content picks up momentum, it goes viral. Word-of-mouth marketing is the discipline dedicated to promoting products or content through the engagement and promotion of the people; it's intended to benefit, educate, enlighten, or entertain.

Notes

■ **CHAPTER 1 THE SOCIAL MEDIA MANIFESTO: ENGAGE OR DIE**

1. Taken from Wikipedia.
2. Taken from Learnthat.com.
3. Wiktionary.org.
4. Http://vlib.anthrotech.com/guides/anthropology.shtml.

■ **CHAPTER 2 THE CASE FOR SOCIAL MEDIA, BY THE NUMBERS**

1. Internet Usage Statistics, www.internetworldstats.com/stats.htm.
2. "Russia Has World's Most Engaged Social Networking Audience," comScore (July 2, 2009),www.comscore.com/Press_Events/ Press_Releases/2009/7/Russia_has_World_s_Most_Engaged_Social_ Networking_Audience.
3. "Global Faces and Networked Places," Nielsen (March 2009), http://server-uk.imrworldwide.com/pdcimages/Global_Faces_ and_Networked_Places-A_Nielsen_Report_on_Social_Networkings_ New_Global_Footprint.pdf.
4. Jeremiah Owyang, "Social Media Playtime Is Over," Forrester Research (March 16, 2009), www.forrester.com/Research/ Document/Excerpt/0,7211,47665,00.html.
5. "Is Social Network Advertising Ready for Primetime?" eMarketer (July 9, 2009), www.emarketer.com/Article.aspx?R=1007165.
6. Shar VanBoskirk, "Interactive Marketing Nears $55 Billion; Advertising Overall Declines." Forrester Research (July 7, 2009), http:// blogs.forrester.com/marketing/2009/07/interactive-marketing- nears-55-billion-advertising-overall-declines.html.

7. Josh Bernoff, "People Don't Trust Company Blogs. What You Should Do about It," Forrester Blogs (December 9, 2008), http://blogs.forrester.com/groundswell/2008/12/people-dont-tru.html.

8. Jose A. del Moral, "Facebook Becomes the Main Social Network in Most Countries, but in Asia and Latin America," Social Networks Alianzo's Blogs (February 22, 2009), http://blogs.alianzo.com/socialnetworks/2009/02/22/facebook-becomes-the-main-social-network-in-most-countries-but-in-asia-and-latin-america/.

■ CHAPTER 4 NEW MEDIA UNIVERSITY: SOCIAL MEDIA 201

1. Josh Bernoff, "Time to Rethink Your Corporate Blogging Ideas," Forrester Research (December 2008), www.forrester.com/Marketing/Campaign2/1,6538,1946,00.html.

2. Jeff Jarvis, "Dell learns to listen," *BusinessWeek* (October 17, 2007), www.businessweek.com/bwdaily/dnflash/content/oct2007/db20071017_277576.htm.

3. "The Infinite Dial 2009," Edison Research (2009), www.edisonresearch.com/Infinite%20Dial%202009%20Presentation.pdf.

4. Definition of Virtual World from ZDNet, http://dictionary.zdnet.com/definition/virtual + world.html.

■ CHAPTER 7 NEW MEDIA UNIVERSITY: SOCIAL MEDIA 301

1. "12% of Americans Bought Virtual Goods in Past 12 Months: Survey," GigaOM (July 30, 2009), http://gigaom.com/2009/07/30/12-of-americans-bought-virtual-goods-in-past-12-months-survey/.

2. Mark Zuckerberg, "Governing the Facebook Service in an Open and Transparent Way," Facebook (February 26, 2009), http://blog.facebook.com/blog.php?post=56566967130.

■ CHAPTER 8 NEW MEDIA UNIVERSITY: SOCIAL MEDIA 302

1. Dan Adler, "In Pictures: 21 Top Twitter Tips," *Forbes.com* (July 31, 2009), www.forbes.com/2009/07/31/top-twitter-tips-entrepreneurs-technology-twitter_slide_2.html.

■ CHAPTER 9 NEW MEDIA UNIVERSITY: SOCIAL MEDIA 303

1. "Web widget," Wikipedia, http://en.wikipedia.org/wiki/Web_widget.
2. "YouTube Surpasses 100 Million U.S. Viewers for the First Time," comScore (March 4, 2009), www.comscore.com/Press_Events/Press_Releases/2009/3/YouTube_Surpasses_100_Million_US_Viewers.

■ CHAPTER 10 NEW MEDIA UNIVERSITY: SOCIAL MEDIA 401

1. "Social theory," Wikipedia, http://en.wikipedia.org/wiki/Social_theory.
2. Bernardo A. Huberman, Daniel M. Romero, and Fang Wu, "Social Networks That Matter: Twitter under the Microscope," Social Computing Laboratory at HP Labs (January 2009), www.hpl.hp.com/research/scl/papers/twitter/.
3. "Folksonomy," Wikipedia, http://en.wikipedia.org/wiki/Folksonomy.
4. Linda Stone, "Continuous Partial Attention—Not the Same as Multi-Tasking," *BusinessWeek* (July 24, 2008), www.businessweek.com/business_at_work/time_management/archives/2008/07/continuous_part.html.

■ CHAPTER 11 NEW MEDIA UNIVERSITY: SOCIAL MEDIA 402

1. Bill McCloskey, "Twitter Surpasses Facebook as Top Link in E-mail," ClickZ, sponsored by StrongMail (July 30, 2009), www.clickz.com/3634551.
2. "Marketers Embrace Twitter over Facebook," eMarketer (August 14, 2009), www.emarketer.com/Article.aspx?R=1007229.
3. "Experiential Marketing," Wikipedia, http://en.wikipedia.org/wiki/Experiential_marketing.

■ CHAPTER 12 NEW MEDIA UNIVERSITY: SOCIAL MEDIA 403

1. "Minimalism," Wikipedia, http://en.wikipedia.org/wiki/Minimalism.

2. "Culture," Merriam Webster, http://www.merriam-webster.com/ dictionary/culture.

■ CHAPTER 13 NEW MEDIA UNIVERSITY: MBA PROGRAM—FIRST YEAR

1. Brian Solis, "Coining the Statusphere: The Social Web's Next Big Thing," Channeling Brian Solis (March 9, 2009), http:// briansolis.tumblr.com/post/85090914/coining-the-statusphere-the-social-webs-next-big.

2. "Attention economy," Wikipedia, http://en.wikipedia.org/wiki/ Attention_economy.

3. Linda Stone, "Continuous Partial Attention—Not the Same as Multi-Tasking," *BusinessWeek* (July 24, 2008), www.businessweek .com/business_at_work/time_management/archives/2008/07/ continuous_part.html.

4. John Freeman, "A Manifesto for Slow Communication," *Wall Street Journal* (August 21, 2009), http://online.wsj.com/ article/SB10001424052970203550604574358643117407778.html.

5. "Rubicon," Dictionary.com, http://dictionary.reference.com/ browse/rubicon.

6. "Network effect," Wikipedia, http://en.wikipedia.org/wiki/ Network_effect.

7. "Network effect," Marketing Terms, www.marketingterms.com/ dictionary/network_effect/.

■ CHAPTER 14 NEW MEDIA UNIVERSITY: MBA PROGRAM—SECOND YEAR

1. Ossi Nykänen, "Semantic Web Definition," Worldwide Web Consortium, www.w3c.tut.fi/talks/2003/0331umedia-on/slide6-0.html.

2. "What Is the Semantic Web?" Altova, www.altova.com/semantic_ web.html.

3. "Lessons from the Ant Colony: Overcoming the Biases of Web 2.0," Read Write Web (April 15, 2009), www.readwriteweb.com/ archives/lessons_from_ant_colony_overcoming_biases_web_20.php.

4. "Augmented Reality," Wikipedia, http://en.wikipedia.org/wiki/ Augmented_reality.

5. Tim O'Reilly and John Battelle, "Web Squared: Web 2.0 Five Years On" (June 2009), www.web2summit.com/web2009/public/schedule/detail/10194.

6. Dion Hinchcliffe, "The Evolving Web In 2009: Web Squared Emerges to Refine Web 2.0," *Social Computing Journal* (June 26, 2009), http://web2.socialcomputingjournal.com/the_evolving_web_in_2009_web_squared_emerges_as_web_20_mai.htm.

■ CHAPTER 15 FUSING THE "ME" IN SOCIAL MEDIA AND THE "WE" IN THE SOCIAL WEB

1. "Butterfly Effect," http://dictionary.reference.com/browse/butterfly+effect.

2. John Hopkins, "Another Story about Getting Fired Because of MySpace?" JohnRHopkins.com (May 4, 2009), http://johnrhopkins.com/another-story-about-getting-fired-because-of-myspace/comment-page-1/.

■ CHAPTER 17 DEFINING THE RULES OF ENGAGEMENT

1. Douglas MacMillan, "A Twitter Code of Conduct," *BusinessWeek* (May 8, 2009), www.businessweek.com/managing/content/may2009/ca2009058_089205.htm?chan=careers_special+report+-+social+media+2009_special+report+-+social+media+2009.

2. "Immediate Ban on Internet Social Networking Sites on Marine Corps Enterprise Network NIPRNET," U.S. Marine Corps (August 3, 2009), www.marines.mil/news/messages/Pages/MARADMIN0458-09.aspx.

3. Noah Shachtman, "Army Orders Bases to Stop Blocking Twitter, Facebook, Flickr," *Wired* (June 10, 2009), www.wired.com/dangerroom/2009/06/army-orders-bases-stop-blocking-twitter-facebook-flickr/.

4. Noah Shachtman, "Marines Ban Twitter, MySpace, Facebook," *Wired* (August 3, 2009), www.wired.com/dangerroom/2009/08/marines-ban-twitter-myspace-facebook/.

5. www.facebook.com/admiralmikemullen.

6. www.facebook.com/RayOdierno.

7. Julian E. Barnes, "What's on the Pentagon's mind? Facebook," *LA Times* (August 5, 2009), www.latimes.com/news/nationworld/nation/la-na-pentagon-facebook5-2009aug05,0,3998956.story.

8. www.drum.army.mil/sites/tenants/division/CMDGRP/CG/CG.htm.

9. Best Buy Connect, http://bbyconnect.appspot.com/tips_and_expectations/.

10. "Guidelines," Best Buy, www.bestbuyinc.com/aggregator/our-guidelines.

11. "Intel Social Media Guidelines," Intel, www.intel.com/sites/sitewide/en_US/social-media.htm.

12. "IBM Social Computing Guidelines," IBM, www.ibm.com/blogs/zz/en/guidelines.html.

13. "Business Conduct Guidelines," IBM, www.ibm.com/investor/corpgovernance/cgbcg.phtml.

14. www.fairwindspartners.com/.

15. Emily Steel, "How to Handle 'IHateYourCompany.com,'" *Wall Street Journal* (September 5, 2008), http://webreprints.djreprints.com/2022491227441.html.

16. Ariel Waldman, "3 Points on Why Government Isn't Ready for 2.0 Yet" (August 14, 2009), http://arielwaldman.com/2009/08/14/3-points-on-why-government-isnt-ready-for-2-0-yet/.

■ CHAPTER 18 THE CONVERSATION PRISM: HOW TO LISTEN

1. Jonathan Whitaker, M. S. Krishnanm and Claes Fornell, "How Offshore Outsourcing Affects Customer Satisfaction," *Wall Street Journal* U.S. (September 13, 2008), http://online.wsj.com/article/SB121441852405104029.html.

2. "Reinforcement.," Wikipedia, http://en.wikipedia.org/wiki/Reinforcement.

3. www.dimihr.com/main-about-katcher.html.

4. Jodi R. R. Smith, "Customer Service Made Simple," Huffington Post (February 25, 2009), www.huffingtonpost.com/jodi-r-r-smith/customer-service-made-sim_b_169827.html.

5. "Ethnography," Merriam Webster, www.merriam-webster.com/dictionary/ethnography.

6. "Boolean Searching on the Internet," Internet Tutorials, www.internettutorials.net/boolean.asp.

7. As defined by Archaeological Institute of America, www.archaeological.org/webinfo.php?page=10299.

8. Brian A. Hoey, "What Is Ethnography?" www.brianhoey.com/General%20Site/general_defn-ethnography.htm.

9. "Emic," Merriam Webster, www.merriam-webster.com/dictionary/emic.

10. "Demographics," Merriam Webster, www.merriam-webster.com/dictionary/demographics.

11. "Psychographics," Merriam Webster, www.merriam-webster.com/dictionary/psychographics.

■ CHAPTER 19   UNVEILING THE NEW INFLUENCERS

1. The following examples are extracted from Sarah E. Needleman, "Relief for Twitter Headaches," *Wall Street Journal* (September 14, 2009), http://online.wsj.com/article_email/SB1000142405297020468320457435644145788488-lMyQjAxMDA5MDEwNDExNDQyWj.html.

■ CHAPTER 20   THE HUMAN NETWORK

1. "Network theory," Wikipedia, http://en.wikipedia.org/wiki/Network_theory.

2. "The Human Network," Cisco.com, www.cisco.com/web/about/humannetwork/index.html.

3. Twitter-Friends, http://twitter-friends.com.

4. NetWiki, http://netwiki.amath.unc.edu.

5. Mailana, http://twitter.mailana.com.

6. Steve Whittaker, Loren Terveen, Will Hill, and Lynn Cherny, "The Dynamics of Mass Interaction," ATT Labs-Research, From Proceedings of the 1998 ACM Conference on Computer-Supported Cooperative Work, http://portal.acm.org/citation.cfm?id=289500.

7. "Participation Inequality," Wikipedia, http://en.wikipedia.org/wiki/Participation_inequality.

8. Christopher Lueg and Danyel Fisher, *From Usenet to CoWebs: Interacting with Social Information Spaces* (New York: Springer, 2003).

9. Mark Granovetter, "The Impact of Social Structure on Economic Outcomes," First appeared in the Winter 2004 *Journal of Economic Perspectives* (Vol. 19, No. 1, pp. 33–50), www.leader-values.com/Content/detail.asp?ContentDetailID=990.

10. F. John Reh, "Pareto's Principle—The 80-20 Rule," About.com, http://management.about.com/cs/generalmanagement/a/Pare to081202.htm.

11. Ben McConnell and Jackie Huba, "The 1% Rule: Charting Citizen Participation," Church of the Customer Blog, www .churchofthecustomer.com/blog/2006/05/charting_wiki_p.html.

12. "Wikipedia's long tail," Joho the Blog (November 1, 2005), www .hyperorg.com/blogger/mtarchive/wikipedias_long_tail.html.

13. Bradley Horowitz, "Creators, Synthesizers, and Consumers," Elatable (February 16, 2006), http://blog.elatable.com/2006/02/ creators-synthesizers-and-consumers.html.

14. Jakob Nielsen, "Participation Inequality: Encouraging More Users to Contribute," Jakob Nielsen's Alertbox (October 9, 2006), www.useit.com/alertbox/participation_inequality.html.

15. Jake McKee, "The 90-9-1 Principle," www.90-9-1.com/.

16. Josh Bernoff, "Social Technology Growth Marches On in 2009, Led by Social Network Sites," Groundswell, Forrester Blogs (August 25, 2009), http://blogs.forrester.com/groundswell/2009/ 08/social-technology-growth-marches-on-in-2009-led-by-social-network-sites.html.

17. Sean Corcoran, "The Broad Reach of Social Technologies," Forrester Research (August 25, 2009), www.forrester.com/ Research/Document/Excerpt/0,7211,55132,00.html.

18. Theodore Levitt, "Exploit the Product Life Cycle," *Harvard Business Review* 43 (November–December, 1965), 81–94.

19. Brian Solis and Deirdre Breakenridge, *Putting the Public Back in Public Relations* (Pearson/Financial Times Press, 2009), p. 190.

20. James Stull and John W Baird, *Business Communication: A Classroom Simulation* (New York: Prentice Hall, 1992).

21. William D. Perreault and E. Jerome McCarthy, *Basic Marketing*, 14th ed. (New York: McGraw-Hill/Irwin, 2003).

22. Don E. Schultz, Stanley Tannenbaum, and Robert F. Lauterborn, *The New Marketing Paradigm: Integrated Marketing Communications* (New York: McGraw-Hill, 1996).

23. Roy McClean, "Marketing 101: 4 Cs versus the 4 Ps of Marketing," FOCUS Marketing Intelligence, www.customfitfocus.com/ marketing-1.htm.

24. "Professor Koichi Shimizu's 7Cs Compass Model," Josai University,www.josai.ac.jp/~shimizu/essence/Professor%20Koichi%20 Shimizu%27s%207Cs%20Compass%20Model.html.

25. Chris Heuer, "Social + Media: What's Needed Next," Drupalcon Keynote (September 3, 2009), Paris.

26. David Armano, "The 4 Cs of Community," Logic + Emotion (November 30, 2008), http://darmano.typepad.com/logic_emotion/2008/11/the-4-cs-of-community.html.

27. "Corporate Title," Wikipedia, http://en.wikipedia.org/wiki/Corporate_title.

■ CHAPTER 21 SOCIAL MARKETING COMPASS: CREATING A SOCIAL MEDIA PLAN

1. David Sifry, "State of the Blogosphere, February 2006, Part 2: Beyond Search," Sifry's Alerts (February 13, 2006), www.sifry.com/alerts/archives/000420.html.

2. "Marketing Plan Outline." Quick MBA, www.quickmba.com/marketing/plan/.

3. William D. Perreault and E. Jerome McCarthy, *Basic Marketing*, 14th ed. (New York: McGraw-Hill/Irwin, 2003).

4. Hugh MacLeod, *Ignore Everybody* (Penguin Group, USA, 2009).

■ CHAPTER 22 DIVIDE AND CONQUER: BUILDING MARKETING AND SERVICE TEAMS AROUND SOCIAL MEDIA PROGRAMS

1. Michael Fitzgerald, "Intel's Hiring Spree," *Technology Review* (February 14, 2006), www.technologyreview.com/InfoTech/wtr_16340,294,p1.html.

2. Ibid.

3. See www.janchipchase.com/.

4. "Meet the Mobile Anthropologist," *Nokia Conversations* (July 2, 2008), www.conversations.nokia.com/2008/07/02/meet-the-mobile-anthropologist/.

5. Jason Palmer, "Interview: The Cellphone Anthropologist," *New Scientist* (June 11, 2008), www.newscientist.com/article/mg19826602.000-interview-the-cellphone-anthropologist.html.

6. Brian Solis, "The State of PR, Marketing, and Communications: You Are the Future," PR 2.0 (June 8, 2009), www.briansolis.com/2009/06/state-of-pr-marketing-and/.

■ **CHAPTER 23 A TALE OF TWO CITIES: SOCIAL CRM AND RELATIONSHIP MANAGEMENT**

1. Bob Thompson, "Social CRM: Strategy, Technology or Passing Fad?" Customer Think (September 16, 2009), www.customerthink .com/blog/social_crm_strategy_technology_or_passing_fad.

2. "CRM 2.0: Creating the New Definition," crm20.pbworks.com/ CRM-2-Definition-%231.

3. William Band, "CRM 2.0: Fantasy or Reality?" Forrester Research (November 13, 2008), www.forrester.com/Research/ Document/Excerpt/0,7211,45753,00.html.

4. Brent Leary, "Social CRM: Not Your Father's Customer Relationship Management," *Small Business Trends* (May 14, 2008), http://smallbiztrends.com/2008/05/social-crm.html.

5. Filiberto Selvas, "Are the Cool Kids Leaving Facebook? So What?" www.socialcrm.net/.

6. Ross Mayfield, "The Social C.R.M Iceberg," Ross Mayfield's Weblog (August 11, 2009), http://ross.typepad.com/blog/2009/ 08/crm-iceberg.html.

7. Jeremiah Owyang, "The Future of Twitter: Social CRM," Web Strategy by Jeremiah Owyang (March 22, 2009), www.web-strategist .com/blog/2009/03/22/the-future-of-twitter-social-crm/.

8. Brian Solis, "Twitter and Social Networks Usher in a New Era of Social CRM," PR 2.0 (March 20, 2009), www.briansolis .com/2009/03/twitter-and-social-networks-usher-in/.

9. Paul Greenberg, "Time to Put a Stake in the Ground on Social CRM," PGreenblog (July 6, 2009), http://the56group.typepad .com/pgreenblog/2009/07/time-to-put-a-stake-in-the-ground-on-social-crm.html.

10. Jon Swartz, "Businesses Use Twitter to Communicate with Customers," *USA Today* (June 26, 2009), www.usatoday.com/tech/ news/2009-06-25-twitter-businesses-consumers_N.htm.

11. Dion Hinchcliffe, "Using Social Software to Reinvent the Customer Relationship," ZDNet (August 18, 2009), http://blogs.zdnet .com/Hinchcliffe/?p=699.

12. See www.kluster.com/.

13. Shel Israel, "Twitterville: How Businesses Can Thrive in the New Global Neighborhoods," *Portfolio* (September 2009), http:// redcouch.typepad.com/weblog/twitterville.html.

14. Christopher Carfi, "VRM: Vendor Relationship Management," *The Social Customer Manifesto* (December 18, 2006), www .socialcustomer.com/2006/12/vrm_vendor_rela.html.

15. Doc Searls, comment to Christopher Carfi's post, "Vendor Relationships Management" (Dec 19, 2006), www.socialcustomer.com/2006/12/vrm_vendor_rela.html.

16. Gillmor Gang, http://cyber.law.harvard.edu/projectvrm/VRM_discussion_in_podcasts.

17. Paul Greenberg, comment to Christopher Carfi's post, "Vendor Relationships Management" (Dec 18, 2006), www.socialcustomer.com/2006/12/vrm_vendor_rela.html.

18. About VRM Labs, www.vrmlabs.net/about/.

19. About Project VRM, http://cyber.law.harvard.edu/projectvrm/About.

20. Project VRM Main Page, http://cyber.law.harvard.edu/projectvrm/Main_Page.

21. Paul Greenberg, *CRM at the Speed of Light: Social CRM 2.0 Strategies, Tools, and Techniques for Engaging Your Customers*, 4th ed. (New York: McGraw-Hill Osborne Media, 2009).

22. Frederick F. Reichheld, "One Number You Need to Grow," *Harvard Business Review* (December 1, 2003), http://harvardbusiness.org/product/one-number-you-need-to-grow/an/R0312C-PDF-ENG.

23. Frederick F. Reichheld, *The Ultimate Question* (Cambridge, MA: Harvard Business Press, 2006).

24. Werner Reinartz and V. Kumar, "Mismanagement of Customer Loyalty," *Harvard Business Review* (July 1, 2002), http://harvardbusiness.org/product/mismanagement-of-customer-loyalty/an/R0207F-PDF-ENG.

25. V. Kumar, *Managing Customers for Profit: Strategies to Increase Profits and Build Loyalty*, (Wharton School Publishing, 2008).

26. Joshua Weinberger, "Social Media Maturity Model: 30 Posts, 30 People, 30 Days," Destination CRM Blog (June 1, 2009), http://www.destinationcrmblog.com/2009/06/01/social-media-maturity-model-30-posts-30-people-30-days/.

■ CHAPTER 24   THE CONTRAST BETWEEN EARNED AND PAID: WHEN PAYING FOR FRIENDS MAKES CENTS

1. "Hashtags," Twitter Fan Wiki, http://twitter.pbworks.com/Hashtags.

2. Douglas Quenqua, "MTV Plays Telephone with Twitter," ClickZ (May 1, 2009), www.clickz.com/3633603.

3. Abbey Klaassen, "Twitter Proves Its Worth as a Killer App for Local Businesses," *Advertising Age* (May 18, 2009), http://adage.com/digital/article?article_id=136662.

4. "FTC Publishes Final Guides Governing Endorsements, Testimonials," Federal Trade Commission (October 5, 2009), www.ftc.gov/opa/2009/10/endortest.shtm.

5. "Twitter Followers 'Can Be Bought,'" *BBC* (July 2, 2009), http://news.bbc.co.uk/2/hi/technology/8130456.stm.

■ CHAPTER 25   THE NEW MEDIA SCORECARD: MEASURING INVESTMENT RETURNS

1. "Social Media Measurement Lags Adoption." eMarketer, September 22, 2009. http://www.marketer.com/Article.aspx?R=1007286#.

2. Nick Saint, "Twitter Users Are an Advertiser's Dream Come True," *Silicon Valley Insider* (September 25, 2009), www.businessinsider.com/twitter-users-are-an-advertisers-dream-come-true-2009-9.

3. K.D. Paine, "Establishing the ROI of Social Media," *KDPaine's Measurement Standard* (May 2008), www.themeasurementstandard.com/issues/5-1-08/painelet5-1-08.asp.

4. "Return on Investment," *The Free Dictionary*, http://financial-dictionary.thefreedictionary.com/Return + on + investment.

5. Brian Solis, "The Essential Guide to Social Media: A Free eBook," PR 2.0 (June 9, 2008), www.briansolis.com/2008/06/essential-guide-to-social-media-free/.

6. "Public Relations Measurement 2010: Five Things to Forget & Five Things to Learn," *MetricsMan* (July 29, 2009), http://metricsman.wordpress.com/2009/07/29/public-relations-measurement-2010-five-things-to-forget-five-things-to-learn/.

7. K.D. Paine, "What's Important about Social Media Is What Happens Because of It," *KDPaine's Measurement Standard* (July 2009), www.themeasurementstandard.com/issues/7-1-09/painelet7-1-09.asp.

8. K.D. Paine, "The All-Purpose, One-Size-Fits-All Public Relations Measurement Program Checklist," The Measurement Standard Blog Edition (March 11, 2009), http://kdpaine.blogs.com/themeasurementstandard/2009/03/the-allpurpose-onesizefitsall-public-relations-measurement-program-checklist.html.

9. Pat LaPointe, "Twittering Away Time and Money," *Marketing Measurement Today* (July 24, 2009), http://marketingmeasurement today.blogspot.com/2009/07/twittering-away-time-and-money .html.

10. Chris Lake, "10 Ways to Measure Social Media Success," eConsultancy (March 5, 2009), http://econsultancy.com/blog/3407-10-ways-to-measure-social-media-success.

11. Chris Lake, "Q&A with Zappos CEO Tony Hsieh," eConsultancy (November 27, 2008), http://econsultancy.com/blog/2955-q-a-with-zappos-ceo-tony-hsieh.

12. "CPM," Marketing Terms, www.marketingterms.com/dictionary/cpm/.

13. "Cost-per-Click," Marketing Terms, www.marketingterms.com/dictionary/cost_per_click/.

14. "Click-Through Rate," Marketing Terms, www.marketingterms .com/dictionary/clickthrough_rate/.

15. Eric von Coelln, "After the Tweet: Exploring Twitter Click Through Rate Benchmarking to Measure Engagement," Voncoelln.com (June 3, 2009), www.voncoelln.com/eric/2009/06/03/after-the-tweet-exploring-twitter-click-through-rate-benchmarking-to-measure-engagement/.

16. "Cost-per-Action," Marketing Terms, www. marketingterms.com/dictionary/cost_per_action/.

17. David Berkowitz, "CPSA: The New Pricing Model For Social Media?" *Social Media Insider* (August 4, 2009), www.mediapost .com/publications/?fa=Articles.showArticle&art_aid=111081.

18. Suzanne Bearne, "Cover Story: P&G to Pay Publishers Based on Online Engagement," *New Media Age* (September 17, 2009), www.nma.co.uk/news/pg-to-pay-publishers-based-on-online-engagement/3004452.article#.

19. "P&G to Pay Publishers Based on Online Engagement," Mad.co.uk (September 16, 2009), www.mad.co.uk/Main/News/Articlex/038 fc4206a70425095eae37466f7ef37/PG-to-pay-publishers-based-on-online-engagement.html.

20. Suzanne Bearne, "Cover Story: P&G to Pay Publishers Based on Online Engagement," *New Media Age* (September 17, 2009), www.nma.co.uk/news/pg-to-pay-publishers-based-on-online-engagement/3004452.article#.

21. "The 100 Top Brands," *BusinessWeek*, http://images.businessweek .com/ss/08/09/0918_best_brands/index.htm.

22. ENGAGEMENTdb 2009 Report, www.engagementdb.com/Report.

23. Charlene Li, "New Study: Deep Brand Engagement Correlates with Financial Performance," *The Altimeter* (July 20, 2009), www.altimetergroup.com/2009/07/engagementdb.html.

24. The Razorfish Social Influence Marketing Report, http://fluent .razorfish.com/publication/?m=6540&l=1.

Index